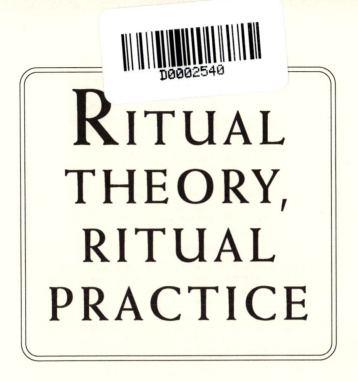

RITUAL THEORY, RITUAL PRACTICE

Catherine Bell

New York   Oxford
Oxford University Press
1992

Oxford University Press

Oxford   New York   Toronto
Delhi   Bombay   Calcutta   Madras   Karachi
Petaling Jaya   Singapore   Hong Kong   Tokyo
Nairobi   Dar es Salaam   Cape Town
Melbourne   Auckland

and associated companies in
Berlin   Ibadan

Copyright © 1992 by Catherine Bell

Published by Oxford University Press, Inc.

198 Madison Avenue, New York, New York 10016-4314

Oxford is a registered trademark of Oxford University Press

Library of Congress Cataloging-in-Publication Data
Bell, Catherine M., 1953–
Ritual theory, ritual practice / Catherine Bell.
p. cm.
Includes bibliographical references and index.
ISBN 0-19-506923-4
ISBN 0-19-507613-3 (pbk.)
1. Ritual.   2. Anthropology—Methodology.   I. Title.
BL600.B46   1992
291.3'8—dc20   91-16816   CIP

8 9 7

Printed in the United States of America
on acid-free paper

"...I take ritual to be *the* basic social act."   R. RAPPAPORT[1]

"Ritual is pure activity, without meaning or goal."   F. STAAL[2]

This [interpretation] has allowed the scholarly fantasy that ritual is an affair of the *tremendum* rather than a quite ordinary mode of human social labor."   J.Z. SMITH[3]

"Ritual [is] like a favoured instance of a game...."
C. LEVI-STRAUSS[4]

"In ritual, the world as lived and the world as imagined... turn out to be the same world."   C. GEERTZ[5]

"[There is] the widest possible disagreement as to how the word ritual should be understood."   E. LEACH[6]

"The more intractable puzzles in comparative religion arise because human experience has been... wrongly divided."
M. DOUGLAS[7]

Preface

This book is the result of a longstanding curiousity about ritual and our notions of ritual. The problems and issues engaged here were first formulated for a dissertation chapter, but since then they have continued to intrude on several very different projects. I could no longer resist the temptation to follow through on a few key ideas and see what might emerge, although I knew that as a book on ritual, the project would display one obvious idiosyncrasy: rather than contributing to the conceptual integrity and scope of the notion of ritual, this book is designed to be something of a lightning rod for the dilemmas of theory, analysis, and practice. The concept of ritual is not destroyed in the process, but I hope this study succeeds in shaking it up a little.

Several very different scholars of religion and ritual have influenced my particular formulation of the "problem" of ritual. Durkheim was the first such influence since I was exposed to the full sweep of his *Elementary Forms of the Religious Life* very early in my education. In defining religion as a formal object of theoretical and comparative analysis, Durkheim laid out categories that I could use to locate my own experience of religion in the schools and churches of pre–Vatican II Catholicism. Nonetheless, these categories did not always fit, and I have argued with Durkheim in my head ever since. In the end, it is with Durkheim's pragmatic formulation of religion as a matter of primary beliefs and secondary rites that the battle is joined and my analysis of ritual begins. I have enjoyed the prospect of a subsequent and complementary study giving full attention to the problem of 'belief'.

The pedagogy and essays of Jonathan Z. Smith have been a second influence. Many years ago, his argumentative assertion that "ritual is *work!*" raised innumerable questions for me about the construction and use of categories in the study of religion.[8] The element of surprise in his statement came, of course, from the emphasis on ritual as labor in contrast to the tendency to see ritual in terms of symbolic or idealized expression. Aside from provocative connections to Marxist theories of labor, his inversion ultimately suggested that the more common perspective was supported by an unexamined logic, which made it seem immediately convincing and right. I began to trace how the categories and rhetoric mobilized in standard approaches to ritual functioned to substantiate larger entities such as religion, society, or culture. Since then the "dismantling" of concepts like ritual and other deconstructive impulses has become more fashionable.

Another set of issues crystallized for me around the recent emergence of ritual studies as an independent and interdisciplinary field of study. As both an observer and participant at many conference panels I have been intrigued with the swelling of interest in ritual. The development of ritual studies as a distinct focus is clearly due in great part to the vision and efforts of a few individuals, particularly Ronald Grimes. His sense of intellectual purpose and wide-ranging inquiry has effectively encouraged a dialogue among quite different types of scholars. Yet the emergence and appeal of ritual studies must also be rooted in other forces operative within academic life. In the course of various formal discussions of ritual, I became curious about the intellectual and practical imperatives that would foster the construction of a category, such as 'ritual', in such a way as to organize and legitimize an independent discourse, expertise, and scholarly identity. I wondered if ritual studies as such could survive a major reorganization of the notion of ritual.

Writing this book has answered some but not all of the questions I brought to the project. In the end I have been content to make two main arguments about ritual activity. First, after tracing some of the connections that can make a discourse on ritual seem so compelling and useful to studies of cultural activity, I contend that few if any of the current theories of ritual avoid a rather predetermined circularity. This circularity functions to constitute ritual as an object of analysis in such a way as to mandate a particular method, expertise, and way of knowing. Perhaps a similar conclusion could be reached about many other topics of study, but ritual is an interesting case study of these practices for several reasons. Most simply, ritual is so readily cast as action in opposition to thought and theory that the structuring effect of assumptions about thought and action can be traced with great clarity. Moreover, ritual studies, as a recent mode of discourse, has claimed an odd exemption from the general critique that scholarship distorts and exploits, tending to see itself, by virtue of its interest in ritual performances per se, as somehow able to transcend the politics of those who study and those who are studied.

My second argument attempts to break free of the circularity that has structured thinking about acting by undermining the very category of ritual itself. I abandon the focus on ritual as a set of special practices in favor of a focus on some of the more common strategies of "ritualization," initially defined as a way of acting that differentiates some acts from others. To approach ritual within the framework of practical activity raises, I suggest, potentially more fruitful questions about the origins, purposes, and efficacy of "ritualized actions" than are accessible through current models.

My critical appraisal of the theoretical literature on ritual and the subsequent sketch of an alternative direction of inquiry attempt to address an impasse in ritual theory not unrecognized by others. It is probable that my alternative framework does not fully succeed in breaking free of the structures that have shaped thinking about ritual. Yet I suspect that even this failure will illuminate something basic about the constraints that are intrinsic to scholarly discourse on ritual and to the more general strategies by which we define and structure an authoritative interpretation. In any case, for reasons spelled out in the chapters that follow, I am not interested in presenting a systematic critique of all work on ritual or a new theory of ritual in general. Neither am I concerned to make any pronouncements on the intrinsic value of studying ritual per se. Rather, I am launching an analytical exploration of the social existence of the concept of ritual, the values ascribed to it, and the ramifications of these perspectives for scholarship.

Preliminary versions of certain sections of this book appeared elsewhere. Sections of Part I appeared in "Discourse and Dichotomies: The Structure of Ritual Theory," *Religion* 17, no. 2 (1987):

95–118. Some of the material in Part II concerning ritual change and the Christian liturgical tradition was presented in "Ritual, Change and Changing Rituals," *Worship* 63, no. 1 (1989): 31–41. Ideas on the ritual body and power (discussed in Parts II and III) were first formulated for the second of two conferences on ritual sponsored by the Department of Religious Studies at the University of California at Santa Barbara. The paper I presented there was subsequently published as "The Ritual Body and the Dynamics of Ritual Power," *The Journal of Ritual Studies* 4, no. 2 (Summer 1990): 299–313. Two papers presented in 1987 and 1988 to the Group on Ritual Studies of the American Academy of Religion gave me the opportunity to lay various arguments out before a very responsive set of colleagues. I am grateful for the encouragement extended by those involved in these projects.

Several people have directly affected this book, but none more than Steven Gelber, who patiently read the manuscript at each juncture, always improving the prose and the sense. I would also like to thank Richard Gardner and Ronald Grimes for their careful reading, critical feedback, and encouragement. Santa Clara University and the National Endowment for the Humanities provided some of the time and resources needed to complete this project.

Santa Clara, Calif.   C. B.
May 1991

Contents

RITUAL
THEORY,
RITUAL
PRACTICE

Introduction

In the last twenty years a number of diverse fields have found ritual to be an important focus for new forms of cultural analysis. Besides anthropologists, sociologists, and historians of religion, there are sociobiologists, philosophers, and intellectual historians who have turned to ritual as a "window" on the cultural dynamics by which people make and remake their worlds. The result has been a relatively broad and interdisciplinary conversation known as "ritual studies." Certainly the notion of ritual has been central to research in religion and society since the late nineteenth century, and few other single terms have been more fundamental in defining the issues basic to culture, society, and religion. Now, however, ritual has become a topic of interest in its own right, not merely a tool for understanding more embracing social phenomena. Indeed, ritual has simultaneously become an object, a method, and even something of a style of scholarship on the American academic scene.

Given both the history and scope of the appeal to ritual as a category of experience and analysis, the term is overdue for an extended critical rethinking. Jack Goody first addressed the state of ritual theory in a definitive study published nearly thirty years ago. Yet when he last addressed it in 1976, he expressed a dramatic loss of confidence in the formal category of ritual.[9] Aside from his comments, there has been no sustained analysis of the term that evaluates its role in our thinking on religion, society, and culture.[10] Nor has there been any concomitant assessment of the underlying problems engaged by the term 'ritual' and the structure this category imposes on theoretical discourse.

This book undertakes such an analysis in two ways: first, through a critical reading of how the notion of ritual has been used in the study of religion, society, and culture; and second, through an attempt to carve out an approach to ritual activities that is less encumbered by assumptions about thinking and acting and more disclosing of the strategies by which ritualized activities do what they do. I do not provide a comprehensive history of the term, a review of the most famous ethnographic examples, or a revised theory of ritual—useful though these projects might be. The purpose of this book is both more ambitious and more pragmatic—to reassess what we have been doing with the category of ritual, why we have ended up where we are, and how we might formulate an analytic direction better able to grasp how such activities compare to other forms of social action.

The sections that follow concentrate on a broad but selective set of influential theories about ritual. My discussion remains focused on an explicitly theoretical level of reflection about ritual rather than one more linked to ethnographic data. While many theories come embedded in particular ethnographic studies, none confine themselves to interpreting just the rites of a particular group. They all generalize in order to discuss ritual action per se. Since I am concerned with the most basic assumptions and tendencies in thinking about ritual activities, the analyses that follow also remain rather abstract. My starting point is not some objective instance of ritual activity that I attempt to interpret, such as Vedic ritual or the garden magic of the Trobriand Islanders. Rather, my starting point is an exploration of what makes us identify some acts as ritual, what such a category does for the production and organization of knowledge about other cultures, and how we might assess the assumptions that create and constrain the notion of ritual. Truly thick ethnographic descriptions of particular rites rarely succumb to the systematic division of human experience evidenced in theoretical studies. When they do, it is frequently due to the influence of categories developed to empower theoretical discourse. The divergence between theoretical formulations and descriptive studies is germane to the issues raised here, but a fuller treatment is regrettably beyond the scope of this book.[11]

In addition to analyzing the category of ritual and proposing another framework within which to assess ritual activity, this book has a third level of concern. In arguing how categories of ritual practice have been used to define objects and methods of theoretical practice, I raise questions about the dynamics of theoretical practice as such. By dismantling ritual as a theoretical construct, it is possible to uncover some of the more hidden but decisive practices by which a body of theoretical knowledge is generated and theoretical activity is differentiated from other forms of social activity. As part of its exploration of ritual, therefore, this book initiates a foray beyond the customary confines of ritual theory to suggest some of the strategies basic to other forms of practice and the social relationships these practices support.

The intellectual framework for 'doing theory' has shifted dramatically in the last twenty years. The premises and boundaries of the theoretical enterprise have undergone a wave of challenges, a periodic but no less traumatic experience, leaving us to wonder how and what we can know. This series of challenges has generated an open debate on the social and political ramifications of particular forms of knowing.[12] Some consensus has emerged from this debate that critical analysis of a theoretical perspective must look not only to the logic of the set of ideas under scrutiny, but also to the history of their construction.[13] In addition, a critical analysis must also incorporate a reflexive awareness of the conditions under which it operates to constitute meaningful interpretation.[14] In this era of theoretical practice, therefore, we are "rethinking" entire conceptual constructions handed down within our fields of inquiry.[15] Any thorough process of rethinking these basic concepts appears to involve three closely related operations: first, a deconstruction of the historical definitions of the problem or issue and a delineation of the circumstances under which the problem has been *a problem for us;* second, the proposal of an interpretive perspective on the issue that enables our cultural categories seriously to engage and be engaged by the material addressed; and third, an extension of this perspective to real applications and examples in order to explore relationships among hitherto unrelated issues.[16]

In rethinking ritual these operations form three stages of the argument that spans the following sections. The first stage discloses the construction of ritual as an object of analysis and thereby reveals the problems for us that have been embodied in the term and discourse on it. The second stage formulates an interpretation of this problem that reflexively provides an analysis of its own conditions as an interpretation. And the third stage, by applying this interpretation to a field of interrelated issues, attempts to generate an open but coherent framework for seeing new relationships among traditional issues, without losing sight of the contingent and determined nature of this framework.

More specifically, the chapters in Part I take up the initial task of a critical theory of ritual by addressing the construction of the category itself and the role this construction has played in organizing a broad discourse on religion, society, and culture. Despite the differences among historians of religion, sociologists, and anthropologists, their theories of ritual all similarly function to resolve the complex problems posed by an initial bifurcation of thought and action. Indeed, theoretical discourse about ritual is organized as a coherent whole by virtue of a logic based on the opposition of thought and action. This argument suggests that, historically, the whole issue of ritual arose as a discrete phenomenon to the eyes of social observers in that period in which 'reason' and the scientific pursuit of knowledge were defining a particular hegemony in Western intellectual life.

Given such a sociohistorical and logical-practical context for the term "ritual" as a category of experience and of analysis, a question arises: Can there be any argument for continuing to ascribe validity to the term? Goody, as noted earlier, sees no further usefulness in a "global construct" like ritual and has seriously called for its retirement in favor of a revitalizing "paradigm shift."[17] Although it is interesting to imagine a paradigm shift, any number of problems beset the attempt to jettison an older category, whether it be to impose a new one or simply to clear the field. There is hardly a consensus, first of all, about the inadequacy of the term ritual. It is still being used widely both by the general public and by many academic disciplines less immediately concerned with the problems that attend it. In fact, the popularity of the term and the topic, evidenced in ritual studies, reflects the very success scholars have had in securing the retirement of older and more obviously problematic terms. That is, ritual has replaced terms such as 'liturgy' versus 'magic', which were used to distinguish high religion from primitive superstition or *our* ritual from *theirs*. To try to discard the term ritual just when scholars have been successful in popularizing its use would imply a desire for esoteric categories accessible only to the cognoscenti.

Such housecleaning could also undermine any thorough exploration of how and why the term has become problematic. It is far from clear that a quickly summoned paradigm shift could solve either our immediate problems or the more buried ones they rest upon. Many attempts to produce a paradigm shift end up simply repackaging older problems in new jargon. Rather than eventually find that the disgraced presuppositions of the abandoned term have resurfaced in a newly deployed set of categories, it seems more responsible to hold on to our battered terminology, just as we hold on to the artifacts of our own personal histories no matter how difficult they might become. They ensure that we do not forget where we come from. They curb our pretenses. We may decide to tailor our terms with annotations or hyphenations, but it would be ill-advised to pretend to abandon what has been so well internalized. A real revolution will not be accomplished by a mere change of terms, nor will it be held off by modifying older ones. I *do* intend to modify the term ritual to function as something other than a "global construct" or "a key to culture."[18] Yet my close reliance upon current and preceding scholarship ensures continuity with the commonsense notion of ritual while making explicit some of the assumptions and perspectives built into it. Given the analysis of discourse on ritual presented in Part I, it becomes apparent that rethinking ritual will yield less rather than more—less generality, less universality, and perhaps less of the trappings of persuasive, explanatory power. This 'less-ness' may ultimately be more effective in spurring a shift of paradigms than the introduction of newly designed terms.

Part II, which takes on the second task of critical theorizing, proposes that so-called ritual activities be removed from their isolated position as special paradigmatic acts and restored to the context of social activity in general. Some attempts to see ritual as social praxis are analyzed, as are the stubborn difficulties encountered by 'practice theory' in its attempt to transcend only the most obvious forms of the thought–action dichotomy. In response, I propose a focus on 'ritualization' as a strategic *way* of acting and then turn to explore how and why this way of acting differentiates itself from other practices. When analyzed as ritualization, acting ritually emerges as a particular cultural strategy of differentiation linked to particular social effects and rooted in a distinctive interplay of a socialized body and the environment it structures. The confusions that accompany attempts to distinguish clearly between rite and non-rite—those perennial obstacles to neat definitions and classification—are revealed to be highly significant for understanding what ritualization does.

Part III addresses the large body of theories that discuss ritual as a form of social control. In so doing it attempts to fulfill the third task of a critical theory by applying an interpretation of ritualization as a culturally strategic way of acting to several classic issues within the traditional study of ritual, namely, belief, ideology, legitimation, and power. The main argument suggests that ritualization is a strategy for the construction of a limited and limiting power relationship. This is not a relationship in which one social group has absolute control over another, but one that simultaneously involves both consent and resistance, misunderstanding and appropriation. In exploring how ritualized ways of acting negotiate authority, self, and society, I attempt to delineate something of the social dynamics by which all activity reproduces and manipulates its own contextual ground.

As a particular reading of much of what has been written on ritual, this book is neither an objective nor a systematic review designed to evaluate each contribution in its own context and on its own merits. On the contrary, I have read to discover the cracks, instabilities, and manipulated themes in order to undo the process by which the notion of ritual has been constructed and to illuminate dynamics basic to how we think about the actions of others. At the risk of making the reading more difficult than it needs to be, I have tried to quote or paraphrase terms and descriptions as much as possible, since much of my argument rests on the subtle ways in which language is used.

Fredric Jameson introduced a recent study by calling attention to its "organizational fiction," the textual ploy that implies the existence of a problem the study will resolve.[19] The problem of ritual is, of course, just such an organizational fiction. This book is organized around a problem it first constructs and then solves—the problem of how the notion of ritual orders a body of theoretical discourse. I must first convince you that there is a problem and that the nature of it is such that you will find the proposed solution suitable. This is a strategy of scholarly production, aspects of which are common to other forms of socially effective action. It is my hope that this book, by virtue of its arguments about ritual theory *as well as* its own performance as a piece of theoretical practice (with all its schemes, feints, and blind spots), will contribute to a discussion of the activities of understanding.

Notes

Epigraphs

1. Roy A. Rappaport, *Ecology, Meaning and Religion* (Richmond, Calif.: North Atlantic Books, 1979), p. 174. Emphasis in the original.
2. Frits Staal, "The Meaninglessness of Ritual," *Numen* 26, no. 1 (1975): 9.
3. Jonathan Z. Smith, "The Domestication of Sacrifice," in *Violent Origins,* ed. Robert G. Hamerton-Kelly (Stanford: Stanford University Press, 1987), p. 198.
4. Claude Lévi-Strauss, *The Savage Mind,* trans. George Weidenfeld and Nicolson Ltd. (Chicago: University of Chicago Press, 1966), p. 30.
5. Clifford Geertz, *The Interpretation of Cultures* (New York: Basic Books, 1973), p. 112.
6. Edmund R. Leach, "Ritual," in *The International Encyclopedia of the Social Sciences,* vol. 13, ed. David L. Sills (New York: Macmillan, 1968), p. 526.
7. Mary Douglas, *Purity and Danger* (New York: Praeger, 1960), p. 28.

Preface

8. On ritual as work, see Victor Turner, "Variations on a Theme of Liminality," in *Secular Ritual,* ed. Sally F. Moore and Barbara G. Myerhoff (Amsterdam: Van Gorcum, 1977), pp. 39–41. Rappaport also talks of rituals as "public work" and "spirit work" (p. 177).

Introduction

9. Jack Goody, "Religion and Ritual: The Definitional Problem," *British Journal of Sociology* 12 (1961): 142–64; and "Against 'Ritual': Loosely Structured Thoughts on a Loosely Defined Topic," in Moore and Myerhoff, pp. 25–35.
10. A number of writers provide useful overviews of ritual. Among these the best are Gilbert Lewis, *Day of Shining Red: An Essay on Understanding Ritual* (Cambridge: Cambridge University Press, 1980); William G. Doty, *Mythography: The Study of Myth and Rituals* (University: University of Alabama Press, 1986); and Brian Morris, *Anthropological Studies of Religion* (Cambridge: Cambridge University Press, 1987).
11. Others have explored this issue, even contending that anthropology and ethnology constitute two distinct disciplines. See Dan Sperber's essay entitled "Interpretive Ethnology and Theoretical Anthropology," in *On Anthropological Knowledge* (Cambridge: Cambridge University Press, 1985), pp. 9–34. For another perspective on the gap between theory and ethnography, or research and writing, see Johannes Fabian, *Time and the Other: How Anthropology Makes Its Object* (New York: Columbia University Press, 1983), pp. ix, 21, and Chapter 3. In their critique of anthropological writing, George E. Marcus and Michael M. J. Fischer (*Anthropology as Cultural Critique* [Chicago: University of Chicago Press, 1986]) find the gap between fieldwork and writing to be the object of much reflection (pp. 5, 12–13, 16). In his analysis of theory in the hard sciences, Wolfgang Stegmüller (*The Structure and Dynamic of Theories* [New York: Springer-Verlag, 1976]) also distinguishes two distinct "languages," one theoretical and the other observational (p. 3).
12. See Fredric Jameson, *The Prison-House of Language* (Princeton: Princeton University Press, 1972); Edward W. Said, *Orientalism* (New York: Pantheon, 1978); Jean-François Lyotard, *The Postmodern Condition: A Report on Knowledge,* trans. Geoff Bennington and Brian Massumi (Minneapolis: University of Minnesota Press, 1984), originally published in 1979; James A. Boon, *Other Tribes, Other Scribes* (Cambridge: Cambridge University Press, 1982); James Clifford and George E. Marcus, eds., *Writing Culture: The Poetics and Politics of Ethnography* (Berkeley: University of California Press, 1986); Marcus and Fischer; and James Clifford, *The Predicament of Culture: Twentieth-Century Ethnography, Literature and Art* (Cambridge, Mass.: Harvard University Press, 1988).
13. Well-known examples include Michel Foucault, *The Order of Things,*

trans. Alan Sheridan (New York: Pantheon, 1970), and *The Archeology of Knowledge,* trans. A. M. Sheridan (New York: Pantheon, 1972); Roy Wagner, *The Invention of Culture,* rev. ed. (Chicago: University of Chicago Press, 1981); and Fabian.

14. For a discussion of critical theorizing, see Raymond Geuss, *The Idea of a Critical Theory* (Cambridge: Cambridge University Press, 1981); and Michael T. Taussig, *The Devil and Commodity Fetishism in South America* (Chapel Hill: University of North Carolina Press, 1980).

15. To mention some of the more obvious titles in this vein, see Edmund Leach, *Rethinking Anthropology* (London: Athlone Press, 1961); Dell Hymes, ed., *Reinventing Anthropology* (New York: Random House, 1969); Dan Sperber, *Rethinking Symbolism* (Cambridge: Cambridge University Press, 1974); Miriam Levering, ed., *Rethinking Scripture* (Albany: State University of New York Press, 1989); and E. Thomas Lawson and Robert N. McCauley, *Rethinking Religion: Connecting Cognition and Culture* (Cambridge: Cambridge University Press, 1990).

16. The stage of application does not necessarily imply a holistic structure of understanding of the type that has been criticized as a matter of "totalizing" explanations reaching for "absolutism." See Fredric Jameson's discussion of totalization in theory and "master narratives" in *The Political Unconscious* (Ithaca, N.Y.: Cornell University Press, 1981), pp. 27, 50ff; and in his introduction to Lyotard's *The Postmodern Condition,* pp. ix–xi. These three features of a critical theory are based in part on Geuss, pp. 1–3, and Stegmüller, pp. 14–16.

17. Goody, "Against 'Ritual'," pp. 27, 29, 34–35.

18. Goody, "Against 'Ritual'," p. 32.

19. Jameson, *The Political Unconscious,* p. 9.

I

THE PRACTICE OF RITUAL THEORY

Theories about ritual come fully embedded in larger discourses. Whether ritual is depicted as a universal phenomenon or merely an applied theoretical construct, the concept of ritual both exemplifies and supports the discourse within which it is elaborated.[1] In the past, scholars concerned with maintaining the objectivity of definitions of ritual—in the face of what they recognized to be powerful interpretive biases—have tended to warn us that the notion of ritual is a mere tool for analysis. As a tool, it must be kept from slipping out of the analyst's hand and into the objective data he or she is trying to interpret. Yet it has become increasingly obvious that a tighter hold on the term does not seem to prevent such "slippage" or maintain the clarity of the boundary between theory and data.[2] To understand this interpretive slippage as well as the variety of positions taken with regard to ritual, it is necessary to inquire into the larger discourses of which ritual is a part.

In the last quarter of a century scholars have discovered that theoretical categories are more than mere tools that can be wielded with control or carelessness. Thomas Kuhn's reappraisal of paradigms in scientific inquiry, for example, began to disclose how analytical categories serve more embracing models of the universe and of knowing.[3] More recently, Michel Foucault's historical archeology of discontinuous discourses suggests that analytical tools do not simply slip from a state of objectivity to which they can be returned, but that the nature of objectivity itself rests on historical paradigms and strategies of human inquiry effective within a specific

13

milieu. Subsequent attempts to relegitimate knowledge have made
even more apparent the dynamics involved in the production of
particular bodies of knowledge based on particular relationships
between subject and object.[4] Thus, it is no longer so easy to argue
that we can establish adequate categories merely by defining them
as objective analytical tools. They will not stay neutral. Rather, they
will conform to whatever subtle purposes the larger analysis serves.
We have learned that such categories are merely the most visible
of those pieces put into play within discourses whose boundaries,
objectives, and rules retreat from our conscious grasp. To challenge
the adequacy of our categories today, scholars must attempt to
track the dynamics of the discourse in which they operate and the
discursive logic by which they function.[5]

The notion of ritual first emerged as a formal term of analysis in
the nineteenth century to identify what was believed to be a universal category of human experience. The term expressed, therefore,
the beginnings of a major shift in the way European culture compared itself to other cultures and religions. Since then many other
definitions of ritual have been developed linked to a wide variety
of scholarly endeavors. Many myth-and-ritual theorists, for example, looked to ritual in order to describe 'religion'. Later social
functionalists, in contrast, explored ritual actions and values in
order to analyze 'society' and the nature of social phenomena. More
recently symbolic anthropologists have found ritual to be fundamental to the dynamics of 'culture'. From W. Robertson Smith to
Clifford Geertz, the notion of ritual has been meaningful precisely
because it functioned as much more than a simple analytical tool.
Rather, it has been integral to the mutual construction of both an
object for and method of analysis.

In debates about the relationship of myths (or beliefs) and rites,
ritual was used to elucidate the social existence and influence of
religious ideas. The theories of Max Müller, Edward Tylor, Herbert
Spencer, James Frazer, Rudolf Otto, William James, and E. O.
James, among others, all stressed the primacy of religious ideas,
born of pseudoscientific explanations or emotional experiences, as
the basis of religion. Ritual, as exemplary religious behavior, was
the necessary but secondary expression of these mental orientations.[6] This understanding of ritual accompanied a primary focus

on religion, as having to do with the sacred, which is still seen in the work of phenomenologists of religion today.[7]

Fustel de Coulanges and Robertson Smith explored other nuances of ritual as a category of human experience, coming to see it as more basic than beliefs and integral to the social dimensions of religion.[8] This perspective received it fullest formulation in Emile Durkheim's *The Elementary Forms of the Religious Life*, where religion is analyzed as both beliefs and rites: rites could be defined only with regard to their object, whereas in beliefs "the special nature of this object" was expressed.[9] Although Durkheim gave an analytic primacy to beliefs, ritual, in the guise of "cultus," played a dynamic and necessary role in social integration and consolidation. Henri Hubert and Marcel Mauss, who demonstrated how ritual activities effectively sacralize things, people, or events, inverted earlier perspectives by tracing how religious phenomena and ideas derived from social activities.[10] In the process, ritual was reinforced as both a central sociological concept *and* a universal category of social life.

In the development of the legacy of Mauss and the other *Annales* theoreticians, ritual's effect on social cohesion and equilibrium came to be interpreted in terms of other, seemingly more basic functions such as symbolization and social communication. This perspective coincides with the emergence of culture as a category of analysis. The analysis of culture, as opposed to society and religion per se, gave a particularly critical place to ritual. The prominence of ritual in the work of cultural anthropologists such as Victor Turner, Clifford Geertz, Edmund Leach, and Marshall Sahlins fueled the emergence of a focus on ritual itself in the cross-disciplinary endeavor of ritual studies.

The prominence of ritual in cultural theories has also occasioned some speculation. George Marcus and Michael Fisher note that description and analysis of ritual have been a popular device for organizing ethnographic texts. This is due, they reason, to ritual's public nature, whereby rituals are "analogous to culturally produced texts" that can be systematically read to endow "meaning upon experience."[11] This understanding appears to have promoted the study of ritual in a variety of areas in recent years, particularly in historical studies, communication the-

ory, theater studies, and social psychology—disciplines whose
practitioners see them, or are beginning to see them, as primarily
'interpretive' endeavors. A recent consensus has emerged that ritual, aside from its role in illuminating religion, society, or culture, should be studied in itself and for itself.[12] The development
of ritual studies as an independent and interdisciplinary area of
scholarly research evinces, perhaps, the final result of the complex coexistence of ritual as an analytical tool and as a universal
human experience—its universality is taken to ensure its usefulness and primacy as analytical concept.[13]

Although these theories have formulated the interrelationships
of religion, society, and culture in a variety of ways, in each case
ritual is seen as a definitive component of the various processes
that are deemed to constitute religion, or society, or culture.
Moreover, despite the variety of avowed methodological perspectives and ramifications, there is a surprising degree of consistency in the descriptions of ritual: ritual is a type of critical
juncture wherein some pair of opposing social or cultural forces
comes together. Examples include the ritual integration of belief
and behavior, tradition and change, order and chaos, the individual and the group, subjectivity and objectivity, nature and
culture, the real and the imaginative ideal. Whether it is defined
in terms of features of 'enthusiasm' (fostering groupism) or 'formalism' (fostering the repetition of the traditional), ritual is consistently depicted as a mechanistically discrete and paradigmatic
means of sociocultural integration, appropriation, or transformation. Given the variety of theoretical objectives and methods,
such consistency is surprising and interesting.

The following chapters analyze this consistency in the theoretical
depiction of ritual. I will show theoretical discourse on ritual to be
highly structured by the differentiation and subsequent reintegration of two particular categories of human experience: thought and
action. An exploration of the internal logic of this differentiation
and reintegration of thought and action in ritual theory suggests
that the recent role of ritual as a category in the study of culture
has been inextricably linked to the construction of a specifically
'cultural' methodology, a theoretical approach that defines and addresses 'cultural' data. That is, the problems we face in analyzing
ritual, as well as the impetus for engaging these particular problems,

have less to do with interpreting the raw data and more to do with the manner in which we theoretically constitute ritual as the object of a cultural method of interpretation. The implicit structure of ritual theory, while effective in identifying a distinctive phenomenon for cultural analysis, has imposed a powerful limit on our theoretical flexibility, our divisions of human experience, and our ability to perceive the logical relations inscribed within these divisions.

1

Constructing Ritual

Theoretical descriptions of ritual generally regard it as action and thus automatically distinguish it from the conceptual aspects of religion, such as beliefs, symbols, and myths. In some cases added qualifications may soften the distinction, but rarely do such descriptions question this immediate differentiation or the usefulness of distinguishing what is thought from what is done. Likewise, beliefs, creeds, symbols, and myths emerge as forms of mental content or conceptual blueprints: they direct, inspire, or promote activity, but they themselves are not activities.[14] Ritual, like action, will act out, express, or perform these conceptual orientations. Sometimes the push for typological clarity will drive such differentiations to the extreme. Ritual is then described as particularly *thoughtless* action—routinized, habitual, obsessive, or mimetic— and therefore the purely formal, secondary, and mere physical expression of logically prior ideas. Just as the differentiation of ritual and belief in terms of thought and action is usually taken for granted, so too is the priority this differentiation accords to thought. For example, Edward Shils argues that ritual and belief are intertwined and yet separable, since it is conceivable that one might accept beliefs but not the ritual activities associated with them. He concludes that logically, therefore, "beliefs could exist without rituals; rituals, however, could not exist without beliefs."[15] Claude Lévi-Strauss takes this logic much further when an initial distinction between ritual and myth eventuates in a distinction between living and thinking.[16]

Aside from this basic structural pattern in which ritual is differentiated from mental categories as readily as action is differentiated from thought, there is a second structural pattern in theoretical discussions of ritual. This second pattern describes ritual as a type of functional or structural mechanism to reintegrate the thought–action dichotomy, which may appear in the guise of a distinction between belief and behavior or any number of other homologous pairs. Both of these structural patterns—the differentiation of ritual as action from thought and the portrayal of ritual as a mechanism for integrating thought and action—can be demonstrated in several representative approaches to ritual.

Durkheim argued that religion is composed of beliefs and rites: beliefs consist of representations of the sacred; rites are determined modes of action that can be characterized only in terms of the representations of the sacred that are their object. "Between these two classes of facts," he wrote, "there is all the difference which separates thought from action."[17] Yet despite the secondary nature of ritual given in these initial definitions, Durkheim's important discussion of cult at the end of *The Elementary Forms* reintroduces ritual as the means by which collective beliefs and ideals are simultaneously generated, experienced, and affirmed as real by the community. Hence, ritual is the means by which individual perception and behavior are socially appropriated or conditioned.[18] In Durkheim's model the ritual activity of cult constitutes the necessary interaction between the collective representations of social life (as a type of mental or metamental category) and individual experience and behavior (as a category of activity).[19]

These two patterns turn up also in another, loosely structural, model employed with great sophistication by Stanley Tambiah but more simplistically by many others. There ritual is provisionally distinguished as the synchronic, continuous, traditional, or ontological in opposition to the diachronic, changing, historical, or social. However, ritual is also subsequently portrayed as the arena in which such pairs of forces interact. It is the mediating process by which the synchronic comes to be reexpressed in terms of the diachronic and vice versa.[20]

A third model, presented most fully in the early work of V. Turner, also portrays these two patterns. Turner initially described ritual as the affirmation of communal unity in contrast to the frictions, constraints, and competitiveness of social life and organization.[21] ~~Rite affords a creative~~ 'antistructure' that is distinguished from the rigid maintenance of social orders, hierarchies, and traditional forms. However, when subsequently portrayed as embodying aspects of both structure and antistructure, he describes rituals as those special, paradigmatic activities that mediate or orchestrate the necessary and opposing demands of both *communitas* and the formalized social order.

Each of these examples employs the two structural patterns described previously: ritual is first differentiated as a discrete object of analysis by means of various dichotomies that are loosely analogous to thought and action; then ritual is subsequently elaborated as the very means by which these dichotomous categories, neither of which could exist without the other, are reintegrated. These two structural patterns are rarely explicit and the first, in particular, in which ritual is differentiated from conceptual categories, is routinely taken for granted. However, the relationship that develops *between* these two patterns when they are simultaneously operative in a theoretical description of ritual is even less acknowledged and much more powerful. In effect, the dichotomy that isolates ritual on the one hand and the dichotomy that is mediated by ritual on the other become loosely homologized with each other. Essentially, as I will demonstrate, the underlying dichotomy between thought and action continues to push for a loose systemization of several levels of homologized dichotomies, including the relations between the ritual observer and the ritual actor. It is this invisible process of 'homologization', driven by the implicit presence of an opposition between conceptual and behavioral categories, that begins to construct a persuasive and apparently logical body of discourse.

Dichotomies and Dialectics

Jameson analyzes a type of logical structure within linguistical theory that is similar to the two patterns sketched out earlier for ritual theory.[22] The structured argument that he isolates provides a useful contrast to the one I am recovering here. Jameson points to a logical structure in which an initial differentiation, originally proposed to enable the theorist to concentrate on just one of the differentiated terms, surfaces again and again within subsequent analysis of that term. Specifically addressing Ferdinand Saussure's system of linguistics, Jameson shows that an initial distinction between structure and history (synchrony and diachrony) enables Saussure to focus upon and systematically elucidate one aspect of language, the synchronic or structural aspect. However, Saussure never resolved or transcended the dichotomy between synchrony and diachrony but reproduced it even in the final terms of his system.[23] How did such a replication occur?

In reaction against historicism in linguistics, Jameson explains, Saussure attempted to talk about the nonhistorical aspects of language. On a primary level, he distinguished between diachrony and synchrony, thereby providing himself a clear focus on the synchronic side of linguistics as opposed to the other side, where, he argued, everyone else was working. On a second level, and therefore within the synchronic system itself, Saussure also distinguished between *langue* and *parole* in order to further differentiate synchronic language from speech. He therein had his first internal replication of the original opposition. On yet a third level, Saussure took *langue* as a system and within it distinguished two ways in which signs are related, the syntagmatic and the associative (or paradigmatic), replicating his original dichotomy for a second time within the system as a whole.[24] The original differentiation between diachrony and synchrony was applied, through various pairs of categories, to three levels of analysis. In other words, the continual application of the dichotomy between synchrony and diachrony systematically generated successive and homologous levels of analysis.

At this point, Jameson suggests that it becomes quite "problematical to what degree the object of study is the thought pattern of the linguist himself, rather than that of the language." Moreover, this is also the point at which the originality of Saussure's initial distinction becomes a constraint on the whole system he has generated from it. Saussure's "initial repudiation of history," remarks Jameson, "which at the very outset resulted in an inability to absorb change into the system as anything but a meaningless and contingent datum, is now reproduced, at the very heart of the system itself, as an inability to deal with syntax as such."[25]

Theoretical discourse on ritual displays a similar logical structure: a distinction between belief and rite, made as readily as the heuristic distinction between thought and action, clears the way to focus on ritual alone. This is the first structural pattern noted previously. Ritual, however, becomes in turn a new starting point at which to differentiate once again between conceptual and behavioral components. This is the second structural pattern described earlier. However, ritual theory goes on to do something that Saussure, in the rigor of his focus and logic, according to Jameson, failed to do, namely, provide a stage of synthetic integration. Differentiated from belief in the first structural pattern, ritual becomes a second point at which to distinguish thought and action. Yet at this second stage ritual is seen as synthetic, as the very mechanism or medium through which thought and action are integrated. The elaboration of ritual as a mechanism for the fusion of opposing categories simultaneously serves both to differentiate and unite a set of terms. That is, the second structural pattern in ritual theory, in which ritual mediates thought and action, posits a dialectical relation between the differentiated entities instead of replicating an unmediated dichotomy. Ritual emerges as the means for a provisional synthesis of some form of the original opposition.

Saussure generated his linguistic system by positing an initial distinction, the successive and systematic replication of which rendered the distinction an ahistorical, nondialectical, or pure opposition.[26] Most ritual theory avoids this by incorporating the notion of dialectic or synthesis: ritual is a dialectical means for the provisional convergence of those opposed forces whose interaction is seen to constitute culture in some form.

The three representative theories of ritual briefly described clearly present ritual as just such a medium of integration or synthesis for opposing sociocultural forces. These are not isolated examples. There is a strong impetus within theoretical studies of religion and culture for this type of dialectic. This impetus can be seen, for example, in contemporary evaluations of Durkheim's theory of ritual. Some argue that his notion of ritual contains a dialectical mediation of the social and the individual; others argue that its fundamental weakness is precisely that his notion of ritual lacks such a dialectic. E. E. Evans-Pritchard has pinpointed Durkheim's theory of ritual as the central but "most obscure" and "unconvincing" part of his notion of society and religion.[27] Nancy Munn, on the other hand, has found it to be of "signal importance" for ritual studies today.[28] She argues that Durkheim developed a model of "social (ritual) symbolism as the switch point between the external moral constraints and groupings of the socio-political order, and the internal feelings and imaginative concepts of the individual actor."[29] Although it is precisely the nature of this switch point that Evans-Pritchard finds obscure, Munn is clearly attempting to find rooted in Durkheim a dialectical relationship between two irreducible entities, the individual's subjective state and the communal order, a dialectic mediated therefore by the collective representations generated and appropriated in the cult.

Sahlins has also looked for a synthetic reintegration of thought and action, self and society within Durkheim's theory and not found it. He argues that Durkheim's collective representations fail to mediate at all. Rather, as idealized representations of social values and structures, they merely act upon subjective states to mold them. For Sahlins, Durkheim's collective representations are unable to mediate or rearticulate individual experience within social categories; all they can do is simply appropriate and organize it into a "metalanguage."[30] In a somewhat similar argument, Lévi-Strauss suggested that Durkheim lacked an "adequate" notion of a symbol and symbolic action.[31] That is, in contrast to how symbols function, Durkheim's collective representations are mere signs, idealizations of the forms of social morphology that have become independent of these forms, and thus act solely to subordinate and structure individual perception and experience.[32]

Ultimately, Sahlins and Lévi-Strauss find Durkheim's theory of cult and ritual action less than complete for two reasons: first, it does not generate a level of cultural analysis as such; and second, it does not overcome the fundamental duality that resurfaced for Durkheim even in his portrayal of human nature itself. "This is the objective foundation of the idea of the soul: Those representations whose flow constitutes our interior life are of two different species which are irreducible one into another. Some concern themselves with the external and material world; others, with an ideal world to which we attribute a moral superiority over the first." For Durkheim, therefore, "we are really made up of two beings facing in different and almost contrary directions, one of whom exercises a real pre-eminence over the other. Such is the profound meaning of the antithesis which all men have more or less clearly conceived between the body and the soul, the material and the spiritual beings who coexist within us."[33]

Whether Durkheim provides a complete notion of ritual or not, we can see in his work and in the arguments of those reading him a tendency to isolate two types of sociocultural processes or entities and then to seek in ritual theory a model of their necessary reintegration. Indeed, given any initial avowal or assumption of such differentiated processes, a theoretician would have to come up with some phenomenon structured to mediate them if it did not already exist. Hence, I am suggesting that descriptions of how rituals work have been constructed according to a logic rooted in the dynamics of theoretical speculation and the unconscious manipulation of the thought–action dichotomy is intrinsic to this construction.

Saussure could not see how his initial distinctions radically limited the descriptive power of his system. Likewise, we do not see how such dichotomies as continuity and change, individual experience and social forms, and beliefs and behavior invoke an assumption about thought and action that runs particularly deep in the intellectual traditions of Western culture. We do not see that we are wielding a particularly powerful analytical tool, nor do we see how our unconscious manipulation of it is driven not only by the need to resolve the dichotomy it establishes, but also simultaneously to affirm *and* resolve the more fundamental opposition it poses—the opposition between the theoretician and the object of theoretical discourse. In other words, we do not see how such dichotomies contribute to the relational definition of a knower, a known, and a particular type of knowledge.

Geertz and the Window of Ritual

To clarify the relationship between dichotomies and dialectics within the structure of ritual theory, a fuller example is needed to demonstrate how a coherent discourse on ritual is generated. The work of Geertz provides an excellent extended illustration for this purpose. Geertz has been a major influence in the study of religion and ritual, as well as a navigator for many through the shoals and reefs of various methodological issues. This is due in part to the symmetry of his terminology, its appeal to common sense, and his richly anecdotal ethnographies in which texture and nuance appear to defy ethnographic reductionism.

Geertz maintains that the thrust of his theoretical approach is the explanation of "meaning" in cultural phenomena.[34] With this focus he wishes to go beyond the functional or mechanistic analyses of human activity that he correlates with the reductionism of subordinating either the social to the cultural or vice versa.[35] Basic to this project is a distinction between "ethos" and "worldview." Ethos designates the moral and aesthetic aspects of a culture—a people's "underlying attitude toward themselves and their world."[36] Elsewhere Geertz describes ethos in terms of "dispositions," defined not as activity but as the likelihood of activity taking place under certain circumstances. Such dispositions are, in turn, further differentiated into two kinds: moods and motivations.[37] Worldview, on the other hand, indicates for Geertz the "cognitive, existential aspects" of a culture, a people's sense of the really real, their most comprehensive idea of a general order of existence.[38] Understood in this way, these two terms clearly lend themselves to a polarization in which ethos is to worldview as action is to thought.

At times Geertz explicitly correlates religious ritual with ethos and religious belief with worldview, thus invoking the first structural pattern in which ritual is taken for activity in contrast to belief as thought.[39] At other times he presents ethos and worldview as synthesized, fused, or stored in symbols that are arranged in various systems, patterns, or control mechanisms such as ritual, art, religion, language, and myth.[40] However, these systems do not only store a synthesis of ethos and worldview; they are also seen to effect it. Geertz argues with regard to ritual that "any religious ritual no matter how apparently automatic or conventional... involves this symbolic fusion of ethos and world view."[41] Here the second structural pattern appears in which ritual involves the integration of thought and action categories.

The dialectical nature of this fusion of ethos and worldview is made clear in Geertz's related discussion of symbolic systems, such as religion, which involve both "models for" and "models of" reality. These systems are "culture patterns." That is, they "give meaning... [or] objective form, to social and psychological reality both by shaping themselves to it and by shaping it to themselves."[42] With regard to ritual per se, Geertz suggests that "it is in some sort of ceremonial form—even if that form be hardly more than the re- citation of a myth, the consultation of an oracle, or the decoration of a grave—that the moods and motivations which sacred symbols induce in men and the general conceptions of the order of existence which they formulate for men meet and reinforce one another." He goes on: "In ritual, the world as lived and the world as imagined, fused under the agency of a single set of symbolic forms, turns out to be the same world."[43]

Here the simplest ritual activities are seen to "fuse" a people's conceptions of order and their dispositions (moods and motiva- tions) for action. For Geertz, this opposition of conceptions and dispositions, or the world as imagined and the world as lived, con- stitutes cultural life per se. Moreover, our perception and analysis of their opposition and resolution constitute a theoretical expla- nation of 'meaning' in culture. Indeed, failure to grasp the inter- action of these two fundamentally differentiated categories— conceptions and dispositions—is tantamount to the reductionism that Geertz specifically decries, the reductionism of the social to the cultural or the cultural to the social.[44] Thus, the dichotomous nature of conceptions of order (worldview) and dispositions for action (ethos) is fundamental to Geertz's approach, as is their resolution in such symbolic systems as ritual. The temporary resolution of a dichotomy is cast as the central dynamic of cultural life.

So far this analysis of Geertz has simply invoked the two struc- tural patterns discussed earlier. However, Geertz also reveals a third pattern and the further implications of his model of ritual. He goes on to explain that cultural performances such as religious ritual are "not only the point at which the dispositional and conceptual as- pects of religious life converge *for the believer,* but also the point at which the interaction between them can be most readily examined *by the detached observer.*"[45]

What does he mean by this? Since ritual enacts, performs, or objectifies religious beliefs (action gives expression to thought) and in so doing actually fuses the conceptual and the dispositional as- pects of religious symbols (ritual integrates thought and action), Geertz must be concluding that ritual offers a special vantage point for the theorist to observe these processes. Why and how, we might ask, does ritual work to facilitate the theorist's project? The answer is left implicitly in Geertz's text. To answer explicitly, we need to retrace the homologizations that silently push his argument forward.

Outsiders, states Geertz, will see in ritual only the mere presentation of a particular religious perspective which they may appreciate aesthetically or analyze scientifically.[46] Neither response, he implies, penetrates to the real meaning and dynamics of such a cultural phenomenon. For participants, on the other hand, rites are "enactments, materializations, realizations" of a particular religious perspective, "not only models of what they believe, but also models for the believing of it."[47] Thus, the outsider has only conceptual categories with which he or she approaches the ritual activity. Participants, in contrast, actually experience in the rite the integration of their own conceptual framework and dispositional imperatives. In this argument, Geertz is setting up a third structural pattern and a third permutation of the thought–action dichotomy. That is, ritual participants act, whereas those observing them think. In ritual activity, conceptions and dispositions are fused for the participants, which yields meaning. Meaning for the outside theorist comes differently: insofar as he or she can perceive in ritual the true basis of its meaningfulness for the ritual actors—that is, its fusion of conceptual and dispositional categories—then the theorist can go beyond mere thoughts about activity to grasp the meaningfulness of the ritual. By recognizing the ritual mechanism of meaningfulness for participants, the theorist in turn can grasp its meaningfulness as a cultural phenomenon. Ritual activity can then become meaningful to the theorist. Thus, a cultural focus on ritual activity renders the rite a veritable window on the most important processes of cultural life.[48]

Slipping in by virtue of its homologization with the other two structural patterns, the third one organizes the argument in such a way that the theoretical explanation of 'meaning' is itself a fusion of thought and action—the theorist's thought (conceptual categories) and the activity of the ritual participants (which is also a fusion of conceptions and dispositions in its own right). Herein lies the implicit structural homology: the fusion of thought and action described within ritual is homologized to a fusion of the theoretical project and its object, ritual activity. Both generate meaning—the first for the ritual actor and the second for the theorist.

Another example of an argument for a particular relationship between the project of the outside observer and the project of the ritual is laid out by Theodore Jennings.[49] Jennings describes ritual as, first of all, a display to an observer (god, theorist, etc.) or observers (the community itself) and, second, as an epistemological project. Both of these dimensions of ritual act as a "point of contact" between the rite and the attempt by outside observers to grasp a "theoretical-critical understanding of it."[50] We need not castigate our pursuit of the meaning of ritual as "voyeurism or whoring," Jennings asserts, since our cognitive concerns are simply an "extension" of those of the ritual we are "invited" to watch.[51]

All the delicate assumptions of Jennings's approach find their inevitable contrast in Stephen Greenblatt's account of the epistemological project of the amateur ethnographer Captain John G. Bourke. Bourke "witnessed among the Zuñi Indians extreme and simultaneous violations of the codes governing food and waste, and hence experienced extreme disgust." His reaction, Greenblatt speculates, was "not simply an occupational hazard; after all, it is the ethnographer's nausea that gives him his particular discursive field." The parameters of Bourke's lengthy 1891 opus, *Scatologic Rites of All Nations,* were defined, asserts Greenblatt, "precisely by the rising of his gorge." "It would be absurd," he continues, "to conclude that a similar, if better disguised, revulsion lies at the constitutive moment of *all* ethnography, but one may easily find other and more respectable instances than the work of Captain Bourke, in which aversion serves to transform behavior and material substances into the objects of representation and interpretation."[52]

Greenblatt suggests that Bourke instinctively depended on his revulsion to define his epistemological project and the 'otherness' it both required and established. Geertz and Jennings, in contrast, would have us depend on the essential congruity or likeness of doing ritual and generating theoretical interpretations of ritual to establish both our difference from and access to the "other."

2

Constructing Meaning

The result, for Geertz, of the convergence of concepts and dispositions effected by ritual is the theorist's understanding of the cultural meaning of a ritual. What is this meaning exactly? What does it render meaningful and meaningless? Citing Milton Singer, Geertz suggests how the convergence effected in ritual enables one to understand the way in which people regard their religion as "encapsulated" in specific performances that can be performed for visitors and themselves.[53] He quotes with much approval a well-known passage by Singer: "Whenever Madrasi Brahmins (and non-Brahmins, too, for that matter) wished to exhibit to me some features of Hinduism, they always referred to, or invited me to see, a particular rite or ceremony in the life cycle, in a temple festival, or in the general sphere of religious and cultural performances. Reflecting on this in the course of my interviews and observations I found that the more abstract generalizations about Hinduism (my own as well as those I heard) could generally be checked, directly or indirectly, against these observable performances."[54]

Singer's comments are presented as the discovery of an insightful method. They are also, however, an excellent example of the naturalness of the thought–action dichotomy in ritual discourse. First, in regard to Hinduism, he says that the Hindus have rites which they can enact or exhibit, whereas the researcher has concepts which can be thought or talked about. As a consequence of this distinction, the particularity of any one local ritual is contrasted with the more embracing, abstract generalizations of the researcher. Second, such rites are seen not only as very particular

30

enactments of that abstract totality, Hinduism, but they are also portrayed as enactments exhibited *to others* for evaluation or appropriation in terms of their more purely theoretical knowledge. Third, because enactment of the rite is already implicitly construed as effecting an integration for participants between a supposed conceptual totality (Hinduism) and the practical needs of a particular time and place (the dispositions within the ritual context), the researcher easily sees in the exhibition of these rites for theoretical interpretation an equally effective convergence of theory and practice on another level—our conceptual abstractions integrated with their specific practices.

Thus, a model of ritual based upon our two structural patterns—in which ritual is both activity and the fusion of thought and activity—ultimately involves a third pattern, one in which the dichotomy underlying a thinking theorist and an acting actor is simultaneously affirmed and resolved. It is this homologization that makes ritual appear to provide such a privileged vantage point on culture and the meaningfulness of cultural phenomena.

To question Geertz's or Singer's appreciation of the way that ritual obliges the detached observer is to discover that ritual does so by virtue of those very features with which it has been theoretically constituted in the first place. Again we are faced with the question raised by Jameson: To what extent is the object of study the thought pattern of the theorist rather than the supposed object, ritual?

We have seen in Geertz's work not only the two patterns of the thought–action dichotomy described here but a third one as well. First, ritual was said to dramatize, enact, materialize, or perform a system of symbols. This formulation invokes the notion that activity is a secondary, physical manifestation or expression of thought. Second, by enacting the symbolic system, ritual was said to integrate two irreducible aspects of symbols, the conceptual (worldview) and the dispositional (ethos). In this way a thought–action dichotomy is inscribed within the opposing sociocultural forces that Geertz isolates in order to be subsequently resolved in the performance of the rite. On a third level, or in a third structural pattern, ritual as performance likewise enables the integration of the theorist's abstract conceptual categories and the cultural particularity of the rite. With this third level or pattern, the thought–action dichotomy has differentiated native ritual as activity from the thought of the theorist, while casting the resolution of this thought–action opposition in a theoretical grasp of the meaning of the ritual acts. What constitutes meaning for the ritual actors is seen as the integration of their conceptual and dispositional orientations that takes place in ritual. What constitutes meaning for the theorist is the same model, the integration of his or her conceptual categories with the ritual dispositions of the native actors, an integration afforded by proper analysis of ritual.

To restate the structure of this argument more formally is to make ludicrously explicit a type of logic that is effective only when left unexamined. Most simply, we might say, ritual is to the symbols it dramatizes as action is to thought; on a second level, ritual integrates thought and action; and on a third level, a focus on ritual performances integrates *our* thought and *their* action. The opposition of the theorist and the ritual object becomes homologized with two other oppositions, namely, the opposition that differentiates ritual (beliefs versus activities) and the opposition of two fundamental sociocultural forces that is resolved by ritual (conceptual versus dispositional forces). This homology is achieved by a hidden appeal to a type of common denominator, the opposition of thought and action. In the end, a model of ritual that integrates opposing sociocultural forces becomes homologized to a mode of theoretical discourse that reintegrates the dichotomy underlying the identification of a thinking theorist and an acting object.

This type of expedient logic carries another inevitable corollary, however. That is, theories of ritual which attempt to integrate thought and action in any guise simultaneously function to maintain their differentiation. This type of discourse on ritual not only constructs a model that integrates a thinking observer and an acting object; it simultaneously functions to distinguish them clearly. The resolution of a dichotomy functions to affirm the polarity of the terms involved. The implications, therefore, of differentiating a subject and object on the basis of thought and action are rather striking and present some interesting ramifications to be examined later in the next chapter. At this point, a final example further illustrates the circular logic built up by these homologies and the theory of ritual that emerges.

When Ritual Fails

In his study of a Javanese funeral ceremony, Geertz ventured to analyze "a ritual which failed to function properly."[55] The analysis is simple and compelling. He begins by discussing the inability of functionalism to deal with social change and transformational social processes.[56] The reason for this, he suggests, is the tendency of functional theory to identify social conflict as disintegration and to treat sociological and cultural processes unequally, reducing either one to the other.[57] Such reductionism makes it impossible to articulate social change, which arises in "the failure of cultural patterns to be perfectly congruent with the forms of social organizations."[58]

Thus, to develop theoretical tools capable of analyzing social change, Geertz wishes to distinguish clearly between culture and the social system. He defines culture "as an ordered system of meaning and of symbols, in terms of which social interaction takes place." The social system, on the other hand, is "the pattern of social interaction itself."[59] The conceptual-dispositional nature of this distinction is made apparent when he further describes them as a "framework of beliefs" in contrast to ongoing processes of "interactive behavior." Culture is the set of meaningful terms people use for interpretation and guidance; social system is the actual "form that action takes."[60]

With these categories and a great deal of contextual detail, Geertz analyses the particular failure of funeral services held after the sudden death of a young boy. He considers the funeral rites to have failed for the following reasons: first, they heightened tension and distress in the community rather than producing the usual effects of *iklas,* a detached acceptance of death, and *rukun,* communal harmony; second, the usual Islamic procedures were not followed due to a local officiant's sense of conflict between these practices and the politics of a new group to which the household of the boy belonged; and third, the modifications desperately introduced in order to proceed with a funeral of some sort were ad hoc, unauthorized, and initiated by individual enterprise rather than by consensus.[61]

Geertz concludes that the conflict which surfaced at the funeral was the result of a growing discontinuity between the community's cultural framework of beliefs and the actual patterns of social interaction. That is, community members were urbanites who still thought like villagers, expecting village values to fit increasingly urban forms of organization behind which quite different values were actually operative.[62] Geertz argues that a conflict between the community's cultural categories (beliefs and values) and their customary social behavior (group affiliation) emerged in the funeral.

This example illustrates the expedient homologizing and collapsing of levels of analysis that can make an interpretation appear so effective.[63] Geertz's initial discussion contrasts the functionalism of sociological and social-psychological approaches with an approach that can articulate the dynamics of change in positive terms. Within the space of just a few paragraphs, however, these contrasting analytical perspectives have been rendered loosely equivalent to a distinction between sociological and cultural processes that Geertz argues should be considered independently and treated equally. These processes are then described as the forces that are mobilized and brought to confrontation in ritual. Since a ritual that does not work is identified as one in which cultural and sociological categories are experienced as discontinuous, we are led to assume that successful rituals are those in which these terms or forces are "perfectly congruent."

Geertz has done two things in this analysis. First, the two methodological perspectives (the sociological and the cultural) have been homologized with a pair of analytical categories (culture and the social system, as defined by Geertz), which were then found to be those very sundered forces underlying the dynamics of the unsuccessful ritual. This is a collapse of three levels and an implicit identification of three sets of oppositions. Ultimately, the discontinuity affirmed in the conclusion is a direct replication of the differentiation established in the beginning.

Second, there are some implications for ritual. Geertz's usual model of ritual is upheld in this analysis by the implication that a successful ritual is one in which the differentiated forces of culture and the social system can be effectively integrated. In addition, however, if an unsuccessful ritual effects change, then a successful one maintains stasis or no change. Thus, in Geertz's analysis, ritual as an integrative mechanism is also a synchronic force within the society, rendering it roughly equivalent to what he considers 'culture.' Although it is fairly clear that Geertz wants to conclude that ritual facilitates change, he is logically kept from such a conclusion by the description of this rite as a failure and by the pure oppositions that such an unsuccessful ritual leaves unresolved.

The Myth of the Fundamental Contradiction

There are several other ways in which ritual has been cast as a mechanism for the resolution of basic oppositions or contradictions. The most common approach, I have argued, is exemplified in the work of Geertz. A slightly different form can be seen in the work of Max Gluckman and some of V. Turner's analyses. In this approach ritual is the arena in which purely social conflicts are worked out. In general, they describe how social conflict is recognized within the strategic limits of ritual where it can be systematically subsumed within a reaffirmation of unity.

Gregory Bateson and Lévi-Strauss both employ yet another permutation of the approach. For them, the conflict is not as general as that between ethos and worldview, nor is it as simple and concrete as a social conflict between two parties. The problem is identified as one embedded in the social structure, while the ritual solution is a more or less symbolic one that does not effect any real changes. For Bateson, an outstanding feature of the Iatmul *naven* ceremony was the cross-dressing of particular relatives and the specific sexual gesture of the mother's brother. Analyzing these acts and features led Bateson to conclude that the ritual strengthens the tense and ambiguous relationship between a child and his or her mother's family.[64] For his part, Lévi-Strauss saw in the asymmetrical facial paintings of the Caduveo Indians the attempt to resolve a "lived" contradiction, namely, the dilemma of marriage in a rigidly hierarchical society lacking any institutional structure for unrestricted and egalitarian exchange.[65] He suggested that the facial paintings were the "symbolic" expression of an attempt at a compromise since the Caduveo were never really able to articulate and resolve effectively the contradiction in which they were caught.[66] Lévi-Strauss argued that ritual ultimately seeks the resolution of the inherent conflict of culture and nature.

As with Geertz's approach, these theories see ritual as designed to address fundamental conflicts and contradictions in the society, and there is similarly little evidence that the conflicts so addressed are not simply imposed through the categories of the observer. As we have seen, it is quite common for scholars to see ritual as resolving the conflict between thought and action, particularly in the guise of belief systems in conflict with the real world.

'Contradiction' is, of course, a standard Hegelian and Marxist term that figures prominently in analyses of social process.[67] For Marx, contradiction occurs when the forces of material production begin to outstrip the system of social relations to which they earlier gave rise.[68] Other Marxist analyses suggest that the perception of such contradictions can be repressed by the generation of ideological structures. Thus, cultural artifacts such as Caduveo face paintings or works of literature are seen as expressions of this repressed but lived contradiction, expressions that embody the contradiction while attempting to resolve some version of it. For Marxists and many cultural anthropologists, therefore, a basic contradiction at the root of social experience provides the impulse for the generation of a variety of integral social phenomena—historical change and revolution, or culture itself with its arts and institutions.[69] Whether the emphasis is on how such fundamental contradictions are repressed or expressed, displaced or resolved, they are usually linked to "fissures" of a type that provide the theorist with an interpretive *entré* into the ideological structures of a society, an activity, or a cultural artifact.

Lévi-Strauss and Bourdieu talk of "fundamental oppositions" that generate various oppositional series, which can all be reduced in turn to the most fundamental opposition. In some passages these fundamental oppositions do not seem to mean much in themselves but are effective for the internal organization of taxonomic schemes that generate the sense of a coherent cultural unity.[70] That is, such oppositions are not basic or fundamental in the sense of being underlying or absolute social, metaphysical, or logical values; rather, they are particularly useful tools for invoking and manipulating the taxonomic schemes of a culture. Bourdieu also describes ritual's role in effecting change in terms of how it breaks up the 'natural' taxonomic order so as to impose the reordering of 'culture.' Ritual, he states, always aims to facilitate and authorize passages or encounters between opposed orders, presumably the orders of nature and culture or, equally reified, the old order and the new order.[71]

In this general type of argument the notion of a fundamental social contradiction appears highly suspicious—at least by virtue of the way in which the imposition of a neat logical structure renders ritual action amenable to theoretical analysis. Certainly, the identification of a contradiction *out there* at the root of culture and society also works to construct an object and method of analysis by which theory can be seen to grasp and explain the puzzles that 'the other' simply lives. Roy Wagner states that "anthropology is theorized and taught so as to *rationalize* contradiction, paradox and dialectic."[72] Indeed, contradiction in some form is readily presumed in order to mandate the rational exercises, resolutions, and breakthroughs of theory. The notion that ritual resolves a fundamental social contradiction can be seen as a type of myth legitimating the whole apparatus of ritual studies.

Equally mythical, perhaps, is the notion that there is anything fundamental. As a counterpart in logic to the search for origins in historical studies, the notion of a fundamental force or conflict also functions suspiciously like some key to understanding. In an exasperated tone, Foucault has declared that "nothing is fundamental" and *that,* he continues, is what is really interesting about social phenomena: "There are only reciprocal relations, and the perpetual gaps between intentions in relation to one another."[73]

In the interests of identifying such seductive myths and exploring truly alternative conceptions of ritual activity, it is probably more useful to proceed with the notion that ritual is *not* some basic mechanism for resolving or disguising conflicts fundamental to sociocultural life. However, as I will explore in Parts II and III, the strategies of ritual may well generate the sense of a basic and compelling conflict or opposition in light of which other contrasts are orchestrated.

"Performance" and Other Analogies

In recent years the notion of 'cultural performance' has become increasingly popular as a category and general approach. This popularity appears to have been nourished by a variety of sources. Foremost among these are Kenneth Burke's notion of "dramatism," V. Turner's work on social dramas, the multiplication of categories such as "civil ceremonial" and "secular rites," work on the sociology of role playing along with Erving Goffman's interaction rituals and, last but not least, perhaps, J. L. Austin's and John Searle's analyses of "speech acts."[74]

In its own way, performance theory signals a strong dissatisfaction with the traditional categories brought to the study of ritual. At the same time, however, its focus on ritual, theater, or sports as 'genres' or 'universals' of performance appears to involve the construction of very traditional types of relationships and categories.[75] Some performance theorists have explicitly aspired "to transcend such conventional dichotomies as oral and written, public and private, doing and thinking, primitive and modern, sacred and secular."[76] Clearly these dichotomies have contributed to the perception that theoretical analysis is failing to convey something important about how ritual activities are generated and experienced. Grimes has rued how "foreign" ritual has become for us, while V. Turner echoed D. H. Lawrence's quip that "analysis presupposes a corpse."[77] Turner, in particular, repeatedly argued that a "living quality frequently fails to emerge from our pedagogics."[78] More specifically, Sherry Ortner suggests that frustration with structural linguistics was responsible for this turning to how language communicates via performance.[79] Robert Wuthnow supports this idea by explicitly contrasting dramaturgical and structural approaches to analyzing culture. The former, he argues, which focuses on ritual in the broadest sense, is able to incorporate the social dimension lost to structural analysis.[80] For Wuthnow, the dramaturgical approach recasts the problem of meaning by affording a shift from analysis of the subjective or semantic meaning of symbols to analysis of the conditions under which symbolic acts are meaningful.[81]

Despite their insights into the problems of ritual theory, neither Wuthnow nor the others cited effectively break free of a theoretical framework in which activity is seen as dramatizing or enacting prior conceptual entities in order to reaffirm or reexperience them. Grimes, for example, argues "the primacy of the human body" in ritual studies, but he equates this primacy with the body's "capacity to *enact* social roles and body forth cultural meanings."[82] Although the notion of performance appears to many to offer some solution to the way in which theory fails to grasp action, as a whole the contributions of performance theory and terminology to the formulation of an approach that does not dichotomize doing and thinking remain somewhat obscure. Indeed, the performance approach appears to suggest a further exaggeration of the structured relations between thinking theorist and acting object which I have already examined.

Performance theorists frequently base themselves on two interrelated points originally articulated by Singer. First, as noted previously, people "think of their culture as encapsulated within discrete performances, which they can exhibit to outsiders as well as to themselves." Second, such performances constitute for the outside observer "the most concrete observable units of the cultural structure"—since each performance "has a definitely limited time span, a beginning and an end, an organized program of activity, a set of performers, an audience, and a place and occasion of performance."[83] Although such statements do not constitute an agenda for systematic analysis, they are more than a simple application of the "drama analogy" with its whole system of terms, relationships, and assumptions.[84] Singer did not merely suggest an approach to ritual that guarantees direct access to native units of experience and clear observation of sociocultural processes; he also defined culture itself in terms of those very activities that appear to provide such clear access and observation. That is, cultural performances are the ways in which the cultural content of a tradition "is organized and transmitted on particular occasions through specific media."[85] Thus, these performances are the specific and particular manifestations ('instances') of culture aside from which culture is just an abstract category.[86] However, if culture is the giving of performances, then culture is that which is given to an 'audience' or the outside theorist who has joined it. Researchers and theorists are repositioned in performance theory: no longer peering in through the window, they are now comfortably seated as members of the audience for whom the performance is being presented. As such, the theorist-observer has become an important participant, one who is integral both to the actors' ability to act culturally (i.e., to perform) and to their ability to understand their own culture (since such understanding is the result of expressing their general cultural orientations in discrete ritual activities).

In some cases, performance theory appears to promote an even more intense mode of participation. In discussing ritual and social drama, for example, Turner calls for the "performance of ethnography" by both anthropologists and professional actors.[87] John MacAloon refers to the "performance" given by academic participants at a symposium that resulted in the book he subtitled "Rehearsals Toward a Theory of Cultural Performance."[88] Grimes finds that the activities of scattered experiments in improvisational theater are "crucial both to the practice and study of religion, particularly ritual studies."[89]

This enhanced participation of the scholar-observer takes an interesting form in Grimes's development of the project of "ritual criticism." Ritual criticism is loosely modeled on the relationship of literary criticism to literature and on cultural-critical developments in anthropology (as described by Marcus and Fischer). Moreover, Grimes's critical evaluation of ritual can be conducted in a variety of ways: through indigenous forms of emic criticism, etic forms by scholars or foreign critics, and even criticism of one religious tradition by another. In another formulation, he contrasts the criticism practiced by rites and ritualists themselves with the critical activities of "ritologists."[90] The position of the critical observer, Grimes suggests, should be neither scientifically neutral nor theologically normative; the purpose of critical observation is to aid in the recognition of ritual exploitation on the one hand or appropriate revision and borrowing of ritual practices on the other.[91] It appears that two concerns are central to Grimes's project: first, an appreciation of the inadequacy of earlier models of participant–observer relations and, second, a real sense of shared purpose between participants and critics. What Jennings saw as a shared "epistemological" project, Grimes would appear to embrace as a shared project of both cultural critique and reflexive self-observation.

Performance terminology has been used in a wide variety of ways. By far the most cautious performance position was laid out by the British anthropologist Gilbert Lewis. According to Lewis, our tendency to be preoccupied with the intellectual aspects of responses to ritual (i.e., deciphering the meaning of its coded messages) leads us to overlook more immediate sensory responses. He suggests "likening" ritual to the performance of a play or a piece of music, but he cautions against using such insights into ritual to define it.[92]

If Lewis has been the most cautious of those who invoke performance, then V. Turner was certainly one of the most enthusiastic. Yet Turner's late work on ritual and performance remains fundamentally within the framework of his early theory of ritual as the transformational dialectic of structure and antistructure (or organization and communitas) to serve as a vehicle for unfolding social dramas.[93] Social dramas are embodied in ritual, where they have paradigmatic functions that make clear the deepest values of the culture. In Turner's view, such paradigmatic functions also serve to provide the outsider with a "limited area of transparency in the otherwise opaque surface of regular, uneventful social life."[94] This is the same "window of ritual" evoked by Geertz.

Performance theory probably has one of its most sophisticated presentations in the work of Stanley Tambiah. Tambiah explicitly reacts against the opposition of thought and action and suggests that the devaluation of action embedded in the distinction can be redressed by a focus on performance.[95] Like Ortner and Wuthnow, he argues that the social dimension becomes more accessible through performance theory. Tambiah is particularly concerned, in fact, that the significance of the semantic structure of words and acts not lead us to ignore the significance of social relations both within the ritual itself and within the larger context of the rite.[96] He breaks with the Durkheimian approach developed by Gluckman and V. Turner in arguing that ritual does not evoke feelings or express the mental orientation of individuals in any sort of direct and spontaneous way. Rather, he emphasizes the formalism of ritual as having a distancing effect that serves to articulate and communicate attitudes of institutionalized communication.[97] Tambiah's appreciation for the social dimension also leads him to amend Austin and Searle by explicating the necessary social conditions under which "saying is doing" and ritual is "a mode of social action."[98] Saying is just saying and formalized acts are idiosyncratic, he argues, unless they conform to established social conventions and subject themselves to judgments of legitimacy.[99]

Tambiah distinguishes three ways in which ritual is performative:

(1) it involves doing things, even if the doing is saying in the Austinian sense; (2) it is staged and uses multiple media to afford participants an intense experience; and (3) it involves indexical values in the sense laid out by Pierce. The indexical features of ritual are seen in its graded scale of ostentatiousness, the choice of site, the degree of redundancy or elaboration, and so on, all of which present and validate the social hierarchy indirectly depicted by them. As a system of communication, ritual involves both indexical features that refer to the social hierarchy and symbolic features that refer to the cosmos. Indeed, Tambiah goes on to elaborate a series of opposing features mobilized in ritual, including semantic/referential components versus pragmatic components, form versus content, the cultural and the universal, and indexical symbolism versus indexical iconicity.[100] Thus, despite his focus on performance and his concerns about the thought–action dichotomy, he also is drawn into the familiar dilemma of setting out to transcend one bifurcation only to generate others that find their integration in ritual as a mechanism for fusing theoretical distinctions.[101]

Performance theory rests of course on the slippery implications of an extended metaphor, specifically the analogy between ritual activities and the acts of performing and dramatizing. While it offers a new descriptive vantage point on aspects of ritual activities, as a paradigm or model it is gravely disadvantaged in several ways. First, the increased naturalization of the outside observer that is obtained in the very definition of act as performance takes the relationship between subject and object constructed by the theorist and inscribes it into the nature of the object itself. In other words, ritual comes to be seen as performance in the sense of symbolic acts specifically meant to have an impact on an audience and entreat their interpretive appropriation. Second, the notion of performance as a theoretical tool for approaching certain activities comes to be used as descriptive of the fundamental nature of those activities; in other words, a model of ritual activity provides the criteria for what is or is not ritual. Third, although performance may become a criterion for what is or is not ritual, insofar as performance is broadly used for a vast spectrum of activities, there is no basis to differentiate among ways of performing. An initial focus on the performative aspects of ritual easily leads to the difficulty of being unable to distinguish how ritual is not the same as dramatic theater or spectator sports.[102]

Rappaport attempts to avoid some of these problems when he maintains that ritual is not drama, although performance, like formality, is a sine qua non of ritual.[103] In this way he holds on to the primacy of doing and acting that a performance focus promises, but he does not succumb to the slippage of explaining by analogy. In a somewhat similar vein, Emily Ahern also challenges the description of ritual as a dramatization that is meant to affect the participants as opposed to the external world.[104] In so doing, she points to an interesting problem inherent in the performance metaphor: Since performance theory denies any validity to indigenous claims that certain actions *affect* the gods, the harvest, or anything beyond the dispositions of the actors and audience, how much epistemological sharing can there actually be between Chinese participants and Western interpreters concerning the type of project at stake in a Chinese "soul-settling" ceremony?

Performance theorists, of course, argue that what ritual does is communicate (and hence, it does not secure the intercession of deities, pacify the dead, or encourage rain, etc.) and it is through this function that ritual indirectly affects social realities and perceptions of those realities. However, when performance theory attempts to explain such communication it must fall back on ritual activity as depicting, modeling, enacting, or dramatizing what are seen as prior conceptual ideas and values. The meaningfulness of ritual that such interpretations attempt to explicate has nothing to do with the efficacy that the ritual acts are thought to have by those who perform them. The idiom of communication through symbolic acts maybe a corrective to the notion of magic, but it does little to convey what these acts mean to those involved in them.

In his famous discussion of "blurred genres," Geertz looks at three popular analogies adopted by the social sciences to interpret social behavior.[105] He begins with the "game" analogy, then goes on to explore the "drama" analogy, and finally turns to the "text" analogy. The drama analogy, he suggests, affords an appreciation of certain features of action, specifically its temporality, collectivity, public nature, and power to transmute not just opinions but people themselves. However, it lumps all types of social action together as having the same form without any ability to appreciate the differences in content. The game and text analogies likewise illuminate certain features and confuse others. All of these analogies, he argues, are examples of a cases-and-interpretations approach to social theory, rather than the older laws-and-instances approach. Thus, they are concerned with interpretation and meaning, specifically, what "all the usual objects of social-scientific interest" mean to those who are immediately involved in them.[106] Yet it is not at all clear that this actually is the type of meaning derived from the theoretical deployment of these analogies. While Geertz finds that "religious symbols . . . reek of meaning," Tambiah has his doubts.[107] Tambiah rejects such "intentionality" theories as inadequate to the interpretation of formalized and conventionalized action and finds the various conceptions of meaning in anthropology a "deadly source of confusion."[108] With the exception of Tambiah, however, the popularity of performance metaphors and theories represents something of a consensus about "meaning" as a specifically hermeneutical conception.

In the same vein, Marcus and Fischer suggest that the popularity of ritual as a theoretical focus is based on how readily a public performance can be *read like a text*.[109] The text analogy is used explicitly in Alton Becker's study of Indonesian *wayang* performances as "text-building." It is more implicit in James Fernandez's study (with its echoes of Boas and Burke) of ritual as the strategic deployment of a metaphor.[110] In both cases, however, the interpretative hermeneutic brought to bear on ritual approaches the rite as if it were a text. In his essay "Deep Play," Geertz also explicitly approaches ritualized activities as a text to be decoded.[111] Yet he concludes his later comparison of blurred genres with a recognition of the particular dangers and implausibility of the text analogy. Its application to action is, Geertz argues, an example of "a thoroughgoing conceptual wrench."[112] Hinting at the problems involved in the readiness to decode ritual, Geertz nearly echoes some of Tambiah's reservations after all.

Paul Ricoeur has argued both systematically and pointedly that "meaningful action" is indeed like a text, delineating criteria for textuality that meaningful action also fulfills.[113] For the most part, however, the textual analogy is usually applied with much less clarity. Moreover, the analogy tends to be based not on the assertion of a similarity between texts and rites but on the similarity of the interpretive position of the theorist in each case. In fact, if we think in terms of the mode of interpretation rather than the similarities of such objects as rite, drama, and text, the text analogy can be seen to underlie the drama analogy and be quite basic to performance theory.

Certainly there is a general tendency in the social sciences to 'textualize' the objects of its concern. Such textualization, according to Jameson, is "a methodological hypothesis whereby the objects of study of the human sciences ... are considered to constitute so many texts which we *decipher* and *interpret,* as distinguished from the older view of those objects as realities or existants or substances which we in one way or another attempt to know."[114] We textualize, he implies, not because rites are intrinsically like texts, but because we approach both looking for meaning as something that can be deciphered, decoded, or interpreted. Developing Geertz's contrast between "law-and-instances" and "cases-and-interpretation" styles of analysis, one might suppose that the shift in cultural studies away from the model of science and the dogma of scientific objectivity has been essentially based on an interpretive-textual model.[115]

Yet the interpretive project, whether conducted in literary criticism or anthropology, carries some important assumptions. Foremost among them are the assumptions that the text (rite or another example of meaningful social action) is autonomous and unified on the one hand, and that its latent meaning is fully accessible to a close reading of its manifest form on the other.[116] Both assumptions present problems when it comes to the avowed benefits of a performance approach to ritual. For example, the emphasis on the *activity* of ritual which performance theory attempts to develop may actually be something of an illusion. The interpretive endeavor requires, and assumes, that activity encodes something. As the foregoing thought–action argument illustrated, the assumed existence of such a 'something,' the latent meaning of the act, once again devalues the action itself, making it a second-stage representation of prior values.

It has been suggested that the reasons for the shift to a performance approach, with its underlying interpretive-textual paradigm, are the perceived failures of earlier models and the greater explanative power, particularly in terms of social dimensions, of the new paradigm. The performance paradigm deserves a thorough assessment of its "merits as a concept," as Leach would say, and the results might vindicate this explanation of its popularity. Yet it is also possible to see some basis for its popularity in the distinctive imagery of performance theory (that of a sensitive and appreciative participant interpreter, not a coldly detached, analytic scientist) and in the greater obscurity of the slippage involved (how much more readily 'performance' slips from being a tool for analysis to being a feature of the object and thereby validates an approach and a whole discourse). While it is this type of slippage that affords the expedient logic on which many theories of ritual are based, this imagery is an equally powerful incentive for ritual studies.

3

Constructing Discourse

The preceding chapter suggested that there is a logic of sorts to most theoretical discourse on ritual and that this discourse is fundamentally organized by an underlying opposition between thought and action. Although initially employed to afford a heuristic focus on ritual as a type of activity, this fundamental dichotomy helps to generate a series of homologized oppositions that come to include the relationship between the theorist and the actors. At the same time, ritual is portrayed as mediating or integrating all these oppositions. Constituting ritual in this way involves a particular structuring of the subject's relationship with its object. It is not simply a matter of constituting ritual as an autonomous and general object of study distinct from particular rites—in the way that Saussure constituted linguistics by differentiating language from its actualization or Panofsky established art as objectively distinct from peculiarly valued works.[117] The thought–action dichotomy not only differentiates ritual-as-activity as an object of theoretical attention; it also differentiates a 'thinking' subject from an 'acting' object—or, when pushed to its logical conclusion, a 'thinking' subject from a 'nonthinking' object. Then, in the same way that ritual is seen to reintegrate thought and action in some form, discourse on ritual is seen to afford special access to cultural understanding by integrating the subject's thought and the object's activities.

As demonstrated, this discursive structure can be delineated in a series of three structural patterns. In the first, ritual as activity is differentiated from conceptual categories. In the second, ritual is the cultural medium by which thoughts and acts (or concepts and dispositions, beliefs and behavior, etc.) are reintegrated. In the third, the activities of the object (the actors) and the concepts of the subject (the theorist) are also integrated by means of a discursive focus on the integrative function of ritual. Of course these patterns are not 'logical' in the usual sense of the term. Rather, an initial and often unconscious assumption—to think about ritual as a type of activity—invokes a powerful dichotomy between thought and action that helps in turn to generate a discourse loosely structured but effectively, or persuasively, systematized by the expedient logic of homologized levels of structural patterns.[118]

It is possible that the whole structure of theoretical discourse on ritual primarily serves to solve the problems posed for scholars by their reliance on a distinction between thought and action. It is a distinction used not only to differentiate project and object, method and data, or theory and facts; it also appears to be essential to any so-called theoretical project in the first place and, in a second place, to the generation of meaning or explanation.[119] Thus, an implicit use of the dichotomy may well overdetermine the real problems that remain.

Perhaps the initial generation of polarized distinctions and their subsequent homologous replication is inevitable in the process of analysis or interpretation. Indeed, dichotomization and the systems of practical homologies that such dichotomies can generate are thought to be integral to the fundamental processes of differentiation involved in perception, cognition, and human activity in general. However, a closed and highly structured discourse may be necessary *only* to an attempt to generate and secure bodies of knowledge that have a particular function with regard to the knower and the known: they set up a relationship based on differentiating one from the other while inscribing the basis for this differentiation into the nature of the object itself, that is, the reality of ritual.[120]

In the final analysis the results of such a differentiation between thought and action cannot be presumed to provide an adequate position vis-à-vis human activity as such. Naturally, as many others have argued before, the differentiation tends to distort not only the nature of so-called physical activities, but the nature of mental ones as well. Yet the more subtle and far-reaching distortion is not the obvious bifurcation of a single, complex reality into dichotomous aspects that can exist in theory only. Rather, it is the far more powerful act of subordination disguised in such differentiations, the subordination of act to thought, or actors to thinkers. Indeed, no matter how provisional or heuristic, a distinction between thought and action is not a differentiation between two equally weighted terms. When used, it is rarely intended to be. Despite the seeming equality of abstract distinctions—male–female, black–white, true–false, one–many—such dichotomies are implicitly employed to afford one term some purchase over the other. To perceive this is to grasp differentiation itself *as an activity* and, therefore, to begin to appreciate the strategic activity of theory-making in general.

Let us look at this particular form of theoretical activity more closely. To generate theoretical discourse on culture, or almost any theoretical discourse for that matter, it is necessary to do two things: first, to specify a distinct level or mode of analysis, in this case a 'cultural' level; and second, to identify an object or phenomenon that exists as a 'meaningful totality' only on such a level of analysis. This object will act as the natural object of the specified mode of analysis, although the object so identified is not independent of this analysis; it is constituted and depicted as such in terms of the specified method of analysis. That is, the object and the method are actually intrinsic to each other, one demonstrating the naturalness and validity of the other. As we have seen with ritual, particularly in the extended example drawn from Geertz, the structure of the constituted object is a veritable model of the method of analysis and vice versa.

Mauss provides a particularly clear and concise example of how this process was used to establish a specifically 'sociological' level of analysis, the object of which was, he indicated, "total social phenomena." Mauss argued that his new method sees social systems as wholes, that is, as where "body, soul, society—everything merges." It is only as wholes that the "essence" of the social system is revealed.[121] "We are dealing with something more than a set of themes," he wrote, "more than institutional elements, more than institutions, more even than systems of institutions divisible into legal, economic, religious and other parts. We are concerned with 'wholes', with systems in their entirety." Such wholes cannot be broken down into smaller elements since "it is only by considering them as wholes that we have been able to see their essence, their operation and their living aspect."[122]

Mauss argued that a total social phenomenon such as gift-giving can be analyzed in its totality and essence only through a specifically sociological method of analysis, that is, the study of dynamic metasystems that include legal, economic, religious institutions as well as persons in their sense of themselves as individuals and as a group. It is an inherently circular argument, of course—which is precisely what enables it to demonstrate perfectly the simultaneous construction of an object, a method, and a framework of discourse, all of which reinforce each other.

To establish a level of analysis that is distinctly cultural, one must likewise identify 'cultural facts' that exist as meaningful wholes only on the horizon of this cultural perspective and can be analyzed for the essence of their wholeness only through a specifically cultural method of analysis. We saw that Geertz made "meaning" in "cultural phenomena" the object of his analysis. In his studies this meaning was revealed through a particular method: the initial differentiation of conceptual and dispositional categories, which facilitated a recognition of their fusion (or failure to fuse) in such cultural phenomena as ritual and religion. The method is also a model of the object upon which Geertz focused—namely, ritual as that which fuses conceptual and dispositional categories. Furthermore, the method is the means of identifying a new and specific relationship between a knower and the object known, a relationship that is mediated by a specifically cultural body of knowledge.

The same pattern for constructing object, method, and subject–object relationship can be seen in Hans-Georg Gadamer's or Ricoeur's application of the model of the text to the interpretation of social action.[123] Ricoeur, as noted earlier, specifies four criteria for what constitutes a text: its fixing of meaning, its dissociation from the mental intention of the author, the display of nonostensive references, and the universal range of its addresses.[124] The most pertinent is the objectification that "fixing" in writing brings. Ricoeur goes on to argue that action can be similarly fixed (and it also displays the other three criteria), implying that it is this objectification that renders action open to investigation and hence to meaningfulness. The meaning of the act can be detached from the event of the act in the same way that a text can be detached from its author. This "autonomization," he argues, is the basis of action's social dimension and meaning.[125] As a result, a meaningful action is an action whose importance goes beyond its relevance to its initial situation. In other words, an action can be meaningful only when it is detached from its initial context and objectified as an autonomous entity, and when its autonomous significance is assessed for any relevance or importance that can be addressed to "an indefinite range of possible readers."[126] Ricoeur rightly appreciates how meaning is conferred or awarded when decontextualized entities can prove themselves relevant to the interpreter. And his appreciation of this is based on his understanding of the mediating role of objectification—as the creation of an autonomous "object"—in scientific methodology.

To treat action as a text, Ricoeur argues, is to objectify it and therein disjoin "meaning" from intentionality of the author or actor.[127] This process engenders a first-stage dialectic between *verstehen* and *erklären,* understanding and explanation, guessing and validating, a subjective approach and an objective approach. A second stage involves the reverse dialectic—from explanation to understanding—starting with the referential functions of the action-as-text and moving beyond the ostensive situation (surface-level semantics), via a structural act of distancing, to the depth semantics that will yield an interpretation. For Ricoeur, these depth semantics open up for interpretation the "ultimate referent" of the text action, its "world propositions"—which are not what the text action is saying but what it is talking about.[128] (Note that Geertz also talks about "how the said is rescued from its saying" by the interpreter.)[129] The understanding that results is, of course, "entirely *mediated* by the whole of the explanatory procedures which precede it and accompany it."[130] As a result, this act of hermeneutical understanding does not appropriate a foreign experience; rather, it is an act that appropriates the power to disclose the world that is the true referent of the text.[131]

In this very abbreviated summary, Ricoeur can be seen to lay out the steps for creating an object amenable to a certain type of scrutiny; insofar as the object so constructed and scrutinized is seen to yield a higher, fuller, truer meaning (indeed, its *only* real meaningfulness), it simultaneously constructs and legitimates that method of scrutiny. For Ricoeur, the social dimension of an act is its ability to act outside its initial context and help construct meaningfulness for the interpreter. Ricoeur is very aware that these steps construct a particular discourse, that of hermeneutics per se, and he is self-consciously extending that discourse to address social action. In the end, meaningfulness mediates subject and its object; it constitutes them and is simultaneously constituted by them. The goal of the whole enterprise is clearly the discourse itself, constructed by a winding series of oppositions, homologized, mediated, and redundant. Ultimately, the discourse is a function of meaning and meaning a function of the discourse.

Marcus and Fischer suggest that the trend in anthropology in the last twenty years or so has been a gradual shift away from the construction of grand theories of culture and society to a more interpretive and narrowly focused mode of reflection upon fieldwork, writing, and hermeneutical problems.[132] Quentin Skinner, of course, argues the opposite with regard to the more broadly defined "human sciences."[133] Skinner finds that despite themselves the major "anti-theorists" of the last few decades have generated comprehensive and architectonic theoretical frameworks. Different from the "laws-and-instances" mode of theorizing, as Geertz put it, the more recent style of object-and-discourse construction can appear to its participants as antitheoretical and committed to cultural self-reflection. Indeed, the cultural knowledge constituted in this type of discourse tends to see itself as both salvaging other cultures from Westernization and serving as the basis for the West's own cultural critique.[134]

Roy Wagner, for example, depicts the role of the anthropologist as a "bridge" that mediates two cultures, not merely outsider to both but also inventor of both cultures through the activity of studying and interpreting.[135] In Ricoeur's terms, such a figure is a maker of meaning. For both Wagner and Ricoeur, it is a crucial if slightly melodramatic role. Rereading these types of descriptions, one cannot help but recall Susan Sontag's description of Lévi-Strauss and hear in it more ambivalence today, perhaps, than she intended in 1961.

> He is not, like recent generations of American anthropologists, simply a modest data-collecting "observer." Nor does he have any axe—Christian, rationalist, Freudian, or otherwise—to grind. Essentially he is engaged in saving his own soul, by a curious and ambitious act of

intellectual catharsis.... The anthropologist... acts out a heroic, diligent and complex modern pessimism.[136]

These sentiments are echoed elsewhere: "Anthropology is not the mindless collection of the exotic, but the use of cultural richness for self-reflection and self-growth."[137] Or, "anthropology, reified as the study of man, is the study of men in crisis by men in crisis."[138] "The history of anthropology is a sustained sequitur to the contradiction of its existence as a Western science of other cultures."[139]

Although the question goes beyond the scope of this study, we should make preliminary inquiries into the impetus for this interpretive form of cultural knowledge and discourse. Some possible clues are implicit in the analysis so far. A more or less internal impetus for generating such discourse on culture may well have been the attempt to come to some resolution of the major conflicting forces in the humanities and social sciences in the last three decades. Variously identified, this conflict has usually been seen as a tension between how something functions and what something symbolizes, between intellectualists and symbolists, between utility and meaning, or explanation and understanding.[140] Dell Hymes, for example, has heralded the specific possibility that the study of performance could very well integrate the social sciences and the humanities.[141] Similar sentiments have been expressed by V. Turner and Grimes among others. Yet a sense of commitment to a mode of analysis in which the symbolic tends to dominate the functional is common to most of these theorists.[142] This suggests that the search for integration has been led by the symbolists. We can see in their model of ritual something of the integration they are seeking: apparently equal consideration of differentiated *social* and *cultural* forces illuminates the effective interaction and fusion of these forces within such phenomena as ritual, making apparent the true meaning of cultural phenomena.

An external impetus for cultural knowledge may derive from the fact that the social sciences and humanities are now operating in a world where "the natives" have increasingly freed themselves from colonialism and the cultural assumptions behind it, where local informants have been educated abroad, and peoples deemed to have no history have become quite sophisticated in their manipulation of the media, politics, and sentiments of technologically dominant nations.[143] Within this milieu cultural knowledge may be an attempt to cut a new image or find a new basis between theorist and native actors upon which to continue the traditions of research we inherit. Cultural knowledge constituted through the study of ritual and performance appears to experiment with a new sense of community between theorists and actors, characterized by modest, mutual dependence and shared problems of meaning, epistemology, and critical self-reflection. Yet the domination of the theoretical subject is neither abrogated nor transcended.[144] This domination is maintained and disguised by virtue of the implicit structuring of the thought–action dichotomy in its various forms.[145]

Ritual, I have suggested, has a prominent role in securing this form of cultural knowledge. Although ritual has been perceived in very different ways since the beginnings of the social sciences, it has consistently been a fundamental focus for invoking major issues. Yet something more may well be at work when ritual is declared to be "*the* basic social act."[146] I have tried to suggest that ritual is an eminently suitable device for organizing a theoretical conversation that wishes to uncover cultural meanings through the interpretation of "texts" that "reek of meaning." The construction of ritual as a decipherable text allows the theorist to interpret simply by deconstructing ritual back into its prefused components. The theoretical construction of ritual becomes a reflection of the theorist's method and the motor of a discourse in which the concerns of theorist take center stage.

I. Notes

Introduction

1. For a history of the term, see Leach, "Ritual," pp. 520–23.
2. See Leach, "Ritual," p. 521; and Goody, "Religion and Ritual," p. 156. The phenomenon of "slippage" is described by Pierre Bourdieu in *Outline of a Theory of Practice,* trans. Richard Nice (Cambridge: Cambridge University Press, 1977), p. 29.
3. Thomas Kuhn, *The Structure of Scientific Revolutions,* 2nd rev. ed. (Chicago: University of Chicago Press, 1970).
4. Lyotard, pp. vii–xxi, 6–9, 27–41 passim.
5. My use of the term "discourse" is based on Bourdieu's discussions of "discourse on practice" (*Outline of a Theory of Practice,* pp. 16–22, 168–70, 221 note 26) and Foucault's discussion of discourses as characterized both by the formation of their objects and by their unity (*The Archeology of Knowledge,* pp. 40–49, 72–76).
6. See W. Richard Comstock et al., eds., *Religion and Man: An Introduction* (New York: Harper and Row, 1971), pp. 5–9. Ritual, magic, and taboo, etc., were all identified as types of religious behavior deriving from different intellectual orientations.
7. On the phenomenological approach to ritual, see L. Leertouwer, "Inquiry into Religious Behavior: A Theoretical Reconnaissance," in *Religion, Culture and Methodology,* ed. P. van Baaren and H. J. W. Drijvers (The Hague: Mouton, 1973), pp. 79–80; and Robert D. Baird, *Category Formation and the History of Religions* (The Hague: Mouton, 1971), pp. 82–91. On the lingering concern with the interrelationship of ritual and myth, however qualified, see Jonathan Z. Smith, *To Take Place: Toward Theory in Ritual* (Chicago: University of Chicago Press, 1987), pp. 100–103, 113–17; Doty, espe-

55

cially pp. 35–36; and Burton Mack's introduction to the theories of René Girard, Walter Burkert, and Jonathan Z. Smith in *Violent Origins,* ed. Robert G. Hamerton-Kelly (Stanford: Stanford University Press, 1987), pp. 1–70.

8. N. D. Fustel de Coulanges, *The Ancient City,* trans. Willard Small (New York: Doubleday, 1963), originally published in 1864; and W. Robertson Smith, *The Religion of the Semites* (New York: Schocken Books, 1972), originally published in 1894. As with the current phenomenologists of religion who can be grouped as stressing the primacy of intellectual orientations (belief/myth) over behavior (ritual), there are avowals in anthropology of the primacy of ritual over belief, e.g., Anthony F. C. Wallace's affirmation of Franz Boas's "recognition" of the primacy of ritual and how it is a stimulus for myth (*Religion: An Anthropological View* [New York: Random House, 1966], p. 102).

9. Emile Durkheim, *The Elementary Forms of the Religious Life,* trans. J. W. Swain (New York: Free Press, 1965), p. 51.

10. Henri Hubert and Marcel Mauss, *Sacrifice: Its Nature and Function,* trans. W. D. Hall (Chicago: University of Chicago Press, 1981), originally published in 1898.

11. Marcus and Fischer, p. 61. Also see Doty on the priority given to ritual in contemporary studies (pp. 78–81).

12. I am paraphrasing Claude Lévi-Strauss, *The Naked Man, Introduction to a Science of Mythology,* vol. 4, trans. John Weightman and Doreen Weightman (New York: Harper and Row, 1981), p. 669 (also quoted in the original French in Pierre Smith, "Aspects de l'organisation des rites," in Michel Izard and Pierre Smith, eds., *La fonction symbolique* [Paris: Gallimard, 1979], p. 139).

13. As noted earlier, "ritual studies" can be appropriately, if a bit too simplistically, credited to the work of Ronald L. Grimes, particularly his *Beginnings in Ritual Studies* (Washington, D.C.: University Press of America, 1982) and "Defining Nascent Ritual," *Journal of the American Academy of Religion* 50, no. 4 (1982): 539–55. As a loosely coherent area of research, ritual studies appears to inherit some of the concerns and ambiguities that attended earlier work in "civil religion" (e.g., Robert N. Bellah and W. Lloyd Warner, among others), which attempted to integrate traditional religious values with the values of American sociology. In a similar way, ritual studies seems concerned to integrate liberal religious values with symbolic anthropology. For example, Grimes notes that one major goal of ritual studies is "to mediate between normative and descriptive, as well as textual and descriptive, methods." Other goals are "to lay

the groundwork for a coherent taxonomy and theory that can account for the full range of symbolic acts running from ritualization behavior in animals, through interaction ritual, to highly differentiated religious liturgies and civil ceremonies"; and "to cultivate the study of ritual in a manner that does not automatically assume it to be a dependent variable" ("Sources for the Study of Ritual," *Religious Studies Review* 10, no. 2 (1984): 134.

Chapter 1

14. Gilbert Lewis discusses the general application of the notion of ritual to conduct or behavior rather than thought or feelings in *Day of Shining Red*, pp. 10–11.
15. Edward Shils, "Ritual and Crisis," in *The Religious Situation: 1968*, ed. Donald R. Cutler (Boston: Beacon Press, 1968), p. 736. (This version of "Ritual and Crisis" differs substantially from a paper with the same name included in Sir Julian Huxley, ed., "A Discussion of Ritualization of Behavior in Animals and Man," *Philosophical Transactions of the Royal Society*, series B, 251 [1966]: 447–50.)
16. Lévi-Strauss, *The Naked Man*, pp. 669–75, 679–84.
17. Durkheim, p. 51.
18. Durkheim, pp. 463ff.
19. James Peacock has noted how Weber's model, which he finds to be "the most systematic and comprehensive conceptualization of the relationship between belief and action," contrasts with the Durkheimian model. See Peacock, "Weberian, Southern Baptist, and Indonesian Muslim Conceptions of Belief and Action," in *Symbols and Society: Essays on Belief Systems in Action*, ed. Carole E. Hill (Athens: University of Georgia Press, 1975), p. 82. Action (*Handeln*) is the "fundamental unit" of Weber's sociology, a unit that represents the act *and* its subjective meaning to the actor, which cannot be separated from each other. Hence, for Weber action cannot be analyzed "independently of belief" (Peacock, p. 82). As such, Weberian analysis focuses on the relationship between the individual and his or her acts and involves the interpretation of the meanings of those acts to the actor. It does not focus on the relationship of beliefs to society as in the Durkheimian approach. This Weberian perspective was elaborated into a full theory of action by Talcott Parsons, of course, in *The Structure of Social Action* (New York: Free Press, 1937) and with Edward Shils in *Toward a General Theory of Action* (New York: Harper and Row, 1962).

Yet the objection can be made that the results of both the Durkheimian and the Weberian approaches are rather similar. The Durkheimian is left with a vividly constructed social self (or spiritual being)
oddly contrasted with that other vaguely noted being, the physical
individual self. In his opposition of self and society, the self is left in
somewhat mystical shadows. The Weberian on the other hand is left
with a vivid construction of the subjective meanings attached to the
objective acts of the individual in contrast to the social significance
of these acts. Their social significance, or meaningfulness for others
in the culture, cannot be depicted. Rather their transpersonal significance can be described only in terms of logical and idealized
systems of socioeconomic behavior completely dissociated from real
people and their activities. In both Durkheimian and Weberian con-
ceptualizations, an underlying distinction between the individual and
society, or belief and action, pushes the analysis to a dualism in
which two entities or forces are simply juxtaposed and not really
integrated.

Numerous Durkheimians and Weberians have attempted to
complete the "integration" that their masters left incomplete. See
Robert Wuthnow's discussion of such dualisms and their resolution in *Meaning and Moral Order* (Berkeley: University of California Press, 1987), pp. 23, 26–27, 37–41. For a critique of Parsons
and his separate systems of culture and personality, see Marcus
and Fisher (pp. 9–11) and Sherry B. Ortner, "Theory in Anthropology Since the Sixties," *Comparative Studies in Society and History* 26 (1984): 150.
20. Stanley J. Tambiah, *Buddhism and the Spirit Cults in North-East
Thailand* (Cambridge: Cambridge University Press, 1970).
21. Victor W. Turner, *The Ritual Process: Structure and Anti-Structure*
(Chicago: Aldine, 1966).
22. Jameson, *The Prison-House of Language*, pp. 17–32.
23. Jameson, *The Prison-House of Language*, pp. 18–21.
24. Jameson, *The Prison-House of Language*, pp. 18–39 passim.
25. Jameson, *The Prison-House of Language*, p. 39.
26. Jameson, *The Prison-House of Language*, p. 22.
27. E. E. Evans-Pritchard, *Theories of Primitive Religion* (Oxford: Clarendon Press, 1965), pp. 61–62.
28. Nancy D. Munn, "Symbolism in a Ritual Context," in *Handbook
of Social and Cultural Anthropology,* ed. John J. Honigmann (Chicago: Rand McNally, 1973), p. 583.
29. Munn, p. 583. This is the basis for Munn's own view according to
which "ritual can be seen as a symbolic intercom between the level

of cultural thought and other complex meanings, on the one hand, and that of social action and immediate event, on the other" (p. 579).

30. Marshall Sahlins, *Culture and Practical Reason* (Chicago: University of Chicago Press, 1976), pp. 110–13, especially p. 111.

31. Claude Lévi-Strauss, "French Sociology," in *Twentieth Century Sociology*, ed. George Gurvitch and Wilbert E. Moore (New York: The Philosophical Library, 1945), p. 518.

32. In this context, Sahlins (*Culture and Practical Reason*, p. 111) draws attention to W. Doroszewki's theory of the influence of Durkheim's notion of a "sign" on Saussure, in Doroszewki's "Quelques rémarques sur les rapports de la sociologie et de la linguistique: Durkheim et F. de Saussure," *Journal de Psychologie* 30 (1933): 82–91.

33. Durkheim, p. 298.

34. Geertz, *The Interpretation of Cultures*, p. 89. According to Sperber, Radcliffe-Brown regarded anthropology as a "natural science of society," while Evans-Pritchard put it among the humanities. Geertz, on the other hand, is a major representative of a third approach according to which "the only way to *describe* cultural phenomena is, precisely, to *interpret* them." Sperber goes on to criticize this approach and to "develop a fourth view of anthropological knowledge" (*On Anthropological Knowledge*, pp. 9–10).

35. Geertz, *The Interpretation of Cultures*, pp. 143–44.

36. Geertz, *The Interpretation of Cultures*, pp. 89, 126–27.

37. Geertz, *The Interpretation of Cultures*, pp. 95–97.

38. Geertz, *The Interpretation of Cultures*, pp. 89, 98, 126–27.

39. Geertz, *The Interpretation of Cultures*, pp. 127 and 131.

40. Geertz, *The Interpretation of Cultures*, pp. 44–45, 48, 89, 113, 127, 137, etc.

41. Geertz, *The Interpretation of Cultures*, pp. 113 and 127. Also see Geertz's discussion of how symbols "synthesize" ethos and worldview (p. 89).

42. Geertz, *The Interpretation of Cultures*, pp. 92–93.

43. Geertz, *The Interpretation of Cultures*, pp. 112–13.

44. Geertz, *The Interpretation of Cultures*, pp. 143 and 163.

45. Geertz, *The Interpretation of Cultures*, p. 113. Emphasis added.

46. Geertz, *The Interpretation of Cultures*, p. 113.

47. Geertz, *The Interpretation of Cultures*, p. 114.

48. Frits Staal gives an interesting demonstration of the problems that arise when ritual is seen as "pure activity." By this characterization, made in the context of a clear and complete opposition between thought and action, Staal wishes to maintain the total resistance of pure activity to any theoretical appropriation whatsoever. Thus, Staal

concludes that ritual cannot be understood, that it is "meaningless" ("The Meaninglessness of Ritual," pp. 2–22).

49. Theodore Jennings, "On Ritual Knowledge," *Journal of Religion* 62, no. 2 (1982): 111–27.

50. Jennings, pp. 113, 124.

51. Jennings, pp. 124–27.

52. Stephen Greenblatt, "Filthy Rites," *Daedalus* 111, no. 3 (1982): 3–4.

Chapter 2

53. Geertz, *The Interpretation of Cultures*, p. 113, quoting Milton Singer, *Traditional India: Structure and Change* (Philadelphia: American Folklore Society, 1959), pp. 140–82. Parentheses added by Geertz.

54. Geertz, *The Interpretation of Cultures*, p. 113, quoting Milton Singer, "The Cultural Pattern of Indian Civilization," *Far Eastern Quarterly* 15 (1955): 23–26.

55. Geertz, *The Interpretation of Cultures*, p. 146.

56. Geertz, *The Interpretation of Cultures*, p. 143.

57. Geertz, *The Interpretation of Cultures*, pp. 143 and 163.

58. Geertz, *The Interpretation of Cultures*, p. 144.

59. Geertz, *The Interpretation of Cultures*, p. 144.

60. Geertz, *The Interpretation of Cultures*, pp. 144–45.

61. Geertz, *The Interpretation of Cultures*, pp. 153–62.

62. Geertz, *The Interpretation of Cultures*, p. 164.

63. For an example of Geertz's approach taken on wholesale, see Carole E. Hill, ed., *Symbols and Society: Essays on Belief Systems in Action* (Athens, Ga.: Southern Anthropological Society, 1975), p. 4.

64. Gregory Bateson, *Naven*, 2nd ed. (Stanford: Stanford University Press, 1958), pp. 86–107.

65. Claude Lévi-Strauss, *Tristes Tropiques*, trans. John Weightmann and Doreen Weightmann (New York: Atheneum, 1975), pp. 178–97, especially pp. 196–97. Also see Fredric Jameson's discussion of this story in *The Political Unconscious*, pp. 77–80, as well as Dowling's comments on it (William C. Dowling, *Jameson, Althusser, Marx* [Ithaca, N.Y.: Cornell University Press, 1984], pp. 119–26).

66. This is Jameson's interpretation, which reads a bit more into Lévi-Strauss's account than the latter might have intended.

67. On the notion of contradiction, see Anthony Giddens, *Central Problems in Social Theory: Action, Structure and Contradiction* (Berkeley: University of California Press, 1979), especially pp. 132–45; and also a more recent work, *The Constitution of Society: Outline of a Theory*

of Structuration (Berkeley: University of California Press, 1984), pp. 310–19.

68. In his analysis of the Javanese funeral, Geertz uses a very similar set of categories to generate his notion of social change as the result of a perceived discrepancy between the cultural ideals of a community and the real social relationships among them ("Ritual and Social Change: A Javanese Example," in *The Interpretation of Cultures,* pp. 144–46).

69. It could be argued that this formula is not unique to Marx but underlies much of the reorientation of late nineteenth- and early twentieth-century thought, including the theories of Sigmund Freud, Max Weber, and Emile Durkheim.

70. Bourdieu, *Outline of a Theory of Practice,* pp. 114–24.

71. Bourdieu, *Outline of a Theory of Practice,* p. 120.

72. Wagner, p. x.

73. "Space, Knowledge and Power," an interview with Michel Foucault, in *The Foucault Reader,* ed. Paul Rabinow (New York: Pantheon, 1984), p. 247.

74. Kenneth Burke, *The Philosophy of Literary Form,* 3rd ed. (Berkeley: University of California Press, 1973), originally published in 1941; Victor Turner, *Dramas, Fields and Metaphors* (Ithaca, N.Y.: Cornell University Press, 1974); Sally F. Moore and Barbara G. Myerhoff, eds., *Secular Ritual* (Amsterdam: Van Gorcum, 1977); Erving Goffman, *Interaction Ritual* (Garden City, N.Y.: Doubleday, 1967); J. L. Austin, *How to Do Things with Words* (Cambridge: Harvard University Press, 1962); and John R. Searle, *Speech Acts* (Cambridge: Cambridge University Press, 1969). For a good discussion of the various roots of performance theory, see Lawrence E. Sullivan, "Sound and Senses: Toward a Hermeneutics of Performance," *History of Religions* 26, no. 1 (1986): 2–14.

75. On the various "genres" of performance, see Richard Schechner and Willa Appel, eds., *By Means of Performance: Intercultural Studies of Theatre and Ritual* (Cambridge: Cambridge University Press, 1989), p. 3.

76. John J. MacAloon, *Rite, Drama, Festival, Spectacle: Rehearsals Toward a Theory of Cultural Performance* (Philadelphia: Institute for the Study of Human Issues, 1984), p. 1.

77. Grimes, *Beginnings in Ritual Studies,* introduction, no pagination; Victor Turner, *From Ritual to Theater: The Human Seriousness of Play* (New York: Performing Arts Journal Publications, 1982), p. 89.

78. V. Turner, *From Ritual to Theater,* p. 89.

79. Ortner, "Theory in Anthropology Since the Sixties," p. 144.

80. Wuthnow, pp. 11–15, 343. He also considers two other approaches which he characterizes as subjective and institutional.
81. Wuthnow, p. 344.
82. Ronald L. Grimes, "Ritual Studies," in *The Encyclopedia of Religion*, vol. 12, ed. Mircea Eliade (New York: Macmillan, 1987), p. 423. Emphasis added.
83. Singer, *Traditional India*, p. xiii.
84. On the drama analogy, see Geertz's "Blurred Genres: The Refiguration of Social Thought," in *Local Knowledge: Further Essays in Interpretive Anthropology* (New York: Basic Books, 1983), pp. 19–35.
85. Singer, *Traditional India*, p. xii.
86. In her book *Sherpas Through Their Rituals* (Cambridge: Cambridge University Press, 1978), Sherry Ortner echoes Singer's definitions of culture and provides another very intelligent definition of ritual that is still governed by the three homologized structural patterns.
87. Turner, *From Ritual to Theater*, pp. 89–101.
88. MacAloon, p. 3.
89. Grimes, *Beginnings in Ritual Studies*, p. 53. See Grimes's discussion of the role of the theorist as a critic of ritual in "Ritual Criticism and Reflexivity in Fieldwork," *Journal of Ritual Studies* 2, no. 2 (1988): 217–39.
90. Grimes, "Ritual Criticism," pp. 221 and 235. Also see his recent book *Ritual Criticism: Case Studies in Its Practice, Essays on Its Theory* (Columbia: University of South Carolina Press, 1990).
91. Grimes, "Ritual Criticism," p. 218.
92. Lewis, pp. 8, 22, 33–34, 38.
93. MacAloon, p. 3.
94. Victor Turner, *From Ritual to Theater*, p. 82; and his *Schism and Continuity in African Society* (Manchester: Manchester University Press, 1957), p. 93, quoted in MacAloon, p. 3.
95. Stanley J. Tambiah, "A Performative Approach to Ritual," *Proceedings of the British Academy* 65 (1979): 113–69, particularly p. 120.
96. Tambiah, "A Performative Approach to Ritual," p. 115; also see Stanley J. Tambiah, "The Magical Power of Words," *Man*, n.s. 3, no. 2 (1968): 180, 189.
97. Tambiah, "A Performative Approach to Ritual," p. 124.
98. Tambiah, "A Performative Approach to Ritual," pp. 119 and 122.
99. Tambiah, "A Performative Approach to Ritual," p. 127.
100. Tambiah, "A Performative Approach to Ritual," pp. 153–54, 158, and 166.

101. Tambiah, "A Performative Approach to Ritual," p. 139, on the fusion of form and content.
102. Geertz, *Local Knowledge*, pp. 19–35.
103. Rappaport, pp. 176–77.
104. Emily M. Ahern, "The Problem of Efficacy: Strong and Weak Illocutionary Acts," *Man*, n.s. 14, no. 1 (1979): 1–17.
105. Geertz, *Local Knowledge*, pp. 19–35.
106. Geertz, *Local Knowledge*, p. 22.
107. Clifford Geertz, *Negara: The Theatre State in Nineteenth Century Bali* (Princeton: Princeton University Press, 1980), p. 105.
108. Tambiah, "A Performative Approach to Ritual," pp. 123–24, 132.
109. Marcus and Fischer, p. 61.
110. James W. Fernandez, "Persuasions and Performances: Of the Beast in Every Body . . . And the Metaphors of Everyman," *Daedalus* 101, no. 1 (1972): 39–60 (also published in Clifford Geertz, ed., *Myth, Symbol and Culture* [New York: Norton, 1971], pp. 39–60). Also James W. Fernandez, "The Performance of Ritual Metaphors," in *The Social Use of Metaphor: Essays on the Anthropology of Rhetoric*, ed. J. David Sapir and J. Christopher Crocker (Philadelphia: University of Pennsylvania Press, 1977), pp. 100–131.
111. Geertz, *The Interpretation of Cultures*, pp. 412–53.
112. Geertz, *Local Knowledge*, p. 30.
113. Paul Ricoeur, "The Model of the Text: Meaningful Action Considered as a Text," *Social Research* 38 (Autumn 1971): 529–62.
114. Fredric Jameson, "The Ideology of the Text," *Salmagundi* 31–32 (Fall 1975/Winter 1976): 205.
115. Two recent studies of orality, textuality, and performance highlight some other tensions that come to light in performance theory: while William A. Graham's *Beyond the Written Word: Oral Aspects of Scripture in the History of Religions* (Cambridge: Cambridge University Press, 1987) is concerned to demonstrate the oral and performative dimensions of scriptural texts, Stuart H. Blackburn's *Singing of Birth and Death: Texts in Performance* (Philadelphia: University of Pennsylvania Press, 1988) is concerned to argue the importance of texts for oral performance. If their analyses are correct, the first is a justified corrective to an exaggerated stress on textuality and the second to a similar exaggeration of orality. For a demonstration of a comparable set of emphases in recent interpretations of the Javanese *slametan*, see Mark R. Woodward's corrective to Geertz's approach in "The *Slametan*: Textual Knowledge and Ritual Performance in Central Javanese Islam," *History of Religions* 28, no. 1 (1988): 54–89. Although performance theory does not appear to

offer any resolutions of these oral–text tensions, it may well prove
to be a very useful arena in which the larger issues of orality and
textuality loom more clearly and may be engaged more directly. This
can be seen, for example, in a spate of ethnographies, represented
by Joel C. Kuipers's *Power in Performance: The Creation of Textual
Authority in Weyewa Ritual Speech* (Philadephia: University of Pennsylvania Press, 1990), or M. E. Combs-Schilling's *Sacred Performances: Islam, Sexuality and Sacrifice* (New York: Columbia
University Press, 1989).

116. See Jonathan Culler, *The Pursuit of Signs: Semiotics, Literature and
Deconstruction* (Ithaca, N.Y.: Cornell University Press, 1981), especially Chapter 1. Culler goes on to question "interpretation" as
the goal of a critic's work. Also see Dowling's discussion of Freud's
influence on the notion of latent meaning in Jameson's *The Political
Unconscious* (p. 36).

Chapter 3

117. See Bourdieu's discussion of Saussure and Panofsky in this vein (*Outline of a Theory of Practice,* pp. 23–27).

118. See Bourdieu for a discussion of the expediency and economy of
"practical logic" (*Outline of a Theory of Practice,* pp. 96–97, 109–
10).

119. For a history of the delination of "theory" in contrast to "practice"
see Nicholas Lobkowicz, *Theory and Practice: History of a Concept
from Aristotle to Marx* (Notre Dame, Ind.: University of Notre Dame
Press, 1967).

120. Critiques of this approach to knowing have been assembled in Richard Rorty's study of "representationism" and the claims of knowledge. See his *Philosophy and the Mirror of Nature* (Princeton:
Princeton University Press, 1979).

121. Cited by Claude Lévi-Strauss in "The Scope of Anthropology," *Current Anthropology* 7 (1966): 113; and by Fernandez, "The Performance of Ritual Metaphors," p. 128.

122. Marcel Mauss, *The Gift: Forms and Functions of Exchange in Archaic Societies,* trans. Ian Cunnison (New York: Norton, 1967),
pp. 77–78.

123. See Hans-Georg Gadamer, *Truth and Method,* 2nd rev. ed., trans.
Joel Weinsheimer and Donald G. Marshall (New York: Crossroad,
1989), originally published in 1960; and Ricoeur, "The Model of
the Text." Sullivan links performance theory and hermeneutics in

passing, but primarily as a function of the academic orientation to texts, not as the result of the specific emergence in structural linguistics of a "text"-creating methodology ("Sound and Senses," p. 2).

124. Ricoeur, p. 546.
125. Ricoeur, p. 541.
126. Ricoeur, pp. 543–44.
127. Ricoeur, p. 546.
128. Ricoeur, p. 558.
129. Geertz, "Blurred Genres," p. 32.
130. Ricoeur, p. 561.
131. Ricoeur, p. 558.
132. Marcus and Fischer, pp. 5–16.
133. Quentin Skinner, ed., *The Return to Grand Theory in the Human Sciences* (Cambridge: Cambridge University Press, 1985).
134. Marcus and Fischer, p. 1.
135. Wagner, pp. 8–10.
136. Susan Sontag, "The Anthropologist as Hero," in *Against Interpretation and Other Essays* (New York: Farrar, Straus and Giroux, 1961), pp. 75 and 81.
137. Marcus and Fischer, pp. ix–x.
138. Stanley Diamond, "Anthropology in Question," in *Reinventing Anthropology,* ed. Dell Hymes (New York: Random House, 1969), p. 401.
139. Sahlins, *Culture and Practical Reason,* p. 54.
140. See Marc Augé, *The Anthropological Circle: Symbol, Function and History* (Cambridge: Cambridge University Press, 1982). Also, John Skorupski discusses the "intellectualist" and "symbolist" positions in his *Symbol and Theory: A Philosophical Study of Theories of Religion in Social Anthropology* (Cambridge: Cambridge University Press, 1976). Sahlins raises the issue in terms of "utility" versus "meaning" in *Culture and Practical Reason,* pp. ix, 205–21.
141. Dell Hymes, "Breakthrough into Performance," in *Folklore: Performance and Communication,* ed. Dan Ben-Amos and Kenneth S. Goldstein (The Hague: Mouton, 1975). Cited in Sullivan, "Sound and Senses," p. 3.
142. See MacAloon, p. 2.
143. Grimes notes that his informants interpret their symbols and activities with reference to Mircea Eliade and Carl Jung (Grimes, *Beginnings in Ritual Studies,* p. 6). In *Reflections of a Woman Anthropologist— No Hiding Place* (London: Academic Press, 1982), Manda Cesara uses her own field experiences to argue that the traditional anthropological paradigm of researcher and native not only fails to reflect

actual relationships in the field, but thereby distorts and falsifies the anthropological enterprise.

144. See Geertz, *Local Knowledge,* p. 183, for a discussion of this "community." Foucault's critique of anthropologization and the domination of the individual consciousness (*Archeology of Knowledge,* pp. 12–16) also addresses this issue.

145. Sperber discusses how "relativism" in cultural anthropology is now replacing earlier and more overt notions of superiority with a form of "cognitive apartheid" (*On Anthropological Knowledge,* p. 62).

146. Rappaport, p. 174.

II

THE SENSE OF RITUAL

Part II addresses the kind of activity generally understood to constitute ritual. I first look at two major ways in which ritual is defined as action and then consider various uses of the notion of practice. The term 'practice' brings some correctives and insights to more traditional approaches, yet it often succumbs to the same type of circular argument of theoretical discourse examined in Part I. By building on specific aspects of practice theory, however, I will lay out an approach to ritual activities that stresses the primacy of the social act itself, how its strategies are lodged in the very doing of the act, and how 'ritualization' is a strategic way of acting in specific social situations. The framework of ritualization casts a new light on the purpose of ritual activity, its social efficacy, and its embodiment in complex traditions and systems. This alternative framework for understanding ritual behavior will be developed further in Part III; here I attempt to explicate some basic principles by which to reorient ourselves to ritual activity.

4

Action and Practice

Most attempts to define ritual proceed by formulating the universal qualities of an autonomous phenomenon. They maintain, however provisionally, that there is something we can generally call ritual and whenever or wherever it occurs it has certain distinctive features. Such definitions inevitably come to function as a set of criteria for judging whether some specific activities can be deemed ritual. As a result, these definitions of ritual are not complete when they set up a single universal construct; additional categories are needed to account for all the data that do not fit neatly into the domain of the original term. Definitions of ritual must go on to suggest, explicitly or implicitly, the nature and relation of nonritual activity and various degrees of nearly-but-not-quite-ritual behavior. Hence, a good deal of writing about ritual involves extensive exercises in cleaning up all the data and terms that are not included in the main definition. As a taxonomic enterprise, universal categories have made undisputed contributions to the organization and extension of both empirical observation and particular knowledge systems. Yet with regard to the study of ritual, the initial usefulness of this approach may have begun to give way to a bewildering number of problems.

First of all, categorization develops a dizzying momentum of its own. The plethora of "ritual types," as Grimes points out, demonstrates how little certainty there is "in identifying either ritual's center or boundaries."[1] Distinctions are routinely drawn between ritual studies and liturgics, religious ritual and secular ritual, ritual and ceremonial, secular ritual and secular ceremony, political ritual and civic ceremonial, private ritual and collective ritual, rites of rebellion and rites of solidarity, dramatic performance and ritual performance, the formality of games (in play and organized sports) and the formality of ritual, ritual and festival, festival and holiday, and so on.[2] As distinctions and categories proliferate, scholars begin to talk in rather elaborate circles. For example, Monica Wilson set up an important early model by distinguishing ritual from ceremonial. Goody subsequently recast Wilson's distinction by placing ritual within a more widely embracing understanding of ceremonial. Gluckman, in turn, took Goody's revision of Wilson's categories and inverted it to make ceremonial a subset of ritual.[3]

There is another serious consequence of such definitions of ritual. The categories of activity so defined tend to override and undermine the significance of indigenous distinctions among ways of acting.[4] At best, culturally specific distinctions may be noted in the attempt to discern the nuances of some particular expression of the universal phenomenon, but the 'universal' always impoverishes the 'particular.' In this way, the definitional approach to ritual loses sight of what may be the more useful questions that can be brought to bear on ritual activities of various kinds: Under what circumstances are such activities distinguished from other forms of activity? How and why are they distinguished? What do these activities do that other activities cannot or will not do?

To take up these questions it is necessary to break free of the entrenched tendency to define ritual either as a distinct and autonomous set of activities or as an aspect of all human activity. Yet, as Lewis notes, most influential theories of ritual belong to one of these two camps: some stress the distinctiveness of ritual, how it is clearly different from all other kinds of activity; others stress the congruity of ritual with other forms of human action, usually by seeing ritual as "the expressive, symbolical or communicative aspect" of action in general.[5] The first group usually proceeds by contrasting ritual/magical activity with technical/utilitarian activity. Hence, in ritual activity the relationship between ends and means is described as rule-governed, routinized, symbolic, or noninstrumental. By contrast, technical activity is described as pragmatic, spontaneous, and instrumentally effective.[6] Sometimes ritual is seen to possess both expressive and instrumental aspects simultaneously.[7] Yet even in this last formulation, the expressive aspects of ritual are usually considered to be more authentic to ritual per se than its pragmatic aspects, which may even be characterized as magical.

In descriptions of the noninstrumental nature of ritual activity as symbolic or expressive activity (i.e., communicative in some way), the fundamental contrast of symbolic versus instrumental underscores how ritual activities are seen to differ from more "practical" ones. An interesting use of this perspective can be seen in studies of "rituals of resistance," which are concerned with subcultures and the differentiation of group identities.[8] In exploring "symbolic" forms of resistance to the dominant culture among working-class youth groups in Great Britain, two studies suggest that such symbolic forms effectively constitute group identity and ethos but not politically effective forms of resistance, such as might be found among activists making a real (nonsymbolic?) break with the dominant ideology. That is, apolitical resistance to the dominant ideology is embodied in what the authors see as "rituals of style" in contrast to more politically pragmatic activities.

Despite these sociological uses, the distinction between ritual and instrumental activity can easily collapse into a distinction between the rational and the irrational or the logical and the emotional.[9] Hence, the identification of ritual with symbolic as opposed to instrumental action has also led to descriptions of ritual as cathartic performances that are responses to situations of anxiety or fear.[10] The great debate between Bronislav Malinowski and Raymond Firth on the relationship of ritual and anxiety essentially reflected the need to account for the existence of nonutilitarian practices among people who were incredibly practical in most things.[11] Ritual, as activities that yield no practical result, it was argued, probably function to reduce anxiety. In developing his theory, Malinowski went on to replicate the initial distinction between practical and nonpractical activities by differentiating two forms of ritual as well, magical rites (for which the native can state a practical purpose) and religious rites (for which no practical purpose is given).[12] Another tack suggests that ritual exhibits and exaggerates real conflicts in order to release tensions and afford a type of social catharsis.[13] It was along this line of thinking, of course, that V. Turner developed his early notion of ritual as social drama and helped to usher in a 'performance' approach to ritual.[14]

Among the many problems attending efforts to distinguish ritual from other forms of human activity, most immediate is the fact that a distinction between technical practical and ritual symbolic activities often reflects categories rather alien to the peoples involved.[15] Long ago Mauss pointed to the lack of such distinctions among "primitive peoples" as mandating analysis of the "total man."[16] Aside from how alien the ritual–instrumental distinction may be to many societies and the ease with which this distinction collapses into a problematic dichotomy of rational and irrational behavior, a third and more subtle critique has also been made of these approaches to ritual. It focuses on the tendency to cast activity, ritual or otherwise, as an object and thus as the completed, or "dead," execution of a system.[17] When activity is analyzed and categorized as something already finished, the very nature of activity as such is lost. Although this critique was made by performance theorists, it is also implicit in practice theory, as I will show shortly.

In recent years the second group of ritual theories, those that tend to see ritual as an aspect of all activity, has been dominant in the literature, pushing out the older perspective of ritual as a distinct category of behavior. For example, in his challenge to the "referent" of the term "ritual," Goody points out that " 'routinisation', regularisation, repetition, lie at the basis of social life itself."[18] Others have argued that ritual is a form of communication just like language. Although he describes ritual as noninstrumental, Roy Rappaport also notes that the formality associated with ritual is actually a matter of a continuum of formality found in all behavior. Rappaport uses the term "ritual" in the singular to refer to this formal aspect of all behavior, and "rituals" in the plural for those "invariant events" completely dominated by formality. Ultimately, he argues, rituals communicate by virtue of their formal features, rather than their symbolic and expressive features, although these are the features he finds least distinctive about ritual.[19] Wuthnow invokes a simpler form of Rappaport's argument: he suggests that symbolic and utilitarian activities can be differentiated only in terms of the *degree* to which they are expressive or communicative—and ritual, therefore, as the symbolic and expressive, constitutes some dimension of all social activity.[20] Other theories stress the communicative nature of ritual in terms of either linguistic structures, primarily using Saussurean structuralism, or performative structures, applying the work of Austin and Searle.[21] Mary Douglas, for example, states that "ritual is preeminently a form of communication" composed of culturally normal acts that have become distinctive by being diverted to special functions where they are given magical efficacy.[22] Leach also argues that "we engage in rituals in order to transmit collective messages to ourselves."[23] Elsewhere, he goes further and suggests that "speech itself is a form of ritual."[24] Tambiah's performative approach, noted in Part I, also represents an example of this perspective.

Among the various theories sharing a concern with the ritual dimension of all behavior, ethological studies of ritualization in animals and humans are particularly serious about the universal features of ritual. They cannot claim, however, the unqualified appreciation of other universalists.[25] Sir Julian Huxley first configured the term "ritualization" to indicate "the adaptive formalization or canalization of emotionally motivated behavior, under the teleonomic pressure of natural selection."[26] In Huxley's ethological framework, ritualization among both animals and humans served "to secure more effective communication ('signalling') function, reduction of intra-group damage, or better intra-group bonding."[27] Richard Schechner emphasizes the idea that this ritual form of communication arises in situations where any misunderstanding, or "missignaling," would be catastrophic.[28] The wide variety of activities that have come to be analyzed as ritualized behavior patterns—aggression and combat, song, play, sport, grooming, courting and mating, drama, dance, humor, art, and even thought itself—testifies to the promiscuous tendencies of this approach.[29] It identifies ritual with formal communicative functions and then finds ritual to some degree in all or most activity.[30] Some obvious problems result. Making everything a matter of ritual to some degree broadens the question to proportions impossible to organize. As Meyer Fortes pointed out, it is a short step from the proposition that everything is ritual to the practical reality that nothing is ritual.[31] Playing with the application of a similarly broad-based understanding of ritual, Lévi-Strauss suggested the ludicrous conclusions that alien ethnographers might come to when observing our emotional adherence to the "white line ritual" while driving.[32]

Another example is seen in the curious lengths to which Wuthnow takes his analyses when he focuses on the ritual aspects of signaling a turn in traffic and the collective viewing of a television program.[33]

With these objections an impasse appears to loom. On the one hand there is evidence that ritual acts are not a clear and closed category of social behavior. On the other hand many problems attend the attempt to see ritual as a dimension of all or many forms of social behavior. How can the distinguishing features of so-called ritual activities be approached without cutting ritual off from what it shares with social activity in general? One solution to this impasse would suggest that we refer to the particular circumstances and cultural strategies that generate and differentiate activities from each other. This approach, which assumes a focus on social action in general, would then look to how and why a person acts so as to give some activities a privileged status vis-à-vis others. Rather than impose categories of what is or is not ritual, it may be more useful to look at how human activities establish and manipulate their own differentiation and purposes—in the very doing of the act within the context of other ways of acting.

With this approach in mind, I will use the term 'ritualization' to draw attention to the way in which certain social actions strategically distinguish themselves in relation to other actions. In a very preliminary sense, ritualization is a way of acting that is designed and orchestrated to distinguish and privilege what is being done in comparison to other, usually more quotidian, activities. As such, ritualization is a matter of various culturally specific strategies for setting some activities off from others, for creating and privileging a qualitative distinction between the 'sacred' and the 'profane,' and for ascribing such distinctions to realities thought to transcend the powers of human actors.

Practice Theory

It is not easy to focus on how activity, in the very act, differentiates itself from other activities. One needs a perspective on activity that can facilitate an exploration of the dynamics of social action in general. The notion of 'practice' has been an obvious place to start. Heralded as the "key symbol" of an emerging theoretical orientation in anthropology, practice would appear to be a ready tool to explore ritualization as a way of acting.[34] Ever since Karl Marx the term has been invoked specifically to transcend dichotomies that "wrongly divide" human experience. Nonetheless, the term frequently succumbs to many of the expediencies of theoretical discourse demonstrated in Part I.

Some of the problems with the term go back to Marx and the flexible ways in which he used it.[35] There appear to be two basic senses to the notion of practice in his work. In the first sense the term is explored as descriptive of human nature and all human activity. In a second sense the term appears to be more prescriptive, arguing for the proper way of being theoretical and using theory. In the first, descriptive sense, practice was a methodological focus through which to solve the problems posed by the work of Hegel on the one hand and Feuerbach on the other—namely, the relationship between consciousness and reality, subject and object, idealism and materialism. In that sense, Marx defined practice as "practical activity," a unity of consciousness and social being characterized by the potential to transform real existence. As such, practice was nothing less than the irreducible unity of real human existence itself. In this framework, practice mediates or reintegrates subject and object (consciousness and reality), which is to say that these polarized constructs are thought to exist only as they exist in and through practice. The second, or prescriptive, sense emerges in Marx's other analyses, where practice is seen as inextricably related to theory. Theirs is a dialectical relationship in which practice both actualizes and tests theory while also providing the data for ongoing theory. This dialectical unity of theory and practice was meant to indict the inadequacy of abstract thinking, knowledge, and truth. At the same time, it gave theory an important place in the practice of political activity.

These different uses of the term in Marx crop up again, of course, in the various emphases of more recent studies. Certainly the term has been invoked to redress those "bourgeois categories" that falsely distinguish the individual from society or the sign from the referent.[36] For example, "signifying practices," a term coined by the Tel Quel circle in Paris, not only opposes "the prevailing notion of a transparent relation between sign and referent, signification and reality," but also emphasizes the creativity over and above the mere reproductivity of practice.[37] Language, art, and style, as examples of signifying practices, have been analyzed as active forces that create or transform reality.

Writers only partially aligned with Marxism will also invoke the term practice as a way to evade what they see as the materialist empiricism of much traditional ethnology on the one hand and as the ahistorical abstract idealism of Saussure's or Lévi-Strauss's structuralism on the other. In this context, practice is used to denote a dialectic of the material and the symbolic, the real and the perceived, the structure and the act. That is, practice synthesizes and transcends the materialism and idealism associated with each pole of the dialectic itself. For example, despite his judgment that Marx's praxis concerned only material activity and as such was unable to account for "the symbolic order of culture," Sahlins attempted to rescue the term in the guise of "cultural praxis." The notion of cultural praxis is used to articulate a dynamic at the heart of social and cultural life which cannot be reduced to either pole of the dialectic of which it is composed—*langue* and *parole,* or structure and history.[38]

Whereas Sahlins uses the notion of practice to formulate a theory of culture that can recognize symbolic and historical dimensions, the notion is also used by those concerned with the related issue of social agency. These anthropologists are wont to posit practice in some relation to culture so as to explicate the dynamics by which the social world is both structured and structuring, that is, both shaped by practice and shaping of practice in turn. Hence, Jean Comaroff uses the term to indicate the process of communicative social action by which persons, in acting upon an external and objective order of power relations, construct themselves as social beings, molded but not determined. The construction of social beings is simultaneously the very generation or reproduction of culture.[39] For Ortner as well, the system of structures that are the basis of a culture interact with 'human practice' to yield culture internalized as the 'self' in social actors.[40]

As a term that is designed to represent the synthetic unity of consciousness and social being within human activity, 'practice' appears to be a powerful tool with which to embrace or transcend all analogous dichotomies. And that, of course, is one of its problems. Even in Marx's usage the term comes to play two roles, encouraging a slip from one level of argument to another. In one role practice is seen as the synthetic unity and resolution of the dichotomy of consciousness and social being. Simultaneously, however, practice is also cast in a second role where, as synthetic practical activity, it is contrasted with theory as the *activity of consciousness* (or with "structure," as in Sahlins) with which it forms the poles of another dichotomy. This second dichotomy is frequently invoked in order to resolve it into a third term, the dialectical synthesis of "historical process" (or again, as in Sahlins's analysis, "cultural praxis").

A second problem that afflicts the Marxist usage of the term practice is the inherent privileging of terms afforded by positing fundamental oppositions. One term gradually comes to dominate the other until the first term is seen as the source of the second term. In the extensive literature on formulations of the relationship of base and superstructure in Marxism, for example, consciousness has been variously described as *caused* by practice (e.g., the superstructure caused or produced by the base) or as *expressive* of practice (e.g., the superstructure expresses the real conditions of the base).[41] In both cases, consciousness becomes derivative. In a similar pattern in cultural anthropology the notion of 'structure' often comes to dominate 'act,' rendering activity merely expressive of more primary structures.[42]

The privileged terms in the dichotomies of Marxists on the one hand and cultural anthropologists on the other differ, of course. Anthropological arguments, such as those of Geertz or Sahlins, subtly privilege thought, structure, and the synchronic, thereby rendering act, performance, and the diachronic as secondary and dependent. Marxists, however, with the exception of Louis Althusser, privilege practice, thus appearing to be less committed to the constitution of theoretical discourse and the status of the theorist than to historical process and the importance of political struggle.[43]

A third problem afflicting practice theory arises with the mediating role that practice is meant to play. Practice is said to mediate consciousness and social being, or structure and act, which in turn are said to exist only in and through practice. However, in actual fact, the concept of practice is a secondary and unstable synthesis of these pairs of categories and it tends to keep collapsing into its underlying components. Thus, practice does not really mediate: it is 'constructed' in order to generate a synthetic abstraction that serves as the object and method of a particular discourse. Practice is not deconstructed to see how practical activity itself might give rise to 'consciousness' or 'structure.' Practice continually gets caught in these analytical patterns because it is being used for a particular end, namely, to generate a discourse based upon an object of analysis tied to a concomitant method of analysis. This purposive end is signaled by arguments that explicitly address the need to transcend the dilemma of objectivism and subjectivism.

Jameson's *The Political Unconscious,* a manifesto for neo-Marxist literary analysis, opens with a discussion of the formal dilemma of all cultural study today: "the struggle for priority between models and history," between theory and history, and theory and practice. Jameson maintains that the sterility of theory which rewrites texts in terms of its own aesthetic on the one hand and the inaccessible past of historicism on the other can be transcended only through the practice of Marxist political-historical theory.[44] For Jameson, therefore, in the end it is the theorist's *practice* of Marxist *theory* that is seen to resolve the bifurcations of theory and practice or models and history. We saw a version of this model in the discussion of Geertz in Part I.

Pierre Bourdieu elaborates an influential analysis of practice which also exemplifies the traditional strengths and weaknesses of this term. The opening pages of his *Outline of a Theory of Practice* describe the need to transcend the subjective categories of native experience as well as the objective categories of the outside observer.[45] His science of practice, he argues, will not only overcome the contradictions of objectivism and subjectivism, but it will *save* both by making them into necessary but incomplete stages in the dialectical method of his science.[46] He then defines practice itself in terms of a dialectical relationship between a structured environment (by which he invokes "objectivist structures," which are not necessarily the real world but an agent's practical interpretation of the world) and the structured dispositions engendered in people which lead them to reproduce the environment even in a transformed form. He calls this a "dialectic of objectification and incorporation."[47] Hence, in a second stage, the object of analysis, practice, is also a dialectic, a dialectic of "objectivism" and "subjectivism." The method and the object constitute each other.

Ortner takes a somewhat different approach. She lays out a theory of practice that is "a theory of the relationship between the structures of society and culture on the one hand, and the nature of human action on the other."[48] Practice theory, in this formulation, continuously translates from action to structure and structure to action. Any action is an instance of practice *if* the theorist establishes its relationship to structure. At times it appears that Ortner is not so much proposing a theory of practice, with practice as the object of scrutiny out there, but a way of analyzing that involves the construction of the category of practice. At the root of this distinction is, of course, Marx's two uses of practice—as the nature of all human activity and as a way of doing theory. Ortner does not emphasize how a focus on practice, or even the construct of practice, is a means for appreciating action and structure as a dynamic whole. She is not interested in synthesizing wholes. On the contrary, Ortner creates oppositions (like structure and action, as well as objectivism and subjectivism) and resists any explicit synthesis that resolves or embraces them. She speaks of practice theory as a "controlling framework" in which such real oppositions, which might never be mediated, are "accepted" instead.[49]

In his discussion of *habitus* Bourdieu presents yet another solution to the problem of where and how to formulate practice. This Latin term was first used by Mauss to describe the culturally acquired abilities and faculties associated with his concept of the "total man."[50] For Bourdieu, the habitus is, most simply, the set of habitual dispositions through which people "give shape and form to social conventions."[51] A more complete definition would add that the habitus is the principle by which individual and collective practices are produced and the matrix in which objective structures are realized within the (subjective) dispositions that produce practices. Bourdieu implies that the habitus is an instance of practice, an irreducible 'unit' of culture that cannot be broken down into any autonomous, constitutive forces. In this analysis, practice is real, but action and structure as components of practice would be mere theoretical constructs. That is to say, 'cultural structures' and 'the act itself' exist nowhere except in the theorist's analysis of the habitus. The types of structures that Ortner and Sahlins are concerned to affirm are, in Bourdieu's framework, nothing more than the schemes implicit in practice.[52]

Habitus is an awkward but explicit formulation of the real insight within Bourdieu's work on practice, namely, the need "to confront the act itself." With regard to myth, for example, he argues that we should approach a myth neither as an object (a completed event laid out neatly for analysis) nor in terms of some mythopoeic subjectivity, but as the very act of myth-making. It is possible to confront the act itself in this way, he writes, only by addressing the principle that generates, organizes, and unifies all practices—"the *socially informed body,* with its tastes and distastes, its compulsions and repulsions, with, in a word, all its *senses.*" These senses, Bourdieu goes on to explain, include "the traditional five senses—which never escape the structuring action of social determinisms—but also the sense of necessity and the sense of duty, the sense of direction and the sense of reality, the sense of balance and the sense of beauty, common sense and the sense of the sacred, tactical sense and the sense of responsibility, business sense and the sense of propriety, the sense of humor and the sense of absurdity, moral sense and the sense of practicality, and so on."[53]

In most societies the "sense of ritual" would be a vital addition to this list. It is through a socially acquired sense of ritual that members of a society know how to improvise a birthday celebration, stage an elaborate wedding, or rush through a minimally adequate funeral.[54] Of course, possession of this sense of ritual does not mean that members of a community always agree on how to do a ritual or what to make of it. Disagreements over ritual can be as fierce or as casual as those over honor or artistic beauty. Yet with regard to Geertz's example of the Javanese child's funeral, for example, a focus on the sense of ritual would shift the emphasis from how the rite failed to fulfill Geertz's theoretical model of ritual, as well as Javanese ideals of *iklas* and *rukun,* to how minimal ritual procedures were improvised with sufficient respect for tradition that the child was considered buried more or less satisfactorily.[55]

Confronting the ritual act itself, and therein eschewing ritual as some object to be analyzed or some subjectivity to be fathomed, would involve asking how ritual activities, in their doing, generate distinctions between what is or is not acceptable ritual. From this perspective one could not seek to construct a theory or model of ritual practice. Rather one could attempt to describe the strategies of the ritualized act by deconstructing some of the intricacies of its cultural logic. This is the perspective that will be developed in the rest of Part II.[56] This exploration of the distinctive strategies and cultural logic that lie behind ritual activities may also begin to illuminate the distinctive strategies of theoretical practices.

The Features of Practice

To focus on the act itself practice must be taken as a nonsynthetic and irreducible term for human activity. I will use the term to highlight four features of human activity. Practice is (1) situational; (2) strategic; (3) embedded in a misrecognition of what it is in fact doing; and (4) able to reproduce or reconfigure a vision of the order of power in the world, or what I will call 'redemptive hegemony.' Each of these features will be discussed individually and then used as a basis with which to describe ritual activity.

First, human activity is situational, which is to say that much of what is important to it cannot be grasped outside of the specific context in which it occurs. When abstracted from its immediate context, an activity is not quite the same activity. Practice may embody determinative influences deriving from other situations, but practice is not the mere expression or effect of these influences. Indeed, it can be said that a focus on the act itself renders these 'influences' (structures or sources) nonexistent except insofar as they exist within the act itself.[57]

Jonathan Culler makes this point in a different context when he argues that analysis of "the relationship between a literary work and a social and historical reality is not one of reflected content but of a play of forms" within the work itself. "The interplay between a literary work and its historical ground lies in the way its formal devices exploit, transform, and supplement a culture's way of producing meaning."[58] Yet Culler focuses solely on literary practices within the text as an object and not, as our foregoing analysis demands, on textual practices per se. Therefore, it is useful to turn to Edward Said's example. Said provides a complementary corrective with his description of the "worldliness" of texts, by which he means that texts are cultural entities that act in the world.[59] Internal textual analysis, for which the text is an object, he argues, will lose itself in an "endless deferral of meaning," never grasping that the text is not a disembodied object but a practical set of actions involving the realities of power and authority. Indeed, Said is concerned with "how a text, by *being* a text, by insisting upon and employing all the devices of textuality" functions in the world to "dislodge other texts."[60] His insights into textual practices are useful for thinking about ritual practices as well.

As a second feature of human activity, practice is inherently strategic, manipulative, and expedient.[61] The logic of practice (and there *is* a logic of sorts) is not that of an intellectualist logic, argues Bourdieu. Practice, as real activity in time, by its very nature dodges the relations of intellectualist logic and excludes the questions asked by the analyst.[62] Its practical or instrumental logic is strategic and economic in that it remains as implicit and rudimentary as possible. Practice, therefore, is a ceaseless play of situationally effective schemes, tactics, and strategies—"the intentionless invention of regulated improvisation."[63]

The third feature intrinsic to practice is a fundamental 'misrecognition' of what it is doing, a misrecognition of its limits and constraints, and of the relationship between its ends and its means.[64] An appreciation of the dynamics of misrecognition as such goes back to the Marxist argument that a society could not exist "unless it disguised to itself the real basis of that existence."[65] However, the idea has been developed in a variety of ways—in the notion of *aporia* developed by Jacques Derrida, in Althusser's notion of "a sighting in an oversight," or in Paul DeMan's discussion of "blindness and insight."

Bourdieu provides a clear illustration of this aspect of practice by reexamining the dynamics of gift exchange.[66] To work effectively, the practice of traditional gift-giving presupposes a "deliberate oversight" of the "fake circulation of fake coin" which makes up symbolic exchange.[67] What is not seen by those involved is that which objective analysis takes to be the whole explanation of the exchange, namely, a reciprocal swapping of items with no intrinsic value. Misrecognition is what "enables the gift or counter-gift to be seen and experienced as an inaugural act of generosity."[68] What is experienced in gift-giving is the voluntary, irreversible, delayed, and strategic play of gift and countergift; it is the experience of these dimensions that actually establishes the value of the objects and the gestures. The context of practice, Bourdieu stresses, is never clear cut but full of indeterminacy, ambiguities, and equivocations. Hence, 'theoretical reconstruction,' as a description in terms of general laws, removes the very conditions that afford misrecognition and the social efficacy of gift exchange. By abstracting the act from its temporal situation and reducing its convoluted strategies to a set of reversible structures, theoretical analysis misses the real dynamics of practice.[69]

A fourth characteristic of practice, closely intertwined with the features situationality, strategy, and misrecognition, has to do with the motivational dynamics of agency, the will to act, which is also integral to the context of action. It addresses the question of why people do something or anything, but in a form that attempts to avoid the reductionism of most self-interest theory. This dimension of practice can be evoked through the concept of 'redemptive hegemony,' which is a synthesis of Kenelm Burridge's notion of the "redemptive process" and Antonio Gramsci's notion of "hegemony."[70]

The term hegemony has been used to go beyond more traditional understandings of power and social process, specifically, that ruling power is expressed in direct techniques of coercion, that culture is the 'whole social process,' and that ideology is a system of false meanings expressing the interests of particular classes.[71] Gramsci's term recognizes the dominance and subordination that exist within people's practical and un-self-conscious awareness of the world. It is a term that politicizes our understanding of what David Laitin calls "the symbolic framework that reigns as common-sense."[72] This awareness is a lived system of meanings, a more or less unified moral order, which is confirmed and nuanced in experience to construct a person's sense of reality and identity. As such, this practical awareness of the world is a lived ordering of power, a construal of power that is also, inevitably, a misconstrual since it is power as envisioned and encountered in very particular situations. A lived 'ordering' of power means that hegemony is neither singular nor monolithic; to be at all it must be reproduced, renewed, and even resisted in an enormous variety of practices. Similar to Burridge's concept of the redemptive process, Laitin sees hegemony not only as a lived consciousness and moral order, but also as a prestige order.[73]

Burridge's notion of a redemptive process as the basis of cultural life provides a useful framework for bringing into focus the actual workings of this notion of hegemonic power. Burridge defines the redemptive process as that process by which, in a given context of assumptions about power, persons "attempt to discharge their obligations in relation to the moral imperatives of the community."[74] This redemptive process, he suggests, not only involves assumptions about power and the moral order; it appears to enable people both "to perceive the truth of things" and to be guaranteed that "they are indeed perceiving the truth of things."[75] An insight basic to Burridge's formulation is the idea that people construe power relations in such a way that (1) these power relations are reproduced in various ways, (2) people have a sense of their place in some ordering of relations, and (3) they can envision the efficacy of acting within that ordering of relations. People reproduce relationships of power and domination, but not in a direct, automatic, or mechanistic way; rather, they reproduce them through their particular construal of those relations, a construal that affords the actor the sense of a sphere of action, however minimal.

As a practical construal or consciousness of the system of power relations and as a framework for action, redemptive hegemony suggests that human practice is characterized by relations of dominance and subjugation. These relations, however, are present in practice by means of the practical values, obligations, and persistent envisioning—as both an assumption and an extension of the system—of a state of prestige within this ordering of power. This vision exists as a practical consciousness of the world (common sense) and a sense of one's options for social action. It is also a vision of empowerment that is rooted in the actor's perceptions and experiences of the organization of power. Although awkward, the term 'redemptive hegemony' denotes the way in which reality is experienced as a natural weave of constraint and possibility, the fabric of day-to-day dispositions and decisions experienced as a field for strategic action. Rather than an embracing ideological vision of the whole, it conveys a biased, nuanced rendering of the ordering of power so as to facilitate the envisioning of personal empowerment through activity in the perceived system. The truism that "every established order tends to produce . . . the naturalization of its own arbitrariness" indicates a process in which agents not only accede to a shared sense of reality but also effectively reproduce that reality in ways that continue to empower them to act.[76]

Gramsci proposed that hegemonic ordering of power requires people both to envision and to suppress, to self-censor and to appropriate liberties to themselves. He argued that ruling classes establish dominance not merely through overt mechanisms of control but through a climate of thought to which the oppressed classes subscribe. This theory of ideology suggests what has been called a general "strategy of containment."[77] It also implies what others have made explicit, that ideology is not a disseminated body of ideas but the way in which people live the relationships between themselves and their world, a type of necessary illusion.[78] To maintain and adapt their assumptions about the order of reality persons and groups engage in degrees of self-censorship or misrecognition, as well as legitimization and objectification in the guise of more stable social structures.

In sum, a redemptive hegemony is not an explicit ideology or a single and bounded *doxa* that defines a culture's sense of reality. It is a strategic and practical orientation for acting, a framework possible only insofar as it is embedded in the act itself. As such, of course, the redemptive hegemony of practice does not reflect reality more or less effectively; it creates it more or less effectively. To analyze practice in terms of its vision of redemptive hegemony is, therefore, to formulate the unexpressed assumptions that constitute the actor's strategic understanding of the place, purpose, and trajectory of the act.

Although tailored to the needs of this inquiry into ritual, the concept of redemptive hegemony is akin to several other theories of practical activity. David Cannadine and Simon Price imply a similar notion when they ask how activity projects images of cosmic order on to the plane of human experience.[79] Leach's idea that "social structure in practical situations (as contrasted with the sociologist's abstract model) consists of a set of ideas about the distribution of power between persons and groups of persons" also bears on the discussion here.[80] Similarly, when Geertz argues that any understanding of the Balinese *negara* would have to elaborate not just structures of action or thought but a poetics of power as opposed to a mechanics of power, he also implies a strategic sense of the ordering of power.[81]

Jameson stresses the interaction of misrecognition and something like redemptive hegemony in his description of the method underlying hermeneutical analysis of cultural objects as socially symbolic acts.[82] Such analysis, he argues, must first undertake the essentially "negative" hermeneutical task of unmasking or demystifying the ways in which a cultural artifact fulfills a specific ideological mission, namely, its resolution of real contradictions in disguised forms. Yet that alone will not suffice. Hermeneutical analysis must also undertake the second, "positive" task of determining how that artifact simultaneously projected a type of Utopian power by symbolically affirming a specific historical and class form of collective unity.[83]

Althusser's analytical method gives particular attention to the third feature, the strategic blindness of practice. In his determination the fundamental principle of action is the "problematic" (*problématique*).[84] The problematic is essentially the cultural-historical limits within which practices operate—that is, within which practices address the particular problems posed for them (for the superstructure, the dominant ideology) by the historical moment (or the infrastructure).[85] As such, Althusser's problematic may be compared to (but not equated with) Bourdieu's habitus, described as the set of structured and structuring dispositions in dialectical interaction with the conditions in which these dispositions are operating (the latter being the particular state of the habitus at any one moment).[86] However, Althusser's term also suggests an implicit notion of redemptive hegemony with its description of the 'lived' ordering of power which actors see themselves addressing or countering, but which is reproduced in a transformed way in their actions.

According to Althusser, to understand a set of practices it is necessary to question the relationship of those practices to their intent or object.[87] In looking at someone doing something, for example, we should ask about the relationship between 'the doing' and 'the something.' This is to question the particular object of the practice as well as the particularity of the practice's relationship to this object. In Althusser's words, one puts to practice the question of the specific difference between itself and its "object-intent." That is, with regard to the unity of the practice with its object-intent, one asks what distinguishes this particular unity from the unity of other practices and their object-intent. This is to question the 'object-unity' of a particular action.[88]

There are really two 'questionings' involved in this inquiry into the unity of practice and its intent. The first questioning asks what the practice 'sees,' that is, its conscious 'given,' the questions it asks or situations it addresses, its objective or avowed purpose—in other words, the 'something' in 'doing something.' The second questioning, which Althusser calls "symptomatic," is different.[89] It questions not the 'something' of 'doing something,' but the 'doing.' Althusser argues that to question the 'doing' is to question the "oversights" of a practice, what a specific practice does not see, what it cannot see—namely, the problem or situation that "is only visible in so far as it is invisible."[90] A practice does not see itself do what it actually does. This oversight does not concern the object-intent consciously sighted by the practice but the very ability to see practice itself.

In simpler terms, we can say that practice sees what it intends to accomplish, but it does not see the strategies it uses to produce what it actually does accomplish, a new situation. Althusser shows that practice will give an answer to a question that was never posed: the effectiveness of practice is *not* the resolution of the problematic to which it addresses itself but a complete change in the terms of the problematic, a change it does not see itself make.[91]

To understand how there can be an oversight in the act of sighting, or an 'undoing' in the act of doing, it is necessary to reorganize our traditional concept of knowledge and its "mirror myths of immediate vision" and think of knowledge also as practice or production. Practice sees the problem it is intent upon; it does not see what it itself produces in the very operation of practice: it does not see the production process which constitutes the 'object.' For example, as demonstrated in Chapter 1, ritual theory, a form of practice, does not see how it creates its own object, 'ritual,' in the very course of determining a method appropriate to some object thought to exist independently of theory, method, and discourse. Practice "does not see what it does: its production of a new answer without a question, and simultaneously the production of a new latent question contained by default in this new answer."[92]

Practice, continues Althusser, sees itself as generated by a problematic, but it produces a new problematic without knowing it, usually convinced indeed that it is still on the terrain of the old one. "Its blindness and its 'oversight' lie in this misunderstanding, between what it produces and what it sees, in this 'substitution,' which Marx elsewhere calls a 'play on words' (Wortspiel) that is necessarily impenetrable to its author."[93] Why is practice blind to what it produces? Because it is still fixed on the old question, the old horizon, on which the new problem is not visible. Furthermore, he points out, "what is at stake in the production of this new problem contained *unwittingly* in the new answer is not a particular new object which has emerged among other, already identified objects, like an unexpected guest at a family reunion; on the contrary, what has happened involves a transformation of the *entire* terrain and its *entire* horizon, which are the background against which the new problem is produced."[94] Just as Bourdieu sees practice as the continual production of a new state of the habitus which generates new practices in turn, so Althusser sees practice as the constant production of a new problematic out of an old one.[95]

Ritual necessarily shares these four features of practice. More to the point, the practical logic by which ritual acts are generated vis-à-vis other ways of acting, ritualization, will be more visible in terms of these four features.

Ritualization

The term 'ritualization' has some pertinent history that needs to be reviewed. Two main schools employ the term: the first has developed from the work of Gluckman; the second is more or less linked to the ethological perspective pioneered by Huxley. Nearly forty years ago, Gluckman contrasted the "ritualization" of social relationships with "ritualism" in order to extend the notion of ritual beyond a narrow and somewhat traditional connection with organized religious institutions and formal worship.[96] His work inspired a great deal of sociological literature on ritualization in nonreligious frameworks, such as Murray Edelman's study of ritualization in the political conflicts attending industry–labor union negotiations. Edelman refines the notion of ritualization to describe a process to which a conflicted relationship is subjected in order to facilitate both the escalation *and* resolution of a struggle that otherwise would destroy the relationship.[97]

In the second school, Huxley's use of the term has also served to extend the traditional notion of ritual. Through his influence, ritualization has been adopted both by those who explicitly acknowledge the relevancy of ethology for the study of human ritual, such as Rappaport, and by those who do not make any such acknowledgments, such as John Beattie.[98] For others not directly concerned with Gluckman's or Huxley's lines of thinking, the term is used somewhat more simply to emphasize ritual as activity. This is true for Frits Staal's arguments about the meaning of ritual residing in the structure of the act itself. Yet it is also true for Mary C. Bateson, who uses the term to describe both the development of rituals on the one hand and a particular mode of action on the other. In the latter sense Bateson argues against the effectiveness of a delimited category of action called "ritual," as I did earlier, pointing out that ritualization is a "more-or-less phenomenon" that should be compared to other types of social interactions in terms of "texture," not "structure."[99]

Ritualization is now frequently the preferred term particularly for studies focusing on ritual in technologically advanced societies. Eric Hobsbawn speaks of ritualization to describe the process of "inventing traditions" in modern societies.[100] Crystal Lane's analysis of the development of modern Soviet ritual explicitly adopts the term from Gluckman's work to denote the acting out of social relationships in ritual form in order to express and alter them.[101] Common to most of these perspectives is an appreciation of the emergence of ritual forms for the purpose of social control and/or social communication. Ritual forms of behavior are seen to control by defining, modeling, and communicating social relations.[102] Hence, these studies call attention to the conscious or unconscious deployment of ritual as a type of social strategy. Indeed, for most studies that use the term, ritualization is seen to involve the formal 'modeling' of valued relationships so as to promote legitimation and internalization of those relations and their values.

My use of the term 'ritualization' will build on some of these implications while attempting to focus more clearly on (1) how ritualization as practice distinguishes itself from other practices and (2) what it accomplishes in doing so.

Semiologically speaking, just as a sign or a text derives its significance by virtue of its relationship to other signs and texts, basic to ritualization is the inherent significance it derives from its interplay and contrast with other practices.[103] From this viewpoint, there would be little content to any attempt to generate a cross-cultural or universal meaning to ritual.[104] Likewise, this view suggests that the significance of ritual behavior lies not in being an entirely separate way of acting, but in how such activities constitute themselves as different and in contrast to other activities. Even in theoretical analysis, ritual should not be analyzed by being lifted out of the context formed by other ways of acting in a cultural situation. Acting ritually is first and foremost a matter of nuanced contrasts and the evocation of strategic, value-laden distinctions.

Viewed as practice, ritualization involves the very drawing, in and through the activity itself, of a privileged distinction between ways of acting, specifically between those acts being performed and those being contrasted, mimed, or implicated somehow. That is, intrinsic to ritualization are strategies for differentiating itself—to various degrees and in various ways—from other ways of acting within any particular culture. At a basic level, ritualization is the production of this differentiation. At a more complex level, ritualization is a way of acting that specifically establishes a privileged contrast, differentiating itself as more important or powerful. Such privileged distinctions may be drawn in a variety of culturally specific ways that render the ritualized acts dominant in status.

For example, distinctions between eating a regular meal and participating in the Christian eucharistic meal are redundantly drawn in every aspect of the ritualized meal, from the type of larger family gathering around the table to the distinctive periodicity of the meal and the insufficiency of the food for physical nourishment. It is important to note that the features of formality, fixity, and repetition are not intrinsic to this ritualization or to ritual in general. Theoretically, ritualization of the meal could employ a different set of strategies to differentiate it from conventional eating, such as holding the meal only once in a person's lifetime or with too much food for normal nourishment. The choice of strategies would depend in part on which ones could most effectively render the meal symbolically dominant to its conventional counterparts. The choice would also depend on the particular 'work' the ritualized acts aimed to accomplish in a situation. Given this analysis, ritualization could involve the exact repetition of a centuries-old tradition or deliberately radical innovation and improvisation, as in certain forms of liturgical experimentation or performance art.

An even simpler example might contrast the routine activity of buying some regularly used article of clothing for a spouse or child (such as gym socks) and the ritualized version of buying a similar but different article (argyle socks) and giving it as a gift. These activities are differentiated in the very doing and derive their significance from the contrast implicity set up between them. Routine giving plays off ritualized giving and vice versa; they define each other. The Christian mass and the gift are not models for a normal meal or family shopping; they are strategic versions of them. Yet this is not to say that ritualization is simply acting differently. Otherwise, buying mismatched socks at a bargain table—an act that may communicate simply insofar as it differs from a routine set of expectations—would qualify as ritual.

This foregoing elaboration of the basic principle of privileged differentiation expressed in what and how something is done is not the sole characteristic of ritual action. I regard it as basic here for how it highlights a fundamental strategic and contextual quality of ritual action. By virtue of this quality, what is ritual is always contingent, provisional, and defined by difference.

From the perspective of ritualization the categories of sacred and profane appear in a different light. Ritualization appreciates how sacred and profane activities are differentiated in the performing of them, and thus how ritualization gives rise to (or creates) the sacred as such by virtue of its sheer differentiation from the profane.[105] Whereas Durkheim defined religion and ritual as that which is addressed to the sacred, the approach presented here is an inverse of his, showing how a particular way of acting draws the type of flexible distinctions that yield notions and categories like 'ritual' or 'religion.' The relative clarity and flexibility of the boundaries, of course, are also a highly strategic matter in a particular cultural community and are best understood in terms of the concrete situation.[106]

There is little explicit consensus concerning the intrinsic features of ritual, and some do not believe there to be *any* features intrinsic to ritual.[107] Nonetheless, certain features—formality, fixity, and

repetition—have been consistently and repeatedly cited as central
to ritual and ritualization. Almost all theorists of ritual start with
one or more of these obvious physical characteristics and attempt
to link it to any of a variety of authoritative or communicative
functions also ascribed to ritual. Formality as a matter of embel-
lishment or repetition as a matter of redundancy has each been
defined in turn as central to the communicative functions of ritual.
Rituals come to be defined as a particularly intensive form of communication by virtue of their formality and repetition.[108] Fixity of
the times and places of ritual activities, as well as the exact gestures
to be enacted, also tends to be linked to the authoritative modeling
of ritual.[109]

Yet if ritual is interpreted in terms of practice, it becomes clear
that formality, fixity, and repetition are not intrinsic qualities of
ritual so much as they are a frequent, but not universal strategy for
producing ritualized acts. That is to say, formalizing a gathering,
following a fixed agenda and repeating that activity at periodic
intervals, and so on, reveal potential strategies of ritualization because these ways of acting are the means by which one group of
activities is set off as distinct and privileged vis-à-vis other activities.
Yet in a different situation, informality might be stressed to dominate other ways of acting. For example, the formal activities of
gathering for a Catholic mass distinguish this 'meal' from daily
eating activities, but the informality of a mass celebrated in a private
home with a folk guitar and kitchen utensils is meant to set up
another contrast (the spontaneous authentic celebration versus the
formal and inauthentic mass) which the informal service expects to
dominate. It is only necessary that the cultural context include some
consensus concerning the opposition and relative values of personal
sincerity and intimate participation vis-à-vis routinized and impersonal participation.

Since practice is situational and strategic, people engage in ritualization as a practical way of dealing with some specific circumstances. Ritual is never simply or solely a matter of routine, habit,
or "the dead weight of tradition." Indeed, routinization and ha-
bitualization may be strategies in certain cultural situations, but so
might the infrequent yet periodic reproduction of a complex ritual
tradition. Similarly, ritualization may maximize or minimize its
differentiation from other forms of practice. The degree of differ-

entiation is itself strategic and part of the logic and efficacy of the act. Hence, ritualization can be characterized *in general* only to a rather limited extent since the idiom of its differentiation of acting will be, for the most part, culturally specific.[110]

Aside from the drawing of a contrast between the ritualized activities that are being performed and other forms of social behavior, another feature is also fundamental to the practice of ritualization per se. The strategies of ritualization are particularly rooted in the body, specifically, the interaction of the social body within a symbolically constituted spatial and temporal environment. Essential to ritualization is the circular production of a ritualized body which in turn produces ritualized practices. Ritualization is embedded within the dynamics of the body defined within a symbolically structured environment. An important corollary to this is the fact that ritualization is a particularly 'mute' form of activity. It is designed to do what it does without bringing what it is doing across the threshold of discourse or systematic thinking.

5

The Ritual Body

In the last ten years the 'body' has emerged as a major analytic focus in a number of disciplines. The reasons for this perspective may involve the development and interaction of several lines of thought: the rich tradition of anthropological studies of the body; the critique of traditional objectivism and its "mentalist" or "mind-centered" notions of knowledge; and the impact of feminist and gender studies, which, in some circles, have inspired a new "erotics" of interpretative practice.[111]

Anthropological exploration of the codes and classification systems of body symbolism has vividly illustrated how social categories shape the decoration, perceptions, and dispositions of the body. In contrast to the Darwinian argument that bodily expressions, particularly facial expressions, are genetically determined and therefore both natural and universal, a series of early studies by Durkheim, Mauss, and Robert Hertz demonstrated that bodily expressions are social and learned.[112] Although the debate on the biological or social origins of human behavior and classification was just getting under way at that time—and is far from over—this early stage of research identified the body as a social construction in the image of society and a microcosm of the universe.[113]

More recently, Douglas explored the social body as "a highly restricted medium of expression" and a key to the relationship of self, society, and cosmos.[114] V. Turner pushed the primacy of the body further by arguing that it is the human organism itself, and not society, that is the *fons et origo* of all classification.[115] Goffman, in turn, examined the molding of the body into a nearly mnemonic encapsulation of the cultural principles that organize society.[116] Some have seen the body as mediating the simple dialectical interaction of the individual and society; others have explored how the construction of cultural reality focuses on the body, which in turn experiences that construction as natural.[117] Still others see the body as the "foremost of all metaphors" for a society's perception and organization of itself.[118] Certainly a consensus of sorts has emerged granting the body a critical place in the social construction of reality.[119]

A second line of thinking about the body emerged in connection with a concern to undermine the framework of 'disembodied' objectivism that has constituted the dominant model used in the humanities and social sciences. After years of guerrilla activity against the dualities of mind–body, individual–society, and message–medium, this concern is now readily articulated in many fields. One hears of the "embodied" mind, the "socially embedded" or "socially constituted" person, not to mention the "media-massaged" message. The works of Richard Rorty in philosophy and of George Lakoff and Mark Johnson in linguistics, or Gilles Deleuze and Felix Guattari's critique of psychoanalysis and capitalism, are just a few influential examples of this movement.[120]

Lakoff provides a particularly provocative formulation of this perspective, one with relevance for the issue of ritual action. Interspersed with a careful critique of traditional objectivism, Lakoff demonstrates how the concepts and conceptual categories that both comprise and organize knowledge are neither abstract in nature nor independent of the body. Instead, they are directly or indirectly "embodied."[121] Similarly, Johnson has countered the claims of objectivism by exploring "the indispensable forms of imagination" that emerge from "bodily experience" and profoundly affect human reasoning.[122]

Lakoff's argument, for example, presumes the anthropological analyses noted previously and opposes them in several important ways. He cites evidence illustrating how classification systems are culturally determined and, in particular, how traditional objectivism in Western philosophy itself constitutes just such a "folk classification system." However, Lakoff also finds that the body is not a *tabula rasa* upon which society can inscribe anything it wishes. Without attempting to distinguish between the social and biological experiences of the body, he describes a preconceptual structuring of experience, which in turn structures the conceptual categories with which human beings think.[123] In contrast therefore to Hertz, Mauss, Durkheim, and Douglas, for whom basic logical categories are social in nature and acquired in practice, Lakoff argues that they are fully rooted in the sociobiological body. The import of this approach, which echoes the thrust of V. Turner's argument, suggests both the primacy of the body over the abstraction 'society' and the irreducibility of the social body.

In a third tradition, feminist scholarship has pioneered the recognition of gender as a fundamental condition of experience and as an analytic category for specifically addressing the body's relation to language and identity, writing and power.[124] From the early work of Sandra Gilbert and Susan Gubar, who explored the traditional identification of literary creativity with phallocentric imagery, through the "gynocriticism" of Elaine Showalter, to the more radical work of Hélene Cixous, Julia Kristeva, and *l'écriture feminine*— feminist literary theory has challenged traditional methods to focus on "woman's lived experience" at the center of which is "the Body."[125]

Within the ethos created by these three cross-fertilizing traditions, even relatively mainstream historians are now looking beyond the social construction of institutions to the construction of the 'social bodies' that mandate such institutions.[126] It appears we are now reappropriating the image of the body: no longer the mere physical instrument of the mind, it now denotes a more complex and irreducible phenomenon, namely, the social person.

Not surprisingly, the emergence of a focus on the social body has entailed a close consideration of ritual. Indeed, any discussion of the social body presupposes some theory of how the human psychophysical entity is socialized and therein empowered as a cultural actor. Often a special appeal is made to ritual to 'model' this whole process of socialization as the transformation of nature into culture. It is in this style that Burridge eloquently described how the ritual structure of millenarian activities "recapitulates the process whereby an animal crossed the threshold to become man, and through which one sort of man becomes a new sort of man."[127]

In a more complicated example, Foucault has correlated the various "rituals" of penal discipline with "economies of power" and changing constructions of the human person.[128] For Foucault, the "body" emerged in the late seventeenth century as the arena in which more local social practices were linked to the larger scale organization of power. With examples that range from marking the body with torture to confessional routines and the control of space, Foucault has suggested how "rituals of power" work to forge a specific political "technology" of the body. As *the* medium of the play of power, he argued, the body came to be linked to a new political rationality specifically rooted in the technologies of "biopower."[129] This historical emergence of the body as a focus, moreover, would constitute a new level of analysis located between biology and the institutional vehicles of force, and giving rise to the human sciences themselves.[130]

In a study of the Tshidi of South Africa, Jean Comaroff contrasts the ritual construction of personhood in precolonial ritual life with the very different form of personhood ritually constructed in postcolonial Zionist churches. Comaroff argues that social practices structure the body, thereby constructing "social beings" via the internalization of basic schemes and values. The socialized body in turn gives rise to dispositions that generate similarly, although not identically, structured and structuring practices. Thus, she argues, the body "mediates" all action: it is the medium for the internalization and reproduction of social values and for the simultaneous constitution of both the self and the world of social relations.[131]

Bourdieu's analysis of these dynamics has been, perhaps, the most dramatic. He argues that every social group "entrusts to bodily automatisms" those principles that are most basic to the organization and maintenance of that group. Bourdieu goes further than Douglas, who focused on ritual in terms of how the preservation of the group involves a drive to coordinate all levels of experience and expression by correlating the body with society and the cosmos.[132] Bourdieu explores the mediation of the body via a "dialectic of objectification and embodiment" that makes it *the locus* for the coordination of all levels of bodily, social, and cosmological experience. This coordination is effected only in and through schemes that pass "from practice to practice" without becoming explicit either in personal consciousness or in social discourse.[133]

Despite their differences, these studies constitute a general consensus that the distinctive strategies of ritual action play a major role in the construction of the social body. Unfortunately, however, when discussing the ritual construction of the social body, Foucault, Comaroff, and Bourdieu all slide from a discussion of social practices into a discussion of ritual ones with little if any explication of the implied relation of ritual practices to social practices in general. They appear to mean that ritual practices either 'model' social ones in an extreme way or that ritual practices are particular problem-addressing techniques. Nonetheless, their work provides a useful basis for describing ritualization as strategic social activity and socialization. In the following sections I will rely heavily on their framework and terminology in working out the distinctive object-unity of ritualization as a strategic form of socialization.

The Ritualized Body Environment

The implicit dynamic and 'end' of ritualization—that which it does not see itself doing—can be said to be the production of a 'ritualized body.' A ritualized body is a body invested with a 'sense' of ritual. This sense of ritual exists as an implicit variety of schemes whose deployment works to produce sociocultural situations that the ritualized body can dominate in some way. This is a "practical mastery," to use Bourdieu's term, of strategic schemes for ritualization, and it appears as a social instinct for creating and manipulating contrasts. This 'sense' is not a matter of self-conscious knowledge of any explicit rules of ritual but is an implicit "cultivated disposition."[134]

Ritualization produces this ritualized body through the interaction of the body with a structured and structuring environment. "It is in the dialectical relationship between the body and a space structured according to mythico-ritual oppositions," writes Bourdieu, "that one finds the form par excellence of the structural apprenticeship which leads to the em-bodying of the structures of the world, that is, the appropriating by the world of a body thus enabled to appropriate the world."[135] Hence, through a series of physical movements ritual practices spatially and temporally construct an environment organized according to schemes of privileged opposition. The construction of this environment and the activities within it simultaneously work to impress these schemes upon the bodies of participants. This is a circular process that tends to be misrecognized, if it is perceived at all, as values and experiences impressed upon the person and community from sources of power and order beyond it. Through the orchestration in time of loose but strategically organized oppositions, in which a few oppositions quietly come to dominate others, the social body internalizes the principles of the environment being delineated. Inscribed within the social body, these principles enable the ritualized person to generate in turn strategic schemes that can appropriate or dominate other sociocultural situations.

The importance of the ritual environment has, of course, been elaborated before. Since Arnold Van Gennep correlated spatial or geographical progression with the ritual marking of cultural "passages," many others have developed the idea of "ritual space" in various ways.[136] Mircea Eliade, for example, found ritual inseparable from the delineation of a sacred place and the "regeneration" of time.[137] V. Turner specifically discussed the creation of "ritualized space."[138] Jonathan Z. Smith focused on the ritual dynamics of demarcating a "controlled environment"—to the point of suggesting the role of such places in generating the temporal realities of the ritual calendar itself.[139] Yet a focus on the acts themselves illuminates a critical circularity to the body's interaction with this environment: generating it, it is molded by it in turn. By virtue of this circularity, space and time are redefined through the physical movements of bodies projecting organizing schemes on the space–time environment on the one hand while reabsorbing these schemes as the nature of reality on the other. In this process such schemes become socially instinctive automatisms of the body and implicit strategies for shifting the power relationships among symbols.

Adapting Bourdieu's discussion of practice, we can speak of the natural logic of ritual, a logic embodied in the physical movements of the body and thereby lodged beyond the grasp of consciousness and articulation.[140] The principles underlying this logic can be made explicit only with great difficulty; they are rarely in themselves the objects of scrutiny or contention. And yet, suggests Bourdieu, nothing less than a whole cosmology is instilled with the words "Stand up straight!"[141] Rappaport makes a similar point in describing how the act of kneeling does not so much communicate a message about subordination as it generates a body identified with subordination.[142] In other words, the molding of the body within a highly structured environment does not simply express inner states. Rather, it primarily acts to restructure bodies in the very doing of the acts themselves. Hence, required kneeling does not merely *communicate* subordination to the kneeler. For all intents and purposes, kneeling produces a subordinated kneeler in and through the act itself. On another level of the strategies of ritualization, such an act may in fact set up a bifurcation between the external show of subordination and an internal act of resistance. These more complex dimensions are explored in Part III. For now, what we see in ritualization is not the mere display of subjective states or corporate values. Rather, we see an act of production— the production of a ritualized agent able to wield physically a scheme of subordination or insubordination.

The situational features of ritualization are not exhausted, however, by this consideration of the centrality of the ritual body within a structured environment. The body is always conditioned by and responsive to a specific context. John Blacking underscores this point when he argues that "it is from a specific historical and ethical context that the individual derives the expressive possibilities of his body."[143] Hence, ritualization, as the production of a ritualized agent via the interaction of a body within a structured and structuring environment, always takes place within a larger and very immediate sociocultural situation. Yet just as ritualization is never merely the expression of a subjective state, neither is it merely a spatiotemporal reflection of this larger situation or more encompassing social structures. The relationship between any instance of ritualization and its immediate social and historical situation is, as noted earlier, "not one of reflected content but of a play of forms."[144] Indeed, ritualization is the strategic manipulation of 'context' in the very act of reproducing it. The distinct strategy of ritualization in manipulating its situation will be broken down further in the following chapters. The point to make here is that ritualization cannot be understood apart from the immediate situation, which is being reproduced in a misrecognized and transformed way through the production of ritualized agents.

The opposite view, emphasizing the inherent autonomy of ritual activity and its independence vis-à-vis its context, tends to be adopted by those trying to assess the more complex ritual traditions such as the Catholic mass or the Vedic fire sacrifice. They see ritual as a matter of the exact performance of actions mandated by the authority of history and the sacred. Rappaport, for example, finds that "liturgical orders," by which he means codified ritual traditions such as found in the Christian mass or the Jewish sabbath, do *not* reflect the social–political–ecological relations of their immediate context.[145] Yet if we take seriously the idea that even the exact repetition of an age-old ritual precedent is a *strategic* act with which to define the present, then no ritual style is autonomous. We need tools with which to analyze the particular play of forms of a style that purports to be autonomous.

Ritual Oppositions and Hierarchies

The main strategies of ritualization noted thus far—the generation of a privileged opposition between ritualized and other activities and the production of ritualized agents through the generation of a structured environment experienced as molding the bodies acting within it—appear to involve certain basic dynamics. I will focus on three operations: first, the physical construction of schemes of binary oppositions; second, the orchestrated hierarchization of these schemes whereby some schemes come to dominate or nuance others; and third, the generation of a loosely integrated whole in which each element 'defers' to another in an endlessly circular chain of reference. In this semantic universe, every sign is an implicit set of contrasts and every contrast invokes another. Yet despite the continued juxtaposition of nearly equivalent oppositions, the contrasts are orchestrated so that some come to appropriate, reinterpret, or qualify others. On the one hand, the semantic system evoked is a closed and endlessly self-deferring circular system; on the other hand, the hierarchical orchestration of the contrasts and deferrals generates the sense of a universal totality, a unified and authoritative coherence informing the whole scheme of things.

Returning briefly to the example of the traditional Catholic eucharistic meal, whole sets of oppositions emerge to dominate other sets. The scheme of a central or 'centered' community versus a dispersed population is generated as people congregate together, coming from different directions and situations to assemble at a specific place and time. When they are gathered, this scheme is overlaid with a higher versus lower opposition in which a raised altar and elevated host, the lifting and lowering voices and eyes, as well as sequences of standing and kneeling, and so on, all generate a contrast between a higher reality (spiritual) and a lower one (mundane). However, this scheme is overlaid in turn by an inner versus outer one when the higher reality is internalized through the food shared by participants. Ultimately, the inner–outer scheme comes to dominate the oppositions of higher–lower and centered–dispersed, generating an experience of a higher spiritual authority as an internalized reality.[146]

The importance of oppositions and contrasts in ritual has been apparent since Durkheim's study of ritual's relation to the demarcation of the sacred from the profane. Likewise, a small but critical twist of perspective has suggested that ritual is less concerned to define and proclaim sacrality than it is to assert the contrast between sacred and profane. As J. Z. Smith notes, "Ritual is, above all, an assertion of difference."[147] G. Bateson came to the same conclusion in his early study of the *naven* ceremonies of the Iatmul of New Guinea. He saw these ceremonies as asserting difference, and he coined the term "schismogenesis" to denote the differentiations effected in ritual, where they are also balanced by other processes of integration.[148] Lévi-Strauss also argued for a "unifying" function in ritual that is nevertheless effected through the obsessive ritual process of making countless minute distinctions he termed "parceling."[149]

In practice, however, ritual contrasts are rarely as balanced as these theories suggest. Binary oppositions almost always involve asymmetrical relations of dominance and subordination by which they generate hierarchically organized relationships. Hertz, V. Turner, and Bourdieu have all traced the asymmetrical oppositions that create dominance, hierarchy, and integration among a system of associations. Hertz was the first to describe how the deceptively straightforward oppositions of the body, such as right and left, promoted and rationalized the dominance of the right hand and its analogy in countless homologous contrasts. His insights have been extended by the work of Terence Turner in particular, who argues that formulations of binary oppositions are an elementary means of expressing unity and totality through an implicit hierarchy.[150] Expanding Louis Dumont's work on how the hierarchical caste system of India is rooted in an opposition of purity and pollution, T. Turner concludes that the ritual process of differentiation is simultaneously a process of generating a hierarchical form of unity.[151] Bourdieu likewise describes hierarchization as a strategy of "integration in and through division."[152]

Hertz, V. Turner, and Bourdieu have also remarked upon the manner in which one set of oppositions comes to be related to another set: right–left is analogized to inside–outside or good–evil, while male–female is linked to right–left, front–back, and so on. These relationships both generate and presuppose complex chains of associations and taxonomic relations.[153] Leach and Tambiah explored a similar 'logic' in their appeal to the operations of 'metaphor' and 'metonomy,' which establish relationships between such spheres of reference as one's stomach and one's house or pregnancy and gardening.[154] In addition, Brian K. Smith's discussion of correlation and resemblance in Vedic ritual presents yet another logic by which the transfer of taxonomic schemes defines relationships among every element of the rite and the cosmos.[155]

Bourdieu, in particular, delineates a type of "practical logic" in ritual activities that involves three fundamental operations: (1) positing an initial opposition based upon a fundamental dichotomy; (2) applying different symbolic schemes to a single object or practice (e.g., a girl undergoing initiation will engage in a series of activities organized around such schemes as opening–closing or swelling–shrinking); and (3) applying a single symbolic scheme to different logical universes (e.g., as a world in its own right, a native house may be considered to have male and female parts, but in the context of the whole world outside the house, it will be considered female). Through these operations whole systems of ritual symbols and actions can be generated by means of a small number of oppositions (male–female, within–without) or reduced to a few pairs that appear fundamental—and they all prove to be based on the movements and postures of the body.[156] In addition to the many forms that the basic opposition may take, certain forms tend to act as "switchers" to establish relationships between various homologized activities. For example, 'inside–outside' will come between, and serve to link, 'behind–in front' with 'female fertility–male virility.' Thus, for Bourdieu, the practical logic of ritual is simultaneously logical and biological—or, as Lakoff would argue, "embodied."[57]

This ritual logic is a minimalist logic that generates a 'sense' of logical systematicity while simultaneously facilitating subtle shifts in the ability of some symbols to dominate others. Most important, however, it is by means of these operations that ordinary physical movements generate homologies and hierarchies among diverse levels and areas of experience, setting up relations among symbols, values, and social categories. Homologous oppositions (light–dark, good–evil, male–female) can organize taxonomic sets (the set of light, good, and male, or the set of dark, evil, and female) simply by the juxtaposition of activities that use these oppositions. In actual practice only a few elements from a 'set' need be invoked to imply a whole series of relationships and implications. Such homologized spheres are orchestrated (or confused, or collapsed) so as to produce an experience of their basic identity or coherence.[58] This experience of coherence, however, simultaneously facilitates the emergence of some symbolic terms in a dominant relation to others. The sense of the general identity of the whole naturalizes such hegemony. This is the heart of the not-seeing, the oversight, of ritualization.

In sum, ritualization not only involves the setting up of oppositions, but through the privileging built into such an exercise it generates hierarchical schemes to produce a loose sense of totality and systematicity. In this way, ritual dynamics afford an experience of 'order' as well as the 'fit' between this taxonomic order and the real world of experience.

Internal–External Strategies of Ritualization

The organization of oppositions into hierarchical schemes does not imply the ritual resolution of these oppositions. The type of reintegration effected by hierarchization is based on maintaining and multiplying oppositions. Poststructural linguistics provides some help in seeing how this works. Derrida's critique of structuralism, for example, gave a very different interpretation to the dynamics of binary opposition. Instead of a series of atemporal structural oppositions in which meaning is produced either through the mutual definition of two terms or through their mediation by a third term, Derrida describes a process of *différence*. This is a process of "free play" in which the drawing of distinctions endlessly defers signification, meaning, and reference from the present signifier to a potentially infinite number of signifiers. Not only is 'meaning' never arrived at; it is never present in any sense at all.[159] However, in such a system of endless deferral of reference, meaning may never be given but is always implied.

The open-ended "transcoding" or "rhetoric" of endless *différence* laid out by Derrida is basically at odds with the notion of a fundamental contradiction and the ensuing dialectic that comprise a Marxist style of analysis. Of course a contrast between rhetoric and dialectic dates back to the tensions in ancient Athens between the rhetoric of the Greek Sophists and the dialectic of the Socratic dialogues.[160] More recently, however, such critics of the dialectic as Friedrich Nietzsche and Foucault have attempted to redress its dominance in history and undermine its claims to embody logical reasoning, to reveal meaning, and to ground knowledge. Foucault's critique of the Hegelian dialectic, for example, explicitly challenges how it has served to "organize the play of affirmations and negations, establish the legitimacy of resemblances within representation, and guarantee the objectivity and operation of concepts."[161] Ultimately, a Derridean and rhetorical notion of *différence* would lead an analysis of ritualization in a direction quite different from one that relies on a fundamental conflict and a dialectic of resolution.

Derrida has proposed a "grammatology," or science of signification, whereby signification rests upon the play of differences among related elements. It is clear that ritalization also involves a play of differences. The body produces an environment structured according to a series of privileged oppositions, which in turn is seen to mold and produce a ritualized agent. However, the interaction of body and environment involves a deferral of signification that is not completed or resolved even in the emergence of the ritualized agent. On the contrary, the process of signification is deferred beyond the rite itself, as it must be, into the world at large. Through the production of series of oppositions and the orchestration of these series into dominant and latent schemes, ritualization does not *resolve* a social contradiction. Rather it catches up into itself all the experienced and conventional conflicts and oppositions of social life, juxtaposing and homologizing them into a loose and provisional systematicity. These contraries receive nuances or signification (as male and female will receive the nuancing of right and left) and they defer signification (as female and male nuance the opposition of lowly and mighty). In practice this rhetorical displacement wraps around beyond anyone's ability to follow it fully as the oppositions gradually produce a hierarchical cooptation—as when male–female, deferring to right–left, is then taken up into strong–weak, outward–inward, body–soul. A 'structure' can be said to exist only by freezing or denying this temporal orchestration. Moreover, this orchestrated deferral of signification never yields a definitive answer, a final meaning, or a single act—there is no point of arrival but a constant invocation of new terms to continue the validation and coherence of the older terms. This process yields the sense of a loosely knit and loosely coherent totality, the full potential of which is never fully grasped and thus never fully subject to challenge or denial. One is never confronted with 'the meaning' to accept or reject; one is always led into a redundant, circular, and rhetorical universe of values and terms whose significance keeps flowing into other values and terms.

Yet ritualization does not embrace the lived tensions and values of social life as just one set of terms among others in its taxonomic elaborations. Rather, as the very drawing of a privileged opposition—which differentiates by opposing and unites by dominating—ritualization subjects these tensions, terms, and social bodies to a change in status, or problematic. People do not take a social problem to ritual for a solution. People generate a ritualized environment that acts to shift the very status and nature of the problem into terms that are endlessly retranslated in strings of deferred schemes. The multiplication and orchestration of such schemes do not produce a resolution; rather, they afford a translation of immediate concerns into the dominant terms of the ritual. The orchestration of schemes implies a resolution without ever defining one.

What we might call the 'external strategy' of ritualization, the very drawing of a privileged distinction between its activities and others, parallels what can be called its 'internal strategy,' the generation of schemes of opposition, hierarchization, and deferral by which the body has impressed upon it the schemes that effect the distinctive privileging and differentiation of ritualizing acts themselves. This manner of producing a ritualized agent, as I will argue next, can be seen to be the basic and distinctive strategy of so-called ritual behavior.

Ritual Mastery

The specific strategies of ritualization come together in the production of a ritualized social body, a body with the ability to deploy in the wider social context the schemes internalized in the ritualized environment. The ritualized social body, therefore, is one that comes to possess, to various degrees, a cultural 'sense of ritual.' It is necessary to explore the practical workings of this sense of ritual in order to come to any conclusions about the distinctiveness of ritualization as practice.

Bourdieu speaks of "practical mastery" to indicate the systems of classifying schemes that act as instruments for ordering the world that "every successfully socialized agent" possesses.[162] These schemes of practical mastery are acquired through the interaction of the body with a structured environment. They come to be embedded in the very perceptions and dispositions of the body and hence are known only in practice as the way things are done.[163] I use the term 'ritual mastery' to designate a practical mastery of the schemes of ritualization as an embodied knowing, as the sense of ritual seen in its exercise. Aside from the issue of institutionally recognized ritual experts, which will be considered in the next chapter, ritual mastery can be distinguished from Bourdieu's practical mastery only provisionally, since a cultural sense of ritual cannot be isolated from the other senses of the socialized person. This said, ritual mastery remains a useful term for this analysis in several ways. Most simply, it is a corrective to the habit of thinking about ritual as an existing entity of some sort. Ritual mastery implies that ritual can exist only in the specific cultural schemes and strategies for ritualization (i.e., for the production of 'ritualized' practices) embodied and accepted by persons of specific cultural communities. Ritual mastery also indicates something of the 'work' of ritualization, specifically, the production of a ritualized social agent in whose body lies the schemes by which to shift the organization or significance of many other culturally possible situations. The term should convey an inherently circular phenomenon: the purpose of ritualization is to ritualize persons, who deploy schemes of ritualization in order to dominate (shift or nuance) other, nonritualized situations to render them more coherent with the values of the ritualizing schemes and capable of molding perceptions. Ritualization and ritual mastery are not only circular; they are also an exercise in the endless deferral of meaning *and* purpose. The effectiveness of exercising ritual mastery as strategic practice lies precisely in this circularity and deferral. The following sections attempt to explore several dimensions of this circularity and deferral.

Seeing and Not Seeing

According to our Althusserian model, ritual practices are produced with an intent to order, rectify, or transform a particular situation. Ritualized agents would see these purposes. They would not see what they actually do in ritually ordering, rectifying, or transforming the situation. Foucault implies a similar principle when he notes that people know what they do and they know why they do what they do, but they do not know what what they are doing does.[164] For Althusser, this constitutes the intrinsic "blindness" of practice. For our purposes, it is a strategic 'misrecognition' of the relationship of one's ends and means.

The 'blindness' or 'misrecognition' discussed here should be differentiated from a longstanding tendency toward mystification in the study of ritual in either of two senses: mystifying the phenomenon of ritual or seeing mystification as essential to what ritual does. Whereas theological perspectives tend toward the former, social scientific perspectives tend toward the latter. Marxists combine both by ascribing to ritual an inherent fuzziness that makes it suitable for ideological mystification.[165] Even Rappaport's ecological rationalism succumbs to mystification in some concluding remarks about the study of ritual: "We are confronted, finally, with a remarkable spectacle. The unfalsifiable supported by the undeniable yields the unquestionable, which transforms the dubious, the arbitrary, and the conventional into the correct, the necessary, and the natural. This structure is, I would suggest, the foundation upon which the human way of life stands, and it is realized in ritual."[166]

One might conclude that many theories of ritual argue for the importance of what ritual does by making it as broadly encompassing, important, and mysterious as possible. Nonetheless, with some consistency, ambiguity has also been systematically identified as an important aspect of ritual.[167] Lewis, for example, argues that ritual may emphasize the ambiguity or incoherence of symbols in order to invite speculation or a perception of "a mystery that seems to come within grasp."[168] Valerio Valeri suggests that ritual is much more ambiguous and poetic than linguistic communication since its "grammar" stresses paradigmatic over syntagmatic relations.[169] David Jordan and Fernandez independently explored the ways in which ritual symbols are inherently ambiguous, thereby affording the diverse and nonfalsifiable interpretations they find necessary to the maintenance of community.[170]

These examples suggest that some type of ambiguity or blindness in ritualization is linked to its distinctive efficacy. To pursue this issue more systematically, the Althusserian model would have us pose two questions: first, what does ritualization see and, in seeing it, what does it not see; second, what is the relationship between its seeing and its not-seeing—that is, what is the object-unity of ritualization as practice?

What does ritualization see? It is a way of acting that sees itself as *responding* to a place, event, force, problem, or tradition. It tends to see itself as the natural or appropriate thing to do in the circumstances. Ritualization does not see how it actively creates place, force, event, and tradition, how it redefines or generates the circumstances to which it is responding. It does not see how its own actions reorder and reinterpret the circumstances so as to afford the sense of a fit among the main spheres of experience—body, community, and cosmos.

Ritualization sees its end, the rectification of a problematic. It does not see what it does in the process of realizing this end, its transformation of the problematic itself. And yet what ritualization does is actually quite simple: it temporally structures a space–time environment through a series of physical movements (using schemes described earlier), thereby producing an arena which, by its molding of the actors, both validates and extends the schemes they are internalizing. Indeed, in seeing itself as responding to an environment, ritualization interprets its own schemes as impressed upon the actors from a more authoritative source, usually from well beyond the immediate human community itself. Hence, through an orchestration in time of loosely and effectively homologized oppositions in which some gradually come to dominate others, the social body reproduces itself in the image of the symbolically schematized environment that has been simultaneously established.

As Burridge describes it, ritualization sees the goal of a new person. It does not see how it produces that person—how it projects an environment that, reembodied, produces a renuanced person freshly armed with schemes of strategic reclassification. The complex and multifarious details of ritual, most of which must be done just so, are seen as appropriate demands or legitimate tradition. They are not seen as arbitrary producers of distinctions. Ritualization sees the qualities of the new person who should emerge; it does not see the schemes of privileged opposition, hierarchization, and circular deferment by which ritualized agents produce ritualized agents empowered or disempowered by strategic schemes of practice. Ritualization sees the evocation of a consensus on values, symbols, and behavior that is the end of ritualization. It does not see the way in which the hegemonic social order is appropriated as a redemptive process and reproduced individually through communal participation in the physical orchestration of a variety of taxonomic schemes.[171]

Ritual and Language

Interpretation of the seeing and not-seeing of ritualization is closely linked to interpretation of the communicative function of ritual—an issue around which some controversy has accumulated. When viewed as a form of practice, chosen for its strategic qualites, it becomes more readily apparent that rites take place specifically in lieu of explicit logical speculation.[172] Ritual practices never define anything except in terms of the expedient relationships that ritualization itself establishes among things, thereby manipulating the meaning of things by manipulating their relationships.[173] For Lévi-

Strauss among others, what is distinctive about ritual is not what it says or symbolizes, but that first and foremost it *does things:* ritual is always a matter of "the performance of gestures and the manipulation of objects."[174] Hence, ritualization is simultaneously the avoidance of explicit speech and narrative.

Two issues are involved and often collapsed in any consideration of ritual and language: first, the ritual use of language; and second, the comparison of ritual as a language to verbal or textual languages, in the sense that its activities parallel the communicative functions of the latter.

It has been argued that in ritual words themselves are deeds that accomplish things. This position was pioneered by men like Frazer and Malinowski, who understood most ritual as magic because it assumed an identify between the word and the thing. More recently, Tambiah argued that the notion of ritual language as magical in a causal sense can be retired without losing the importance of words to ritual activity. From his perspective, the distinctive communications of ritual language are not some secondary dimension to the work of ritual but are central to what ritual is.[175]

Tambiah shares with many other ritual theorists a concern to show how ritual communication is not just an alternative way of expressing something but the expression of things that cannot be expressed in any other way.[176] Yet this shared concern has led theorists to widely dissimilar conclusions: that ritual is less ambiguous (i.e., more precise and effective) than ordinary language; that ritual is more ambiguous than ordinary language; and that the development of sophisticated verbal communication actually obliterates the vestigial need for ritual communication.[177]

Some have attempted to show that ritual communicates by 'modeling': strictly speaking, it does not send messages but creates situations.[178] For Valeri, these situations supply the opportunity to infer and master the codes underlying the ostensible activity of the rite. It is a matter of programmed learning that involves the perception and reproduction of concepts or principles.[179] For Tambiah, however, the situations modeled in ritual act either like "signals," which evoke certain responses, or like "signs," which can explain other activities in the same way that

a blueprint can explain a house or the building of a house.[180]
Other formulations have ritual communicate by affording experiences in which underlying cultural premises are verified and
cultural dispositions are reinforced.

Not only has there been criticism of the effort to analyze ritual *as a language* per se; there has also been criticism of the attempt to analyze ritual as communicative in any sense at all.[181]
Bourdieu, who is particularly insistent on this last point, avoids
every semblance of literary or verbal analysis. He eschews, for
example, all use of the terms metaphor, metonomy, and analogy
in describing the operations of ritual practice. Practice qua practice, he insists, remains on the "hither side of discourse," and
that is precisely the key to how it does what it does.[182] Even
those rites that are just a practical *mimesis* of the natural process
to be facilitated are not at all like metaphor or analogy simply
because they are not nearly as explicit. Ritual practice as such is
always much fuzzier, avoiding the distinctive change in state that
occurs when things are brought to the level of explicit discourse.[183] Relatively recent evidence for the existence of nonpropositional schemes and the manner in which they work to
generate a social form of consensual meaning may provide more
support for Bourdieu's position.[184]

Certainly ritualization makes ample use of words in prayers,
vows, recitations, speeches, songs, and the like. Sometimes the
words are considered by those involved to be *the* most critical
elements. Rappaport notes that for thirteenth-century William of
Auxerre, it is the words themselves in the ritual of the Christian
mass that turn physical matter into the sacrament of the body of
Christ.[185] Evidence indicates, however, that this is a historically
defined phenomenon: the words of consecration were formally elevated to this critical position in the Roman rite standardized by
the Council of Trent in 1570 and, significantly, in conjunction with
the formulation of the doctrine of transubstantiation and the enhanced sacramental power of the ordained priest. In the eucharistic
meals of the early Church, on the other hand, the words were of
little significance. The emphasis within those rites was on the doing
of certain actions, specifically those thought to have been done
before by Christ himself.[186]

Even the briefest contrast of these two historical rites, regarded by the Roman church as one and the same liturgical tradition, reveals how strategic the use of language can be. Whereas the use of language or a particular mode of speaking does not appear to be intrinsically necessary to ritual as such, the opposite does hold—namely, that ritualization readily affects the way language is used and the significance it is accorded.[187]

Propositions and formulations occur in many rituals and they may even be the most critical moment, as in the Roman rite's words of transubstantiation or "I do" when one is sworn to tell the truth in a court of law. Verbal formulations with the same performative force can be found even in cultures reputed to be less "logocentric." Yet these formulations themselves do not open a discourse within the rite about what the ritual is doing. They are, in the full sense intended by Austin, performative in their particular context; they are not explicit narrative discourse.[188]

The deconstructive enterprises of Derrida and DeMan have explored nonpropositional meanings and the rhetorical role of metaphorical images in structuring texts. Derrida, as we have seen, points to the endless deferral of meaning both within the text and within the act of interpreting, or transcoding, the text. DeMan, however, calls attention to how deconstruction of the metaphors and tropes structuring the text and thick description of their deferral of signification does not, in the end, begin to grasp the ways in which the text continues to resist reduction to these devices. Said has given this "resistance" a name, calling it "the practical worldliness of the text." He describes this worldliness as a dimension of textuality beyond the free play of grammatology. The practical worldliness of the text is not simply the sociohistorical context of the work or any type of irreducible essence within the work. The practical worldliness of a text is its own practice of the strategies of social action inherent in texts and textualization. Echoing Derrida, Said argues that the text specifically hides how it, in the form of a text, participates in a network of power: "A text is not a text unless it hides from the first comer, from the first glance, the law of its composition and the rules of its game."[189] Again, these laws and rules are not some inaccessible secret within the text but accompany the text as a strategic form of cultural signification and practice.

This example of the resistant text is useful in attempting to explicate the strategies of ritualization. These strategies will inevitably elude full articulation simply by virtue of the fact that full articulation is not a medium that can grasp them. That is to say, within the medium of formally explicit discourse, there is nothing there to grasp, just a variety of culturally instinctive and flexible schemes with which to avoid and undermine everything but the ritual acts themselves.

Redemptive Hegemony and Misrecognition

The relationship between the seeing and the not-seeing of ritual mastery constitutes the particular object-unity of ritualization as a strategic mode of practice. A more familiar example, drawn from theoretical practice, may act as a useful introduction to the notion of an object-unity to ritual practices. Certainly the principles of practice addressed earlier in this chapter can readily be seen to function in the practice of theory as well as ritual. For example, Chapter 1 began by focusing on the strategy of a privileged opposition between thought and action as well as the misrecognition that enables a discourse to identify object, method, and experts as one interdependent and interlegitimizing whole. In the relationship between what theoretical practice sees itself doing and what it does not see (the object-unity of theoretical discourse), one finds the production of systematic and seemingly independent bodies of knowledge. These bodies of knowledge act simultaneously to secure a particular form of authority, a particular autonomous reality for study, and some degree of free competition for access to mastery of theoretical practice. Theorists see the goal of knowledge and the work of research; they do not see the production of a discourse with its objects, subjects, and methods. Nor, as many have described, do they see how this discourse manipulates its own context of power relations. Through appeals to the objectivity attending independent fields of study, such a discourse wins a dominant position by virtue of contrasting itself with more overtly political or coercive practices.

Ritual mastery, like the culturally defined mastery of theorical practice, reveals a specific object-unity characteristic of ritualization as a particular mode of practice. Specifically, its relationship of seeing to not-seeing is the production of agents embodying a sense of ritual constituted by and expressed in particular schemes of ritualization. These schemes act as instruments for knowing and appropriating the world. The deployment of these schemes both structures experience of the world and molds dispositions that are effective in the world so experienced. These structured and structuring experiences of the world appear to guarantee the reality and value of their underlying schemes by means of the sense of fit or coherence between the instincts of the socialized body and the environment in which it acts. And yet ritualization does not simply act, unseeingly, to bring the social body, the community, and the largest image of reality into some reassuring configuration of coherent continuity. More fundamentally, it also appropriates this coherence in terms of the interests of persons or groups. The coherence is rendered and experienced as redemptive for those empowered by the schemes of the ritual.

The distinctive strategies of practices of ritualization—their object-unity, *aporia,* blindness and insight, mastery and misrecognition—must lie beyond the reach of a logical theoretical articulation. The frustration of theorists attempting to grasp the principle of this efficacy is evident in Maurice Bloch's exasperated wail: "How does ritual actually do what we say it does?"[190] Bloch pushes this question, pointing out, for example, that despite the dominance and endurance of Durkheim's analysis of ritual there is still no explanation of *how* ritual makes collective representations come to appear as external to the individual.[191] He similarly critiques Geertz's description of the poetics of power in the Balinese *negara,* arguing that Geertz never really explains *why* the ritual has the power with which he credits it.[192] Bloch himself contributes two valuable answers, "formalization" in one context and the interrelationship of local and central rites in another context.[193] His answers point to important strategies of ritualization but not to their distinctive object-unity. Nor does Bloch's rather functional question ("How does ritual do what we say it does?") adequately allow for the nature of practice. We might better ask, How is it that *ritual* activities are seen or judged to be the appropriate thing to do? This second question gets closer to the dynamics of the 'sense of ritual' and the choice of ritualization strategies over other ways of acting in a given situation.

Nonetheless, using the approach to ritual gradually developed in this chapter, Bloch's question can be answered in part. Ritual does what it does through the privileged differentiations and deferred resolutions by which the ritualized body structures an environment, an environment that in turn impresses its highly nuanced structure on the bodies of those involved in the rite. Strategies, signification, and the experience of meaningfulness are found in the endless circularity of the references mobilized, during the course of which some differentiations come to dominate others. Ritual mastery is the ability—not equally shared, desired, or recognized—to (1) take and remake schemes from the shared culture that can strategically nuance, privilege, or transform, (2) deploy them in the formulation of a privileged ritual experience, which in turn (3) impresses them in a new form upon agents able to deploy them in a variety of circumstances beyond the circumference of the rite itself.

In response to the revised question asked above, it can be said that ritualization is perceived to be the most effective type of action to take in two overlapping circumstances: first, when the relationships of power being negotiated are based not on direct claims but on indirect claims of power conferred; and second, when the hegemonic order being experienced must be rendered socially redemptive in order to be personally redemptive. For example, ritualization is the way to construct power relations when the power is claimed to be from God, not from military might or economic superiority; it is also the way for people to experience a vision of a community order that is personally empowering.

To complete this description of ritualization as a cultural sixth 'sense' for the production of schemes that afford the forging of an experience of redemptive hegemony, it is necessary to explore not the actual contexts of ritualization—that would be a matter of specific cultural communities in history—but at least a more accurate if abstract scope for ritualization, namely, the context of historical traditions and spatiotemporal ritual systems. Few practices of ritualization are effective outside such contexts. While indispensable as context for any act of ritualization, such traditions and systems of ritualized practices are secondary in an analytical sense, since they are themselves constituted by the further play of the strategies of ritualization already discussed. Nonetheless, most

ritual activity not only plays off contrasts with nonritualized behavior; it also plays off other forms and instances of ritual activity.
Thus, the "ritualized ritual" that Douglas sees as defining tradition
is a strategic systemization of ritual schemes to afford a privileged
differentiation of whole institutions and bodies of activities.[194]

6

Ritual Traditions and Systems

Ritualization invokes dynamics of contrast with other forms of cultural activity and, inevitably, with other ritualized acts as well. Indeed, one cannot adequately portray the full dynamics of ritualization except in the larger context of ritual traditions and systems. Several interrelated dimensions of this context can be provisionally distinguished: first, a historical dimension in the sense of traditionally ritualized activities thought to have been handed down from previous generations; second, territorial and calendrical dimensions that include annual cycles of regional ritual activities involving overlapping groups from the domestic to the national; and third, an organizational dimension provided by the presence of ritual experts, their standardization of ritual activities, codification of texts, and elaboration of a discourse on ritual.

The Construction of Tradition

Many theoretical approaches to the notion of 'tradition,' particularly in relation to ritual activities, are structured around the familiar problem of continuity and change. Clearly some things remain sufficiently consistent over time to give people a sense of continuity with what are believed to be precedents; but it is equally clear that traditions change in structure, details, and interpretation and such changes are not always fully recognized by those who live them. Many scholars designate as 'tradition' that which does not change; others attempt to combine change and continuity within the notion of tradition. Taking the latter position, Paul Mus, Tambiah, and J. C. Heesterman have all advanced an understanding of tradition as constituted by a paradox, an "inner conflict" so to speak, between an ideal atemporal order (unchanging structure) on the one hand and the profane world of temporal change and compromise (changing history) on the other. Heesterman, for one, identifies the Vedic sacrifice as the ideal and perfect order of ritual, represented by the brahmin. The brahmin is inevitably locked in struggle with the king, who represents the less than ideal order of the temporal world. Each is differentiated from but dependent upon the other.[195] However, it is hard to see how this analysis of tradition amounts to more than an impressive literary and interpretive device by which theory creates a dialectic of categories by means of which, in this case, structure consistently appropriates history.

Hobsbawn and Terence Ranger also explore the ramifications of tradition as a set of fixed activities and values inherited from the past and scrupulously preserved. But they specifically distinguish tradition from 'custom.' Custom, associated with oral cultures, remains inherently flexible and pragmatic, whereas tradition, by virtue of the role of written records, is a matter of invariant and often impractical routines and conventions.[196] In the spirit of Goody's research on orality and literacy, Hobsbawn and Ranger point to the importance of literacy to any notion of unchanging tradition as well as to the value given 'fixity' as a form of legitimation. "The pastness of the past," Goody and Ian Watt state, " ... depends upon a historical sensibility which can hardly begin to operate without permanent written records."[197] Similarly, the traditional Western distinction between law and custom is one that arises when literacy leads to the distinct fixity of law in contrast to the inherent flexibility of custom—as in ritual, myth, and oratory—in oral cultures.[198]

Rappaport implicitly rejects the typology of literate/tradition and oral/custom. On the one hand it is obvious that literate societies with fixed traditions of law also possess customs transmitted orally. On the other hand, Rappaport argues, even in oral cultures every rite contains some percentage of traditional or unchanging material. He distinguishes these "canonical messages," as he calls them, which derive from the past and do not refer to the current situation in any way, from "indexical" elements, which are shaped by the current context of the rite. Some activities will be primarily canonical while others will be primarily indexical, yet every ritual, he argues, by virtue of being a ritual, contains both indexical and canonical elements.[199] In a similar way, Valeri notes the necessity of a "fixed text" (*langue*) within the ritual activities of tribal cultures as a means by which to establish the authority of a performance. Any ritual performance must be seen as based on and legitimized by the "superior authority" of this very fixity. In oral societies the audience acts as guardians of this superior authority, holding the power to judge a ritual performance and validate its relation to the past and the present. "If the ritual had no fixed text, if it were not law, then authority could not be acquired or denied by virtue of the performance of ritual."[200]

Although these arguments specify slightly different relationships between ritual and fixed tradition, they represent some consensus on two points: first, ritual may be the more fixed expression of a written tradition or the more adaptable expression of flexible custom; second, within itself ritual may also encompass fixed activities as well as acts that reflect changing circumstances. Yet Rappaport's and Valeri's conclusions tend to miss the way in which ritualization actually constructs either fixed traditions or flexible customs— something that Hobsbawn and Ranger explicitly attempt to describe. They look at how ritual "invents" tradition in order to afford a sense of legitimized continuity with the past and to experience tradition as fixed.[201] In the fixity of ritual's structure lies the prestige of tradition and in this prestige lies its power. This type of process is one that P. Steven Sangren finds to be nothing less than the "cultural construction of history."[202]

In his studies of tribal oratory as a form of "social control," Bloch closely analyzes the ritual construction of tradition. He specifically delineates a process of "formalization" that differentiates oratory from more routine ways of communicating.[203] This process of formalization distinguishes some communication by invoking a highly restricted code that purports to be the way the ancestors spoke. As a way of speaking, formalization effectively determines content, transforming the specific into the general terms of a natural and eternally preexisting order. For Bloch formalization not only produces and maintains tradition; it simultaneously produces a form of authority, "traditional authority," rooted in the appeal to the past. The efficacy of formalization is due in part to the fact that it is an intangible form of power. For example, the restrictions on speech and movement that produce formalization are relatively indiscernible as devices, and it is even less obvious that they determine content. Bloch also demonstrates how the formalization of speech can subtly induce a general compliance with what is going on: like the control wielded by the conventions of politeness, formality puts people in a situation that discourages challenge and compels acceptance. "If you have allowed someone to speak in an oratorical manner" in a Merina village council meeting, Bloch notes, "you have practically accepted his proposal." The burden of social control in all societies, he concludes, is borne by the norms of polite behavior.[204]

Yet the effectiveness of formalization as a means of social control is offset by its own built-in constraints. For example, a speaker is very restricted in what he or she can address and say. Often a looser style of speaking must be recognized in order to actually work out real problems, even though its authority is far less than that of the tighter code of formalized speech. Hence, as a strategy of social control, formalization promotes a fairly powerful but constrained voice of authority, one that must in turn delegate authority to lesser voices.[205] In addition, to maintain the authority and prestige of formalized functions there must be restricted access to the necessary skills or training, requiring primarily oral transmission with no written materials to facilitate indiscriminate access. Less vulnerable to overt political challenge than simply to ridicule or denial, traditional authority in general appears most effective when a broad social consensus in a homogeneous society assumes that this authority follows the order of nature.[206]

Bloch's example of the ritual construction of traditional authority demonstrates an important dimension of the construction of tradition. Yet another dimension of constructed tradition concerns the delineation of group identity, which is based not only on generating a shared consensus concerning an authoritative past but also on a set of distinctions, seen as rooted in the past, which differentiates this group from other groups. Staal notes the ability of ritual traditions to "identify groups and distinguish them from one another" by means of distinctions as arbitrary as "meaningless phonetic variations." He cites the example of two Vedic schools of ritual, the Jaiminiya and the Kauthuma-Ranayaniya, who differ from each other only in terms of minor grammatical distinctions with regard to vowel length in their traditional styles of Vedic recitation. Indeed, minor grammatical differences affecting the sounds of ritual chants have always been a basis for distinguishing Vedic ritual traditions. Staal evokes a much larger issue with the observation that "considerations of form and formal derivations and transformations are foremost in the minds of the ritualists," even though these forms may be completely arbitrary.[207] Although they may be arbitrary from some perspectives, such permutations of form are the very stuff of ritually constructed traditions and identities.

Hobsbawn describes the invention of a number of rituals in America in the late nineteenth century that worked to differentiate Americans and Americanism from the ethnicity and "un-Americanism" of the large numbers of immigrants entering the country at the time. Due to this heavy influx of foreigners, he writes, "Americans had to be made."[208] And making Americans was the purpose, in that period, of new public holidays and daily flag rituals in the schools. Likewise, the simultaneous defining of "un-Americanism" generated "an internal enemy against whom the good American could assert his or her Americanism, not least by the punctilious performance of all the formal and informal rituals, the assertion of all the beliefs conventionally and institutionally established as characteristic of good Americans."[209] Hobsbawn concludes that traditions are most effectively invented by appropriating elements that are already closely associated with collective images of the past and the values at stake. When such appropriation involves having to wrest a set of images from the constructed past of another group, then the creation or assertion of tradition can become an arena for dramatic struggles among groups to carve out their own differentiated identities via shared symbols. The examples detailed by Bloch, Staal, and Hobsbawn suggest that the specifically 'ritual' construction of tradition and communal identity may be a powerful and effective strategy for several reasons. It appears to maximize the invocation of authoritative precedent with all its connotations of moralism and nostalgia on the one hand, while recognizing a more flexible level of delegated authority on the other. Similarly, it appears to maximize the perception of consensus based on nonnegotiable values and precedents, while nonetheless tolerating a fair degree of latent conflict in the form of mere compliance, quiet evasion, or idiosyncratic rejection. The construction of tradition may effectively maximize a high-profile identity for a group, even while minimizing any real rift over fundamentals with the neighboring groups.

Tradition, of course, is not created once and then left to its own momentum. Tradition exists because it is constantly produced and reproduced, pruned for a clear profile, and softened to absorb revitalizing elements. Whether it is being performed "for the first time or the thousandth, the circumstance of having been put in the ritual form," write Sally F. Moore and Barbara G. Myerhoff, gives something the effect of tradition.[210] It is possible that in some circumstances, ritualized acts and environments are designed with such rigid schemes of differentiation that the entry of a stray element makes that element a part of the rite forever after—as in the stories from Kafka and Plutarch cited by J. Z. Smith.[211] But a rigid distinction of sacred and profane, and the contamination or appropriation of any profane thing that enters the realms of the sacred, however accidentally, is not particularly common to most traditions of ritualization. It is interesting to speculate what sort of society or community might employ such strategies, but the literary context of both stories suggests further strategies at work, particularly intellectual textual strategies intending to polarize and dominate the realm of such religious practices. Yet Smith uses these stories to talk about routinization, illustrating that ritual is never *simply* the repetition of highly fixed activities or the desultory shouldering of the "dead weight" of tradition. The maintenance of a tradition through exact duplication of fixed activities is an inherently strategic reproduction and valorization of 'tradition'—in contrast not only to the correspondingly demeaned daily activities of the current situation but also, and more pointedly perhaps, to the license to ritualize readily in and from the current situation. Such strict ritualization may produce a pervasive state of cultural stasis, but the ritualization is, in itself, a creative act of production, a strategic reproduction of the past in such a way as to maximize its domination of the present, usually by particular authorities defined as the sole guardians of the past and the experts on ritual.

Theories that have defined ritual activity as first and foremost the reenactment of historical or mythical precedents, such as those formulated by Eliade, risk a certain blindness to a group's constant reinterpretation of what constitutes these precedents and the community's relationship to them. As I indicated earlier, the evocation of tradition differs significantly in the early Christian eucharistic meal, the Roman rite codified by the Council of Trent, and the post–Vatican II folk mass of liturgical renewal.[212] These liturgies display not only different formulations of the significance of Christ's last supper but also different understandings of the relationship existing between the ritual and the original event. Similarly, in each case a different type of community is constituted around different values and forms of authority—and all within a relatively stable liturgical tradition that presents itself as quite fixed.

It cannot be correct therefore to see ritualization as some standardized process of 'traditionalization'—a position that Bloch or Moore and Myerhoff may seem to advocate. Ritual *can* be a strategic way to 'traditionalize,' that is, to construct a type of tradition, but in doing so it can also challenge and renegotiate the very basis of tradition to the point of upending much of what had been seen as fixed previously or by other groups. Examples abound, ranging from the ascetic internalization of the Vedic sacrifice and the iconoclasm of early Ch'an Buddhism to the Reformation's challenge to papal authority through a recreation of the free outpouring of the spirit to the early church. As with the invented traditions described by Hobsbawn and Ranger, various attempts in American society in the last two decades to create new rituals deemed more appropriately symbolic and representative involve renegotiating a repertoire of acknowledged ways of acting ritually. Such innovations may be subtle or dramatic; they may radically reappropriate traditional elements or give a very different significance to standard activities; they may overturn meanings completely through inverted practices. The continuity, innovation, and oppositional contrasts established in each case are strategies that arise from the 'sense of ritual' played out under particular conditions—not in a fixed ritual structure, a closed grammar, or an embalmed historical model.

Spatial and Temporal Systems

The basic logic involved in acts of ritualization is also seen in the ritualized relationships of territorial groups by which they are linked within overarching systems of ritual practices. The internal organization of such a ritual system is usually a complex orchestration of standard binary oppositions that generate flexible sets of relationships both differentiating and integrating activities, gods, sacred places, and communities vis-à-vis each other. Domestic rites contrast with communal rites, male rites with female rites, preliminary rites with culminating ones. Three interrelated sets of oppositions in particular reveal the more systematic dimensions of ritualization: (1) the vertical opposition of superior and inferior, which generates hierarchical structures; (2) the horizontal opposition of here and there, or us and them, which generates lateral or relatively egalitarian relationships; and (3) the opposition of central and local, which frequently incorporates and dominates the preceding oppositions.

Just as strategic differences in ritual traditions can differentiate particular communities, ritualization can also work to integrate communities. Indeed, ritualization appears to be a type of social strategy that can simultaneously do both. This is not due to any synchronic structure it may be said to possess; on the contrary, the integrations and differentiations effected by ritualized activities are closely associated with ritual's temporal dimension. That is, the orchestration of rituals in time, some reproducing local communities, others later integrating them or parts of them into larger communities, enables each unit in the system to experience both its own autonomy and its dependent place within a network of relationships with other groups. This orchestration is not a perfect and holistic order imposed on minds and bodies but a delicate and continual renegotiation of provisional distinctions and integrations so as to avoid encountering in practice the discrepancies and conflicts that would become so apparent if the 'whole' was obvious.[213]

In their respective studies of traditional Hawaiian sacrifice and modern Taiwanese local ritual organizations, Valeri and Sangren each explore the hierarchical systems generated by ritual within which any particular ritual act or occasion is fully embedded. Although they have different positions on the significance of synchronic systems and structures, their ethnographies provide ample evidence of the negotiation of the relationships that comprise the working system. These relationships can be seen to simultaneously differentiate and integrate communities in flexible ways. Valeri finds that a hierarchy of ritual activities corresponds to a clear hierarchy of temples, gods, and social groupings.[214] Sangren, finding the same general principle at work within a more highly stratified society, also shows that the hierarchy of rituals and ritual communities forms a distinct "ritual system" closely related to, but not identical with, the more generally recognized system of marketing communities. He argues that ritually constituted territorial links are so important to Chinese life that no study could afford to focus on one particular village as a microcosm of society.[215]

James Fox's detailed study of the ceremonial system of Savu, an island off the eastern coast of Indonesia, underscores how a relatively complex ritual system is tightly linked with actual territory, with a calendrical cycle variously formulated by the four "states" involved in the system, with the organization of priests, and with the pantheon and its authority. Particularly interesting are his own efforts to compile a "lacuna-free" calendar reconciling differences in practice in terms of some fundamental and underlying structure, despite how his own experiences neatly illustrate the very practical nature of the differentiation and integration afforded by local formulations.[216] When Fox conducted the unprecedented exercise of taking a member of one regional group to view the local rites of another regional group, his Savunese friend was immediately very shocked at the differences. He kept whispering to Fox that something was very wrong in this region. At the same time, in Fox's estimation, his friend was instinctively seeking out the "ritual equivalences" between the local rites going on around him and those of his own region, eventually discovering "the essentials he was looking for." Before long he reassured Fox that the local ritual order "was peculiar but perfectly correct."[217]

Rappaport's exploration of the "ecological processes" involved in ritual cycles is another type of example of a ritually constituted system. Among the Tsembaga of New Guinea, rituals "arranged in repetitive sequences, regulate relations both within each of the [two] subsystems and within the larger complex system as a whole."[218] The first subsystem links the Tsembaga and their nonhuman environment (pigs); the second involves their regional relationships with their human neighbors. Rappaport concludes that it is the ritualization of their relations and interactions that enables them to maintain the environment, limit fighting, adjust the person–land ratios, and facilitate trade and the distribution of surplus pork, assuring sources of protein when they are needed.[219] As such, religious ritual does "more than symbolize, validate, and intensify relationships," he argues; rather, it generates a "ritually regulated ecosystem."[220] Elsewhere Rappaport demonstrates that the ritual cycle not only regulates "social, political and ecosystemic relations," but it also organizes and represents a "hierarchy of understandings" of the ritual activities themselves.[221]

Bourdieu has described ritual systems such as the *kula* ring or the potlach as "consecration cycles" whereby the ritual circulation of goods "performs the fundamental operation of social alchemy, the transformation of arbitrary relations into legitimate relations, *de facto* differences into official recognized distinctions." The transformation of casual relations among arbitrarily distinguished groups into formal relations among officially distinct groups provides the basis for lasting associations.[222] Intrinsic to this process is not simply the differentiation of lateral groups, however, but also the establishment of hierarchical relations among them, even if the higher positions are only temporarily occupied by those in possession of the most valued objects. Hierarchy functions as the indispensable integrative complement to the processes of differentiation of groups and, in practice, the two forms of relationship are usually inseparable. Their appreciation of this principle leads T. Turner and Valeri independently to conclude that hierarchy is intrinsic to ritual and vice versa.[223]

Sangren provides an interesting example of one way in which vertical (hierarchical) and horizontal (egalitarian) systems may interact. He specifically addresses the role of pilgrimage in Taiwan in establishing nonhierarchical, horizontal relations among local communities, particularly pilgrimages related to the cult of the goddess Matsu. A type of patron saint for native Taiwanese identity, Matsu also belongs to a group of mother goddesses who undercut the usual hierarchical pantheon and "may be approached directly by even the most humble pilgrim."[224] However, it becomes readily apparent that despite the egalitarian relations reproduced in the Matsu pilgrimage, her cult depends on various forms of hierarchical integration, most notably in terms of the pilgrims' route, which proceeds up and down a hierarchical ladder of political centers.[225]

In a similar example, Charles Keyes uncovered a traditional pilgrimage system in northern Thailand in which a spatial set of twelve geographical centers on the one hand are coordinated with a temporal cycle of animal years on the other. The twelve centers mark progressively more embracing Buddhist communities beyond the sphere of the local villages. Thus, the eleventh shrine, located in the Tavatimsa heaven, and the twelfth, the site of the Buddha's enlightenment in India, ultimately embrace the whole Buddhist cosmos. These centers are hierarchically ranked according to a scale based on the scope and ultimacy of Buddhist doctrines. On the other hand, the animal year of one's birth directly links a person to one of these pilgrim shrines and the larger Buddhist community it represents. The ultimate result of this system, Keyes suggests, is a series of "moral orders, structured in space and time," linking both local and Buddhist reference systems.[226]

These horizontal and vertical relations played out in time, which are simultaneously the context and the very stuff of ritualization, may also be comprehended in terms of an opposition between central and local. A basic set of dynamics in many (but not all) ritual systems is the construction of central rites from local ones and the construction of local rites from the simplification of central ones. In his study of the royal bath ceremony in Madagascar, Bloch argues that the intrinsic efficacy and compelling quality of the royal ritual derived precisely from the fact that it was composed of local ritual sequences simply rendered more elaborate and complex.[227] Bloch's study of Merina oratory likewise draws attention to how the format of the village council meeting is a particularly elaborate and important version of the format used every day when linked households meet to organize the day's farming activities.[228] This interpenetration of the elaborate and the humble, or the central and the local, is vital to the ritualization of systems and traditions.

In an analysis of the codification of Chinese ritual during the T'ang dynasty (618–906 C.E.), David McMullen shows how central rites were simplified for use in local communities with important ramifications.[229] According to the T'ang code of rites, which was compiled for imperial and official use, the lowest level of official administration and official ritual was the village. The code stipulated that the headman and community of each village should perform an offering to the gods of soil and grain under a sacred tree. At the same time of the year, a more elaborate version of the same offerings were made on the imperial level.[230] A number of other rituals were also repeated down a social hierarchy that was becoming a ritually constituted hierarchy. Intrinsic to this systemization of ritual in the T'ang, McMullen points out, was the way in which rites echoed other rites, implying them, assuming them, extending them.[231] The effects were many: first, in their differences and similarities, ritual activities simultaneously differentiated and integrated the social world; second, replicated and resonating in this way, the logic of these ritual activities would appear to be the very logic organizing the social body and the rhythms of nature; and third, ritual activities and relationships that did not conform to the basic principles echoed throughout the system would immediately stand out as problematic.

The relationship between the Chinese state and local cults is a particularly interesting and complex illustration of the issues attending ritual traditions and systems. Sangren's study of Matsu pilgrimage, for example, also demonstrates how local cults that evoke the unofficial and nonhierarchical imagery of the goddess Matsu are limited in prestige and the ability to grow unless they transcend this basis for local group identity by appealing to various strategies of hierarchization. One such strategy is securing official recognition by the state, which involves the cooptation of the cult by a formal hierarchy of deities, rites, and temples.[232] Yet this cooptation can be wonderfully muted in practice: villagers worship the goddess as they always have, but her official title promotes her cult elsewhere. The official bureaucracy itself has long used the appropriation of local cults into the formal pantheon as a major strategy for extending the control of the central government over outlying areas. At the same time the newly titled local deities legitimated the national pantheon in the eyes of village communities. This "reciprocal authentication of state and local cults," as Sangren describes it, illustrates the role of ritual in constructing center and periphery.[233]

The dynamics of social and cultural integration do not necessarily imply a single, monolithic system of gods, practices, or values accepted in the same way by all groups in the society. It has been suggested that the unity of Chinese culture has lain less in the content than in the form of its cultural practices. While the hierarchies of official and local religion differed, the principle of hierarchy itself, common to all the variant systems, facilitated practices of cultural integration.[234] Such social differentiations and integrations are not hard and fast; they play off each other in a constant give and take.

It is important to emphasize a conclusion implicit in the many examples cited so far: ritual systems do not function to regulate or control the systems of social relations', they *are* the system, and an expedient rather than perfectly ordered one at that. In other words, the more or less practical organization of ritual activities neither acts upon nor reflects the social system; rather, these loosely co-ordinated activities are constantly differentiating and integrating, establishing and subverting the field of social relations. Hence, such expedient systems of ritualized relations are not primarily concerned with 'social integration' alone, in the Durkheimian sense. Insofar as they establish hierarchical social relations, they are also concerned with distinguishing local identities, ordering social differences, and controlling the contention and negotiation involved in the appropriation of symbols.

Ritual Specialists

Relatively little attention has been paid to how the presence of specialists affects ritual practices. Their presence or absence is usually taken simply as an index to the importance of ritual or the stratification of society. In discussing the rise of religious specialists, Joachim Wach notes that the most fundamental differentiations of labor in religious activities are based first on gender, then on age, and finally, in societies with occupational, social, or economic stratification, on a classification of functions, status, and authority.[235] Douglas's typologies have gone further to link the degree and importance of gender and age distinction to Wach's third consideration, the degree of social stratification. Douglas finds ritual specialists in stratified or "high-grid" societies, and she correlates the status of such specialists with a pronounced social hierarchy and a social ethos of piety toward authority.[236] By contrast, for a society in which the social hierarchy is weakly defined, rituals are more likely to be generated without officially trained or designated specialists.[237]

Aside from such correlations of ritual expertise and authority with social divisions of labor and prestige, the most influential attempt to explain the rise of religious and ritual specialists has been Max Weber's theory of rationalization. Implying a developmental process of increasing rationality, Weber distinguished the magician, the priest, and the charismatic prophet as basic types of religious authority.[238] It sometimes appears, however, that increased rationalization does not explain the emergence of these types so much as the interaction of these specialists might explain the development of rationalization.[239] There have been many attempts to reclothe the skeletal outlines of Weber's notion of rationalization, but two in particular are useful for the issues concerning ritualization. The first is a neo-Marxist interpretation represented earliest by Georg Lukacs but recently refitted by Jameson and Bourdieu. For them, rationalization is primarily a process of 'reification' or 'objectification.' A second interpretation is provided by Goody's work on the cultural effects of literacy on social organization and the rise of particular types of authority.

In the Marxist discussion, reification implies that rationalization is accompanied by a process in which the relationships among human beings become objectified as relations among things, most readily seen in the generation of official titles, institutions, personnel, and even official language.[240] Face to face relations among people give way to indirect relations by institutions in addition to concomitant changes in the nature of power and the way it is exercised. The development of a body of specialized agents who possess or control important mechanisms of objectification, such as ritual or educational institutions, is the development of a form of control that can be more total because it is more indirect and invisible. In this development, social control via coercive strategies demanding personal presence and explicit conflict begin to shift to social control via ownership of the means by which 'reality' is articulated for cognitive endorsement by all.[241] This process is inseparable from the development of institutions which ensure that such specialists do not need constant popular support in order to survive. As institutions of specialists take on the formulation of reality, there is a decreased need for personal or collective rituals to assume that function.[242] Ultimately, when the strategies of ritualization are dominated by a special group, recognized as official experts, the definition of reality that they objectify works primarily to retain the status and authority of the experts themselves.[243]

This analysis coincides with many of the conclusions drawn by Goody in his work on the effects of literacy. There is a fair amount of agreement, for example, when both approaches attempt to delineate shifts in the strategies of ritualization that attend the rise of ritual specialists, ritual discourse, and the elaboration of rules and offices. However, when reinterpreted in terms of the impact of literacy upon social relations, rationalization reveals—more fully than in the Marxist discussion—the gradual but total sea change in the nature of almost all social interactions. Goody suggests that when Weber's theory is reanalyzed in terms of the use of writing, some of its most central points—such as the stratification of religious leadership, the emergence of orthodoxy over *doxa,* the rise of ethical universalism, or the generalization of norms—emerge even more clearly. They emerge, moreover, hand in hand with their own inherent historical contradictions, such as the problems that accompany the particular and local application of universalized norms or the difficulties of changing what is fixed as orthodox as it becomes increasingly irrelevant to the community.[244] Goody's approach also complements Douglas's correlation of ethical religions with particular forms of social organization: where belief in rational doctrines takes the place of ritualism, sacraments become mere symbols rather than immediate sources of power and priestly mediation is rejected in favor of the personal commitment of each individual.[245] Douglas effectively correlates such phenomena, but with the exception of "secularism" provides little explanation of how they come about. Goody, on the other hand, illustrates his approach with a description of the development of the priesthood and pantheon in ancient Egypt in terms of the possession and control of writing. Yet this example suggests a lacuna in his overall theory: oral societies also have specialists. His concern with the effects of literacy on religious specialization forces him to give little attention to the organization of ritual specialists in oral societies. Hence, he tends to overestimate writing as a medium uniquely subject to the control of specialists.[246] In fact, Weberian theory and its modern revisions tend to grant enormous power to ritual experts in control of vital media for formulating the nature of reality. Yet the evidence suggests that the relationships within which such experts operate are much more qualified, reciprocal, and strategically defined.

In two examples mentioned earlier, the Savunese of Indonesia described by Fox and the Hawaiians described by Valeri, the systemization of rites is closely linked to the systemization of specialists, the pantheon, the temple network, and the ritual calender. Both forms of systemization can be seen to unfold according to strategies peculiar to ritualization. Although neither ethnography presents much material on the history of the priesthood, both testify to complex systems that simultaneously embody hierarchy and opposition. For example, among the numerous and complex classes of traditional religious specialists, Valeri notes three groups of priests. The first group, the *kahuna pule,* or priests of the central cult, tend to be hereditary priests drawn from the nobility to officiate in the temples of the nobility, for which services they have land rights. There are two important orders, that of the god Ku and that of the god Lono, but the high priest of the Ku order is chaplain to the king and thus has authority over the Lono priests. Indeed, the Ku high priest is integral to the social structure that culminates in the king since he, as high priest, controls the ritual that legitimizes the king. Yet despite his importance, the Ku high priest defers to the king as the true head of the cult and polity.[247]

A second group, whom Valeri calls "professional *kahuna,*" is comprised of a heterogeneous number of ritual and medical specialists, including sorcerers. Sorcerers are excluded from rites of purification and, therefore, are considered impure in contrast to the *kahuna pule.* Their impurity is also associated with various features of marginality, particularly an asocial individualism considered resistant to the social order and an ethos of repressed destructive desires. While their functions are not necessarily antagonistic to the *kahuna pule,* they are likely to be politically contentious. Nonetheless, they are regularly sought out for their skills in healing and wield great influence through these services.[248]

The opposition of the sorcerers and the *kahuna pule* is curiously balanced by another and quite different opposition between the central cult and a third group, the *kaula* prophets. These prophets do not oppose society as the sorcerers do; rather, they transcend it through an individualistic and socially marginal mysticism. According to Valeri, "The *kaula* isolate themselves from society to reach the gods without passing through the social mediation of the human hierarchy or of the specialists."[249] Hence, they have no need to sacrifice and little need for the social order at all. From their direct relationship with the gods, moreover, they are thought to speak for the deity and to possess the ability to predict the fate of the community. Their *mana* is actually greater than that of the *kahuna pule*.

In sum, no one group of ritual experts appears to have unqualified authority. Moreover, the type of authority of any one group seems balanced or even undermined by the very different configurations of power characteristic of the other groups. Clearly priestly authority has been strategically defined and constrained.

Some features appear to be basic to systems of ritual specialists with or without literacy. Most obvious, of course, is how their authority rests on the intrinsic importance of ritual as a means of mediating the relations between humans and nonhuman powers. Yet correct performance of the ritual tends to be critical to its efficacy. An emphasis on the correctness of performance promotes and maintains expertise, but it is not uncommon that other groups, such as the general audience or another lineage of experts, have the right to pass judgment on the performance's correctness. Moreover, the power to do the ritual correctly resides in the specialist's officially recognized or appointed status (office), not in the personhood or personality of the specialist. In this way, the institutionalized office can control, constrain, and pass judgment on a specialist. The separation of the person and the office not only stabilizes the specialist's power and legitimizes it through the social sanctions by which the office is given and recognized; it also controls that power by requiring its conformity to establish models. Indeed, various studies have suggested that the emergence of a priesthood—religious specialists by virtue of holding an office—provides a stabilization and control of religious power not possible with shamanic or mediumistic mediators.[250] While this type of stabilized power is clearly linked to the role of institutions in conferring or authenticating expertise, it is far from obvious that such priests possess the nearly unlimited power to define reality suggested by Weberian theory.

Another feature of the organization of ritual specialists, namely, the ranking of ritual activities, also qualifies their supposed power.

Those rites in which specialists preside are generally seen as more central, powerful, encompassing, and integral to the welfare of the whole than those that employ more locally skilled practioners or none at all. Although ritual practices on this local and immediate level inevitably have less overt prestige, this should not obscure how they can be the backbone of any effective systemization of ritual practices.[251] In Vedic ritual, for example, the hierarchization of ritual activities that relates the domestic *gryha* sacrifice to the central *srauta* or *haviryajna* sacrifice is tightly linked to the emergence of a powerful priesthood and their role in the organization of ritual knowledge and ritual practice.[252] Textual evidence suggests that domestic rites played little if any role in the earliest Vedic sacrifices, but with the composition of the ritual sutras "domestic ritual was included within a totalistic system . . . [and] participated in the web of interrelations linking the components of that system," even though its position was on "the lowest level possible within the Vedic ritual universe."[253] This absorption of domestic ritual appears to have been promoted by brahmins in order to secure their control over all forms of ritual, although the exact history of the phenomenon is not known.[254] As a part of an encompassing ritual system, the domestic rite came to have a complex position. On the one hand, it was the lowest level of ritual and the least amount of knowledge, purity, and status was required—granting, of course, that it could be performed only by a "qualified male, one who has been initiated and has learned some portion of the Veda."[255] In addition, however, it was seen as feminine, simple, weak, and human or earthly as opposed to the virile, complex, powerful, and divine Vedic sacrifice. On the other hand, the fire for the domestic sacrifice was carefully distinguished from the cooking fire and had to be maintained for the duration of the household. Thus, despite its lowliness in the hierarchy, it was clearly distinguished from nonritual activities and thus a part of the system. More to the point, perhaps, the domestic sacrifice was also seen as the basic or "condensed" form of the grandest *srauta* sacrifice, with the latter as an "extension" or elaboration of the domestic. According to B. K. Smith, the domestic rite was *all* sacrifices: "The *srauta* ritual is an 'extended' version of the domestic sacrifice, and the domestic is a condensed counterpart of the *srauta*."[256] Hence, when differentiated as a fire that is *not* the cooking fire, the domestic altar and its activities come to be part of a vast ritual system by virtue of the relational principles of hierarchy, identity, and opposition. The hierarchy can be collapsed into the opposition of male and female, *srauta* and *gryha*. The differentiations can be elaborated to generate the whole hierarchy or to point to the identity underlying all its manifold forms. With all its ranks and complexity, Smith points out, the Vedic system of hierarchy can be completely undone by the egalitarian principle of the fundamental identity of all rituals.[257]

Hence, this systemization is hardly fixed or unambivalent. Its clear hierarchy is built out of basic oppositions that secure the generation of a more or less integrated totality. At the same time, a dynamic principle of identity can demolish even this complex totality into undifferentiated unity. The systemization itself effectively objectifies the status and authority of the brahmin ritual expert as well as the integral place of the domestic rite.[258] A similar ambivalence was seen in Valeri's account of the hierarchy and opposition in the Hawaiian systemization of specialists. The variety of specialists there suggested an inherent structural flexibility. More important, it suggests that the relationships among specialists are themselves an embodiment of the principles manipulated and reproduced in ritual activities. A variety of schemes are held in loose but easily shifting relationships to each other.[259]

The codification of ritual procedures in textual form involves strategies of ritualization different from those effective in primarily oral societies. Indeed, the very act of putting ritual practices into such a format constitutes a tactical recasting of the source and type of authority invoked in ritualization. In general, such textual codification involves a shift from the authority of memory, seniority, and practical expertise (e.g., "traditional authority," according to Weber and Bloch) to the authority of those who control access to and interpretation of the texts.[260]

The fixing of the past in writing can open a gap between the present and the past that appears to demand different forms of mediating authority—perhaps an authority that represents 'sanctified tradition' not through a convincing evocation of the continuity of the past with the present but through privileged access to the 'sources' of the past. Certainly, the influence of literacy and textual models of practice means that the past can no longer be so readily recontextualized in the present. Instead, the past appears to exist independently of the present and in need of reconciliation with it. A textually constituted tradition must continually and simultaneously create both the gap *and* the authority structures that can bridge it. Goody suggests that priestly control of literacy and sacred texts promotes the codification and standardization of 'orthodox' ritual practices in textual form, which in turn establishes a basis for a type of interpretive and exegetical discourse.[261] Such discourse works to constitutes a class of experts and vice versa. These experts maintain both the pastness of the past and their access to it through the elaborate medium of a discipline of interpretion with its methods, skills, first principles, institutions, and credentials.

Standardization has other ramifications for practice. In the ritual systems of primarily oral societies, such as the traditional Hawaiian society described by Valeri, the sense of what is traditional and legitimate stays more or less closely (and homeostatically) related to what is practiced—since both past and present are open for definition. But writing 'fixes' things, turning patterns of custom into preserved models of tradition.[262] As a result, changes are noticed: whether resisted or promoted they generate complex processes of interpretation or even cataclysmic reform, rather than gradual and barely conscious adaptation.[263] Thus, hand in hand with the codification of ritual comes the need to sanction changes in the unchanging. When accomplished through a variety of reinterpretive techniques (juxtaposition of an oral tradition, legal reasoning, theological speculation, etc.) it leads to the proliferation of texts amending the tradition and institutions legitimizing the emendations; when accomplished through the upheavals of reform, invested authority may be painfully recalled only to be lodged more definitively in the text alone.[264]

Textual codification and standardization also open a gap between what is written and what is done by promoting an ideal of uniformity and the elimination or marginalization of alternatives. Frequently the result is a written ideal quite alienated from what is in fact being done in common practice.[265] As a consequence of standardization, the very sense of ritual in a culture may well come to embody forms such as those dominant in the West since the Enlightenment, namely, ritual as a secondary enactment of prior mental states or belief convictions, the rote imitation of prescribed acts, or the performance of a script. From this perspective, rituals without textual roots and textual commentary easily come to be regarded as magical, pseudoscientific, or devotional attempts to achieve direct results. When fixed in writing, prayers are 'repeated' verbatim at the expense of adaptive invention, opening a gap between the language of ritual and the language of daily life. The exaggeration of this gap through the use of archaic language may lead to the emergence of archaicization as a basic strategy of ritualization.[266]

As a formal topic of speculation and the object of an interpretive industry, canonical texts indirectly promote those activities that enhance the status of those reflecting upon, interpreting, and teaching the texts, perhaps at the expense of those more immediately involved in ritual. Goody relates such developments to the emerging importance of internal states of mind. For example, blood sacrifice gives way to the mental concentration of the metaphorical or internal sacrifice.[267] Another example is the development of canonical or ritualized modes of thought.[268] B. K. Smith describes such a phenomenon in Vedic-Hindu culture: While remaining a basic element of Indian life, the system of Vedic ritual is now primarily used as a strategy of "traditionalization," a practical logic of explanatory categories for rendering the new orthodox and canonical.[269]

The textualization of ritual practices has been linked to the promotion of universal values over local ones and the emergence of orthodoxy over orthopraxy.[270] Yet there is little evidence that the emergence of literacy and the textualization of ritual practices moves through history with an inexorable logic and definitive set of effects. Texts appear to be used, and not used, in a wide variety of ways. Kristofer Schipper's analysis of the distinctions among various categories of ritual specialists in Taiwan graphically illustrates assorted strategies for the use of ritual texts and texts in ritual. Written texts read during the ritual performance is one of the features that differentiate the classical rites of the 'Black-head' lineage of Taoist masters, the *tao-shih*, or master of the Tao, from the vernacular rites of the 'Red-head' Taoist masters, the *fa-shih*, or master of the law. The latter may have texts present, almost like props, but he will recite the prayers from memory instead of reading them. Similarly, the classical style of the *tao-shih* specifically emphasizes the universal through an impersonal formality, whereas the vernacular style of the *fa-shih* allows for the particular and the personal. Yet the mere presence of an unread liturgical text in the rites of the *fa-shih* draws an important distinction between these local Taoist specialists and yet another level of ritualist, the local expert in trance and divination. And in the classical lineage of the *tao-shih,* despite his textual differentiation, orally transmitted instructions and information, as well as indecipherable talismanic signs, are integral to his training and easily dwarf the substance of what is actually contained in his texts.[271] Texts are strategic markers of status, scope, and doctrine and are manipulated as such.

James Watson's study of the complex system of types and grades of funeral specialists in Hong Kong presents a similar picture. He found texts present at Cantonese funerals; although none of priests could read them, they pretended to. Cantonese funeral priests appear to be only slightly better educated than the average villager, sufficiently so to be able to prepare the written materials needed for the ritual, but they cannot read most books with any ease. Nonetheless, their prestige and authority rest on their relative degree of literary skill.[272] James Hayes also notes the relative status of a little learning, its role in constituting a "specialist," and the ready appeal to a rich variety of such experts for all types of circumstances.[273] Watson and Hayes both conclude that paid professionals, characterized by some literary skill, are a uniform and universal feature of Chinese ritual. Yet Susan Naquin illustrates something of an opposite impulse when she describes how the public can bypass the experts and clergy by buying specially printed petitions of their own.[274] The availability of printed materials can redefine or undermine liturgical expertise, but appears to do so only as another strategy, coexisting with, not replacing, traditional respect for such expertise. Staal's study of the Nambudiri brahmins of Kerala in southwest India argues that their oral transmission of the Vedas has remained quite independent of the textual tradition that subsequently arose. When scholars would bring out the textual version of a ritual that the Nambudiri were planning to perform and point out the differences, the brahmins would nod politely and go on doing things the way they knew was correct, the way their fathers had taught them.[275] Of course, the rather minimal variations in practice that attend their oral tradition is a well known but still striking phenomenon.

These examples suggest that textualization is not an inevitable linear process of social evolution, as Weber's model of rationalization may seem to imply. The dynamic interaction of texts and rites, reading and chanting, the word fixed and the word preached are practices, not social developments of a fixed nature and significance. As practices, they continually play off each other to renegotiate tradition, authority, and the hegemonic order. As practices, they invite and expect the strategic counterplay.

Rethinking Ritual as Practice

I have not proposed a new theory of ritual because I believe that a new theory of ritual, by definition, would do little to solve the real conundrums that the study of ritual has come up against. Instead, I have proposed a new framework within which to reconsider traditional questions about ritual. In this framework, ritual activities are restored to their rightful context, the multitude of ways of acting in a particular culture. When put in the context of purposive activity with all the characteristics of human practice (strategy, specificity, misrecognition, and redemptive hegemony), a focus on ritual yields to a focus on ritualization.

Ritualization, the production of ritualized acts, can be described, in part, as that way of acting that sets itself off from other ways of acting by virtue of the way in which it does what it does. Even more circularly, it can be described as the strategic production of expedient schemes that structure an environment in such a way that the environment appears to be the source of the schemes and their values.

Ritualizing schemes invoke a series of privileged oppositions that, when acted in space and time through a series of movements, gestures, and sounds, effectively structure and nuance an environment. In the organization of this environment some oppositions quietly dominate others but all also defer to others in a redundantly circular, and hence nearly infinite, chain of associations. The coherence, continuity, and general scope of these associations naturalize the values expressed in the subtle relationships established among oppositions.

This environment, constructed and reconstructed by the actions of the social agents within it, provides an experience of the objective reality of the embodied subjective schemes that have created it. Ritualization as a strategic way of acting does not see the social agent's projection of this environment or his or her reembodiment of the sets of schemes constitutive of it. When these schemes are embodied in a cultural sense of reality and possibility, the agent is capable of interpreting and manipulating simply by reclassifying the very relationships understood as constitutive of reality.

The goal of ritualization as a strategic way of acting is the ritualization of social agents. Ritualization endows these agents with some degree of ritual mastery. This mastery is an internalization of schemes with which they are capable of reinterpreting reality in such a way as to afford perceptions and experiences of a redemptive hegemonic order. Ritualization always aligns one within a series of relationship linked to the ultimate sources of power. Whether ritual empowers or disempowers one in some practical sense, it always suggests the ultimate coherence of a cosmos in which one takes a particular place. This cosmos is experienced as a chain of states or an order of existence that places one securely in a field of action and in alignment with the ultimate goals of all action.

Ritualization is probably an effective way of acting only under certain cultural circumstances. But what counts as ritual can rarely be pinned down in general since ritualized practices constantly play off the field of action in which they emerge, whether that field involves other ritualized activities, ordinary action deemed by the contrast to be spontaneous and practical, or both at the same time.

This description of acting ritually does not necessarily add up to a neat theoretical model that can be readily applied elsewhere to data of various kinds. Rather, it has been an exercise in taking apart one understanding of ritual and putting together a very different context for reflection, one in which ritual as such does not exist. This reorientation to ways of acting allows the blurring of definitions for the sake of mapping strategies. I have tried to suggest the value of a whole series of questions to bring to ritual practices: What activities do they contrast? What schemes come to be embodied as a cultural sense of ritual and how are they effective beyond the rite? What redemptive reordering emerges for the actors as a natural and unsolicited phenomenon? What forms of power are defined in the relationships so redemptively reordered? This last question, the focus of Part III, opens up another dimension to this framework for reconsidering ritual action.

II. Notes

Chapter 4

1. Ronald L. Grimes, *Research in Ritual Studies* (Metuchen, N.J.: Scarecrow Press and The American Theological Library Association, 1985), p. 8.
2. The essays in Moore and Myerhoff, *Secular Ritual,* are a good example of the concern with appropriate and serviceable categories. For a useful summary of many of these distinctions, see Bobby C. Alexander, "Ceremony," *The Encyclopedia of Religion,* vol. 3, ed. Mircea Eliade et al. (New York: Macmillan, 1987), pp. 179–83.
3. See Gluckman's discussion of his revisions of both Wilson and Goody in *Essays on the Ritual of Social Relations* (Manchester: Manchester University Press, 1962), pp. 20–23.
4. See the discussion of the difficulty of applying formal categories as well as the difficulty of using indigenous terms in Crystal Lane, *The Rites of Rulers: Ritual in Industrial Society—The Soviet Case* (Cambridge: Cambridge University Press, 1981), pp. 14–15.
5. Lewis, pp. 6ff. Morris makes a similar contrast in comparing how Durkheim and Leach each approach ritual or symbolic action (p. 220).
6. Mary Douglas, *Natural Symbols* (New York: Random House, 1973), pp. 19–20. Leach, for example, sees ritual as the noninstrumental component of action, the part which primarily communicates symbolically (*The Political Systems of Highland Burma,* 2nd ed. [London: Athlone Press, 1964], p. 13). This approach was also promoted by John H. M. Beattie, who described ritual as expressive versus instrumental behavior in order to avoid categorizing it as either rational or irrational, scientific or practical ("Ritual and Social Change," *Man*

1 [1966]: 60–74; and "On Understanding Ritual," in *Rationality*, ed. Brian R. Wilson [Oxford: Basil Blackwell, 1970], pp. 240–68). Steven Lukes also divides ritual theories into two types, instrumental and noninstrumental, with ritual as expressive and an aspect of all action ("Political Ritual and Social Integration," *Sociology: Journal of the British Sociological Association* 9, no. 2 [1975]: 290–91). In a similar way Richard Schechner distinguishes performances along a binary continuum ranging from efficacy (as in ritual) to entertainment (as in theater) (see *Essays on Performance Theory 1970–1976* [New York: Drama Book Specialists, 1977], p. 75). Valerio Valeri makes a distinction between pragmatic and ritual actions, arguing that although they are not fundamentally different, they are distinct in their degree of order and parallel or complement each other (*Kingship and Sacrifice: Ritual and Society in Ancient Hawaii* [Chicago: University of Chicago Press, 1985], pp. 153–54). This is close to the position of Tambiah on ritual (or magical) activity vis-à-vis technical activity; he argues that ritual activities are a model and/or interpretation of the technical activities with which they have a serial relationship ("The Magical Power of Words," pp. 198–203). Tambiah also argues that sacred and profane language do not fundamentally differ; the former simply involves a heightened use of the features of metaphor and metonomy seen in all language (pp. 182, 184, 186–89). See Goody's discussion of distinctions in the theories of Victor Turner and Stanley Tambiah ("Against 'Ritual'," pp. 27–28).

7. Robin Horton, "A Definition of Religion, and Its Uses," *Journal of the Royal Anthropological Institute* 90 (1960): 222–26, on manipulation and communion.

8. See John Clarke, Stuart Hall, Tony Jefferson, and Brian Roberts, "Subcultures, Cultures and Class: A Theoretical Overview," in *Resistance Through Rituals: Youth Subcultures in Post-war Britain*, ed. Stuart Hall and Tony Jefferson (London: Hutchinson and Company, 1976), pp. 9–74, especially p. 47; and Dick Hebdige, *Subculture: The Meaning of Style* (London: Methuen, 1979), pp. 17–19, 133.

9. This point is also noted by Lewis, p. 13.

10. For example, see Edward Shils, "Ritual and Crisis," in *The Religious Situation: 1968*, ed. Donald R. Cutler (Boston: Beacon Press, 1968), p. 735. Tambiah discusses some examples of this distinction in "The Magical Power of Words," p. 188.

11. See George C. Homans, "Anxiety and Ritual: The Theories of Malinowski and Radcliffe-Brown," *American Anthropologist* 43 (1941): 164–72.

12. Homans, p. 165.

13. Max Gluckman's work was decisive in this regard. See *Order and Rebellion in Tribal Africa* (Glencoe, Ill.: Free Press, 1963], pp. 110–37, and *Politics, Law and Ritual in Tribal Society* (Chicago: Aldine, 1965), especially pp. 250–66. However, Morris cites Gluckman's debt to Meyer Fortes and Gregory Bateson (p. 248).

14. See Victor W. Turner, *The Drums of Affliction* (Oxford: Oxford University Press, 1968), and *Dramas, Fields and Metaphors*.

15. Jack Goody notes that there is no such word as ritual in African languages (*The Logic of Writing and the Organization of Society* [Cambridge: Cambridge University Press, 1986], p. 4). More generally, see Anne-Marie Blondeau and Kristofer Schipper, eds., *Essais sur le rituel* (Louvain: Peeters, 1988), p. viii; and Bourdieu, *Outline of a Theory of Practice*, p. 175.

16. Marcel Mauss, "Techniques of the Body," in *Right and Left: Essays on Dual Symbolic Classification,* ed. Rodney Needham (Chicago: University of Chicago Press, 1973), p. 75, originally published in 1936.

17. Lewis, p. 15; Bourdieu, *Outline of a Theory of Practice*, pp. 1–30; Raymond Williams, *Marxism and Literature* (London: Oxford University Press, 1977), p. 128.

18. Goody, "Against 'Ritual'," p. 28.

19. Rappaport, pp. 174–78.

20. Wuthnow, pp. 99–101, 103, and 109.

21. The use of linguistic models for analyzing ritual behavior goes back to M. Critchley's 1939 study, *The Language of Gesture,* which argued that gestures and movements can be seen as languages. See a discussion of the sources for this approach in Jonathan Benthall and Ted Polhemus, eds., *The Body as a Medium of Expression* (New York: Dutton, 1975), pp. 20ff.

22. Douglas, *Natural Symbols*, pp. 41, 97, 178.

23. Edmund Leach, *Culture and Communication* (Cambridge: Cambridge University Press, 1976), p. 45.

24. E. R. Leach, "Ritualization in Man in Relation to Conceptual and Social Development," in "A Discussion on Ritualization of Behavior in Animals and Man," ed. Sir Julian Huxley, *Philosophical Transactions of the Royal Society,* series b, 251 (1966): 404. Yet, in this article, Leach is still concerned with basic distinctions, for he states that there are three types of behavior: rational technical, signaling-communicative, and magical, associating ritual with the last two (pp. 403–4).

25. See Leach's objections in "Ritualization in Man," pp. 403ff. Also see Lévi-Strauss, *The Naked Man*, p. 682. Huxley's approach has the

support of Frits Staal, particularly in "The Sound of Religion: IV–V," *Numen* 33, no. 2 (1986): 185, 218–19. Although Anthony F. C. Wallace discusses ritual among animals, he does not see ritual as an aspect of all behavior (*Religion: An Anthropological View* [New York: Random House, 1966], pp. 217–24).

26. Sir Julian Huxley, "Introduction: A Discussion on Ritualization of Behavior in Animals and Man," *Philosophical Transactions of the Royal Society*, series B, 251 (1966): 250.

27. Huxley, pp. 258 and 266.

28. Richard Schechner, "The Future of Ritual," *Journal of Ritual Studies* 1, no. 1 (1987): 5.

29. See Huxley, pp. 259, 263–65. In the same volume, see W. H. Thorpe, "Ritualization in Ontogeny, Part 1: Animal Play," p. 311, and Sir Maurice Bowra, "Dance, Drama, and the Spoken Word," p. 387. For more recent discussions of this perspective, see Eugene G. d'Aquili, Charles D. Laughlin, Jr., and John McManus, with Tom Burns, Barbara Lex, G. Ronald Murphy, S.J., and W. John Smith, eds., *The Spectrum of Ritual: A Biogenetic Structural Analysis* (New York: Columbia University Press, 1979). An issue of *Zygon* gathered papers that both develop and reflect upon Huxley's 1965 conference on ritualization; see "Ritual in Human Adaptation," a special issue of *Zygon* 18, no. 3 (1983).

30. For a review of a more recent version of the ethological argument, see Eugene G. d'Aquili, "The Myth–Ritual Complex: A Biogenetic Structural Analysis," *Zygon* 18, no. 3 (1983): 247–69; and Charles D. Laughlin, "Ritual and the Symbolic Function: A Summary of Biogenetic Structural Theory," *Journal of Ritual Studies* 4, no. 1 (1990): 15–39.

31. Meyer Fortes, "Religious Premises and Logical Technique in Divinatory Ritual" in Huxley, p. 410.

32. Lévi-Strauss, *The Naked Man*, p. 670, although his point concerns seeing ritual as involved with emotion.

33. Wuthnow, pp. 111–12, 123–44. Sidney Verba was the first to argue for the ritual nature of collective TV experiences in "The Kennedy Assassination and the Nature of Political Commitment," in *The Kennedy Assassination and the American Public,* ed. Bradley S. Greenberg and Edwin P. Parker (Stanford: Stanford University Press, 1965), pp. 348–60. Verba is also cited in this regard by Lukes, "Political Ritual and Social Integration," pp. 295–96.

34. Ortner, "Theory in Anthropology Since the Sixties," p. 127. Both Jameson and Bourdieu also develop notions of practice, and both suggest that a practice approach does not dispense with other in-

terpretive stances but completes or frames them. See Jameson, *The Political Unconscious,* p. 10; and Bourdieu, *Outline of a Theory of Practice,* pp. 1–4.

35. For a concise but thorough introduction to the history of the term from Aristotle through current Marxist debates, see Gajo Petrovic, "Praxis," in *A Dictionary of Marxist Thought,* ed. Tom Bottomore (Oxford: Basil Blackwell, 1983), pp. 384–89. Lobkowicz provides more detail in *Theory and Practice,* pp. 215–35, 401–26.

36. Williams, p. 28.

37. Hebdige, pp. 117–27.

38. Marshall Sahlins, *Historical Metaphors and Mythical Realities* (Ann Arbor: University of Michigan Press, 1981), pp. 3–8, 67–72.

39. Jean Comaroff, *Body of Power, Spirit of Resistance* (Chicago: University of Chicago Press, 1985), pp. 5–6.

40. Ortner, "Theory in Anthropology Since the Sixties," pp. 152–54.

41. Williams, pp. 75–82; Dowling, pp. 57–75.

42. One term dominates the other by virtue of its replication in homologous oppositions, appearing to become immobilized, reified, and primary, thereby implying an objective and self-legitimating reality. It seems that this type of immobilization can take place despite the original impulse of the theorist to overcome the inadequacy of the two dichotomous abstractions, such as structure and act, with which the analysis began. The reason for this result, as suggested in Part I, appears to be the incredibly persuasive semblance of logical theoretical discourse that results, a semblance dependent upon the nearly hidden rigidification (and absolutization) of one term. When these two roles are played out on various homologized levels of argumentation, the original dichotomy (structure and act) launches the synthesis of a new term (culture), which in subsequent opposition to another version of the original dichotomy (history as the synthesis of structure and act) generates yet another synthetic abstraction (cultural praxis or historical process). When constructed in this way, the last synthetic term is then analyzed by breaking it back down into its components. As an example of this form of argument, see Comaroff's distinction between structure and practice (p. 44), and her discussion of the mediation of structure and practice in ritual (pp. 78–120).

43. See Bourdieu (*Outline of a Theory of Practice,* p. 96) on how Marx's theory addresses the construction of the objects of knowledge. The privileging of practice over consciousness is, for Williams and others, directly stated in Marx: "It is not the consciousness of men that

determines their existence, but, on the contrary, their social existence determines their consciousness" (p. 266).

44. Jameson, *The Political Unconscious*, pp. 13–14, 17–19.

45. Bourdieu, *Outline of a Theory of Practice*, pp. 1–2.

46. Jameson makes the same sort of argument in *The Political Unconscious*, pp. 71–74, when he both rescues and transcends several schema of analysis, such as medieval textual analysis as reprised in the scheme of Northrup Frye.

47. Bourdieu, *Outline of a Theory of Practice*, pp. 3–5, 72, 80, 116, 164.

48. Sherry B. Ortner, *High Religion: A Cultural and Political History of Sherpa Buddhism* (Princeton: Princeton University Press, 1989), p. 11.

49. Ortner, *High Religion*, pp. 17–18.

50. See Mauss, "Techniques of the Body," p. 73.

51. This characterization is given by Anthony Giddens in his review of Pierre Bourdieu's *Distinctions: A Social Critique of the Judgment of Taste* (trans. Richard Nice [Cambridge, Mass.: Harvard University Press, 1984] in "The Politics of Taste," *Partisan Review* 53, no. 2 (1986): 301.

52. Bourdieu, *Outline of a Theory of Practice*, pp. 78–83, 97. Bourdieu's presentation of the notion of habitus is not very clear. Sometimes it sounds like *the* principle of practice; at other times, it is more like one end of a spectrum of forms of objectification on which more explicit cultural schemes, such as law, take up the other end (pp. 18–20). Ortner appears to interpret Bourdieu's habitus not as an instance of practice (embodying her notions of act and structure), but structure; thus she finds his analysis to be ahistorical (*High Religion*, pp. 13, 195–97).

53. Bourdieu, *Outline of a Theory of Practice*, p. 124.

54. Erving Goffman describes "ritual competence as the most fundamental socialization of them all" (cited in Roland A. Delattre, "Ritual Resourcefulness and Cultural Pluralism," *Soundings* 61, no. 3 [1978]: 294). Evan M. Zuesse also discusses aspects of a sense of ritual in his article "Ritual," in *The Encyclopedia of Religion*, vol. 12, ed. Mircea Eliade et al. (New York: Macmillan, 1987), p. 408.

55. See the discussion in Part I, pp. 33–35.

56. The notion of "ritual as practice" is far from new. For example, Ortner writes: "Ritual in fact is a form of practice" ("Theory in Anthropology Since the Sixties," p. 154). Both Comaroff and Bourdieu assume it but do not develop its implications for ritual per se.

57. This would appear to be the sense of Ortner's remarks that the notion

of structure is changed when conjoined with practice, as with Bourdieu's habitus, lived-in and in-lived structure (*High Religion*, p. 13).
58. Culler, p. 13.
59. Edward W. Said, *The World, the Text, and the Critic* (Cambridge, Mass.: Harvard University Press, 1983), pp. 33–35.
60. Said, *The World, the Text, and the Critic*, p. 45.
61. Current use of the term "strategies" probably derives from both Burke's discussions of "situations and strategies" (pp. 1–3, 296–97, 300–304) and Erving Goffman's work on interaction strategies (*Strategic Interaction* [Philadelphia: University of Pennsylvania Press, 1969]). My use of it follows more immediately from Bourdieu (*Outline of a Theory of Practice*, pp. 3–9), who uses it in part to stress how activity is not a matter of following rules of the type amenable to formulation by theorists. In an attempt to depart from the "malfunction" perspective of psychotherapy, R. D. Laing also focused on "strategic" behavior as ways of coping (according to Skinner, p. 9). Ortner discusses a "strategic model" of action in "Theory in Anthropology Since the Sixties" (p. 150). Michel de Certeau distinguishes "tactics" and "strategies" in talking about everyday practices as ways of operating or doing things (*The Practice of Everyday Life*, trans. Steven Rendall [Berkeley: University of California Press, 1984], pp. xvii–xx, and pp. 52–56 for a discussion of Bourdieu's notion of strategic practices).
62. Bourdieu, *Outline of a Theory of Practice*, p. 106.
63. Bourdieu, *Outline of a Theory of Practice*, pp. 79 and 96.
64. Bourdieu discusses how schemes of thought and perception produce objectivity and misrecognition of limits, particularly "oversights" of the real divisions of the social order (*Outline of a Theory of Practice*, pp. 5–6, 163–64). Lane appeals to a slightly more "psychological" version of this notion: she sees a misunderstanding of what is being done and which conflict is being addressed as a "condition" for the ritualization of social relations (p. 13).
65. Sahlins, *Culture and Practical Reason*, p. 220.
66. Bourdieu, *Outline of a Theory of Practice*, pp. 3–15.
67. Bourdieu, *Outline of a Theory of Practice*, p. 6.
68. Bourdieu, *Outline of a Theory of Practice*, p. 171.
69. Bourdieu, *Outline of a Theory of Practice*, pp. 5–6, 14–15. Deconstruction, on the other hand, tends to reveal strategies, but in doing so removes them from the situation in which the strategies are expediently effective. For example, see Said's critique of Derrida (*The World, the Text, and the Critic*, pp. 183–86).
70. Antonio Gramsci, *The Modern Prince and Other Writings*, trans.

Louis Marks (New York: International Publishers, 1957), pp. 174–76 and 186–87; also see Williams, pp. 108–14. Kenelm Burridge, *New Heaven, New Earth: A Study of Millenarian Activity* (New York: Schocken Books, 1969), pp. 4–8. Burridge's notion of the redemptive process can be interpreted as a more dynamic rendering of the notion of cosmology used in history of religions.

71. Williams, p. 108. Stewart Clegg stresses that "hegemony" is not so much a state of mind (and particularly not a matter of a false consciousness) as it is a set of practices (*Frameworks of Power* [London: Sage Publications, 1989], pp. 4 and 15).

72. David D. Laitin, *Hegemony and Culture: Politics and Religious Change Among the Yoruba* (Chicago: University of Chicago Press, 1986), p. 19.

73. Laitin, pp. 19, 107, 183.

74. Burridge, p. 6.

75. Burridge, pp. 6–7.

76. Bourdieu, *Outline of a Theory of Practice*, p. 164.

77. Dowling, p. 83.

78. Louis Althusser and Etienne Balibar, *Reading Capital*, trans. Ben Brewster (London: Verso, 1979), p. 314.

79. David Cannadine and Simon Price, eds., *Rituals of Royalty: Power and Ceremonial in Traditional Societies* (Cambridge: Cambridge University Press, 1987), p. 17.

80. Leach, *The Political System of Highland Burma*, p. 4.

81. Geertz, *Negara*, p. 123.

82. Jameson, *The Political Unconscious*, p. 20.

83. Jameson, *The Political Unconscious*, p. 291.

84. Louis Althusser, *For Marx*, trans. Ben Brewster (London: Verso, 1977), p. 67 note 30 and p. 80 note 45; Althusser and Balibar, pp. 25ff. See Jameson, *The Prison-House of Language*, pp. 106–10, 135–37, and *The Political Unconscious*, pp. 12, 23–25.

85. Based on Jameson, *The Prison-House of Language*, p. 135.

86. Bourdieu, *Outline of a Theory of Practice*, pp. 72–95.

87. Althusser and Balibar, pp. 14–25.

88. Althusser and Balibar, p. 15. My term is based on Althusser's "discourse-object unity."

89. Althusser and Balibar, p. 28.

90. Althusser and Balibar, pp. 19ff.

91. Althusser and Balibar, pp. 21–22.

92. Althusser and Balibar, p. 24.

93. Althusser and Balibar, p. 24.

94. Althusser and Balibar, p. 24.

95. Bourdieu appropriately critiques Althusser for going on to distinguish four types of practices (economic, political, ideological, and theoretical) without specifying the relations among them (*Outline of a Theory of Practice*, p. 83). In addition, however, Althusser could be judged to succumb to what Foucault has called the "will to knowledge/power" when he accords theoretical practice a special legitimacy and truth vis-à-vis the other forms of practice (Althusser and Balibar, p. 316).

96. Max Gluckman, "Les Rites de passage," in *Essays on the Ritual of Social Relations* (Manchester: Manchester University Press, 1962), p. 20.

97. Murray Edelman, *Politics as Symbolic Action* (Chicago: Markham Publishing Company, 1971).

98. John H. M. Beattie, *Other Cultures* (New York: Free Press, 1964), pp. 202–6 (also cited by Hill, p. 8).

99. Staal, "The Sound of Religion: IV–V," pp. 185 and 196; Staal is also sympathetic to Huxley's use of the term. Mary Catherine Bateson, "Ritualization: A Study in Texture and Texture Change," in *Religious Movements in Contemporary America*, eds. Irving I. Zaretsky and Mark P. Leone (Princeton: Princeton University Press, 1974), pp. 150–65. Although Bateson's study is overcomplicated and idiosyncratic, it remains a serious attempt to root ritual action in a theory of practice.

100. Eric Hobsbawn, "Introduction: Inventing Traditions," in *The Invention of Tradition*, ed. Eric Hobsbawn and Terence Ranger (Cambridge: Cambridge University Press, 1983), p. 4.

101. Lane, p. 14.

102. Lane, pp. 25–26.

103. Various studies have remarked on this contrasting function: Douglas, *Natural Symbols*, p. 11; Tambiah "The Magical Power of Words," p. 198; and Lévi-Strauss, who suggested that the problems raised by ritual did not concern its "content" but how rites differ from similar activities in daily life (*The Naked Man*, p. 671). Also see Bourdieu's discussion of how gift-giving contrasts with swapping and lending (*Outline of a Theory of Practice*, p. 5).

104. In addition to Goody's position on this, noted earlier, Douglas also states that it is impossible to have a cross-cultural, pan-human pattern of symbols (*Natural Symbols*, p. 11).

105. Compare Rappaport's reappraisal of "sacredness" and how it arises out of ritual invariance (pp. 208–14).

106. When Lane, for example, picks up the argument as to whether Soviet state ritual is sacred or profane, religious or secular (familiar from

other discussions of Communist, Confucian, and American civic rites), which is a matter of asking which category is most appropriately imposed, she fails to focus on how, why, and to what extent the rites themselves create and manipulate such distinctions (pp. 36, 39, 43).

107. Rappaport argues that "no single feature of ritual is peculiar to it" (p. 175).

108. On formality, see Wuthnow, p. 108; Leach, "Ritualization in Man in Relation to Conceptual and Social Development," p. 408; Moore and Myerhoff, pp. 7–8. On redundancy, see Tambiah, "The Magical Power of Words," p. 192; and Rappaport, pp. 175–79.

109. Valeri, pp. 342–43. For Bourdieu, however, ritualization involves the supposed "necessity" of an assigned but "arbitrary" time (*Outline of a Theory of Practice*, p. 163).

110. There have been various attempts to characterize the distinctiveness of specific ritual traditions. For example, on Chinese ritual, see James L. Watson, "The Structure of Chinese Funerary Rites," in *Death Ritual in Late Imperial and Early Modern China*, ed. James L. Watson and Evelyn S. Rawski (Berkeley: University of California Press, 1988), pp. 3–19; on African ritual, see Evan M. Zuesse, *Ritual Cosmos: The Sanctification of Life in African Religions* (Athens: Ohio University Press, 1979).

Chapter 5

111. For a review of recent literature on the body, see Lawrence E. Sullivan, "Body Works: Knowledge of the Body in the Study of Religion," *History of Religions* 30, no. 1 (1990): 86–99.

112. Darwin's comment, from his *The Expression of the Emotions in Man and Animals* (1873), is cited in Benthall and Polhemus, pp. 15–16. Emile Durkheim and Marcel Mauss, *Primitive Classification*, trans. Rodney Needham (Chicago: University of Chicago Press, 1967), originally published in 1902; Mauss, "Techniques of the Body"; and Robert Hertz, "The Pre-eminence of the Right Hand: A Study in Religious Polarity," in *Right and Left: Essays on Dual Symbolic Classification*, ed. Rodney Needham (Chicago: University of Chicago Press, 1973), pp. 3–31.

113. Hertz, p. 8.

114. Douglas, *Natural Symbols*, pp. 93 and 174.

115. Victor Turner, *Forest of Symbols: Aspects of Ndembu Ritual* (Ithaca, N.Y.: Cornell University Press, 1967), p. 90.

Notes

153

116. Erving Goffman, *Asylum* (Chicago: Aldine, 1962).

117. See Comaroff, pp. 6–7 and 197.

118. Benthall and Polhemus, pp. 10 and 59–73.

119. Grimes notes the primacy of the body in several studies of ritual (*Research in Ritual Studies*, p. 18).

120. Rorty; George Lakoff, *Women, Fire and Other Dangerous Things* (Chicago: University of Chicago Press, 1987); Mark Johnson, *The Body in the Mind* (Chicago: University of Chicago Press, 1987); Gilles Deleuze and Félix Guattari, *Anti-Oedipus: Capitalism and Schizophrenia*, trans. Robert Hurley, Mark Seem, and Helen R. Lane (Minneapolis: University of Minnesota Press, 1983), originally published in 1972.

121. Lakoff, pp. xiv–xv, 12, 56, 112–13, and 154.

122. Johnson, pp. xiv–xv.

123. Lakoff, pp. xiv–xv, 12, 56, 154, 179, 267, etc.

124. See Gabriel Josipovici, *Writing the Body* (Princeton: Princeton University Press, 1982); Ann Rosalind Jones, "Writing the Body: Toward an Understanding of *l'Ecriture feminine*," *Feminist Studies* 7, no. 2 (1981): 247–63 (reprinted in Elaine Showalter, *The New Feminist Criticism* [New York: Pantheon, 1985], pp. 361–78); and Jane Gallop, *Thinking Through the Body* (New York: Columbia University Press, 1988). Feminist psychoanalytic studies by Julia Kristeva and Juliet Mitchell, for example, develop the Freudian notion that the body forms the material basis for the constitution of the self by exploring the emergence of the gendered body physically, psychologically, and linguistically.

125. Sandra M. Gilbert and Susan Gubar, *The Madwoman in the Attic* (New Haven: Yale University Press, 1979). In "The Laugh of the Medusa" (*Signs* 1, no.4 [1976]: 875–93), Hélene Cixous urges women to "write through the body." Elaine Marks and Isabelle de Courtivron, eds., *New French Feminisms* (Amherst: University of Massachusetts Press, 1980). Alison M. Jaggar and Susan R. Bordo, eds., *Gender/Body/Knowledge: Feminist Reconstructions of Being and Knowing* (New Brunswick, N.J.: Rutgers University Press, 1988).

126. For example, see Peter Brown, *The Body and Society: Men, Women, and Sexual Renunciation in Early Christianity* (New York: Columbia University Press, 1988); Bryan S. Turner, *The Body and Society* (New York: Basil Blackwell, 1984); Michael Feher, with R. Naddaff and N. Tazi, eds., *Fragments for a History of the Human Body*, 3 vols. (New York: Zone, 1989).

127. Burridge, pp. 141 and 166.

128. Michel Foucault, *Discipline and Punish: The Birth of the Prison,*

trans. Alan Sheridan (New York: Vintage Books, 1979), originally published in 1975.

129. Michel Foucault, "Body/Power" in *Power/Knowledge: Selected Interviews and Other Writings 1972–77*, ed. Colin Gordon (New York: Pantheon, 1980), pp. 55–62; and *The History of Sexuality, Vol. 1: An Introduction*, trans. Robert Hurley (New York: Vintage Books, 1980), pp. 140–44.

130. Based on Hubert L. Dreyfus and Paul Rabinow, *Michel Foucault: Beyond Structuralism and Hermeneutics*, 2nd ed. (Chicago: University of Chicago Press, 1983), pp. 111–16, 178–83. See Foucault's *Discipline and Punish, History of Sexuality*, and "Body/Power."

131. Comaroff, pp. 5–6, 124.

132. Bourdieu, *Outline of a Theory of Practice*, p. 218 note 44; Douglas, *Natural Symbols*, pp. 95–99.

133. Bourdieu, *Outline of a Theory of Practice*, p. 87.

134. Bourdieu, *Outline of a Theory of Practice*, pp. 87–95, 118–20, 124.

135. Bourdieu, *Outline of a Theory of Practice*, p. 89.

136. Arnold van Gennep, *The Rites of Passage*, trans. M. B. Vizedom and G. L. Caffee (Chicago: University of Chicago Press, 1960), originally published in 1909.

137. Mircea Eliade, *Cosmos and History* (New York: Harper and Row, 1959), and *The Sacred and the Profane* (New York: Harcourt, 1959).

138. Victor W. Turner, "Ritual as Communication and Potency: An Ndembu Case Study," in *Symbols and Society: Essays on Belief Systems in Action*, ed. Carole E. Hill (Athens: University of Georgia Press, 1975), p. 69.

139. Jonathan Z. Smith, *Imagining Religion: From Babylon to Jonestown* (Chicago: University of Chicago Press, 1982), p. 63; and Smith, *To Take Place*, pp. 74–96.

140. Bourdieu, *Outline of a Theory of Practice*, pp. 116–17.

141. Bourdieu, *Outline of a Theory of Practice*, p. 94.

142. Rappaport, p. 200.

143. John Blacking, "Towards an Anthropology of the Body," in *Anthropology of the Body*, ed. John Blacking (London: Academic Press, 1977), p. 4, citing Roger Poole, "Objective Sign and Subjective Meaning," in Benthall and Polhemus, p. 95.

144. Culler, *The Pursuit of Signs*, p. 13.

145. Rappaport, p. 207.

146. For a fuller analysis of this example, see Catherine Bell, "Ritual, Change and Changing Rituals," *Worship* 63, no. 1 (1989): 31–41.

147. J. Z. Smith, *To Take Place*, p. 109. Compare Terence S. Turner, "Dual Opposition, Hierarchy and Value," in *Différences, valeurs,*

hiérarchie: Textes offerts à Louis Dumont, ed. Jean-Claude Galey (Paris: Ecole des Hautes Etudes en Sciences Sociales, 1984).

148. G. Bateson, pp. 175–97.

149. Lévi-Strauss, *The Naked Man,* pp. 669–79. In the same vein, Said observes that culture itself is primarily a system of discriminations, evaluations, and exclusions (*The World, the Text, and the Critic,* p. 11).

150. T. Turner, "Dual Opposition, Hierarchy and Value," pp. 336 and 364.

151. Gloria Goodwin Raheja recently challenged the Dumont thesis that caste is based on a hierarchy of purity–pollution contrasts. She finds that the distinctions of gift-giver and gift-receiver, created in ritualized exchange (*dan*), construct another ordering of relationships according to a pattern of central domination and peripheral subordination. See Gloria Goodwin Raheja, *The Poison in the Gift* (Chicago: University of Chicago Press, 1988).

152. Bourdieu, *Outline of a Theory of Practice,* p. 163.

153. Hertz, p. 13; T. Turner, p. 368; Bourdieu, *Outline of a Theory of Practice,* pp. 114–27.

154. Leach, *Culture and Communication,* pp. 12–16, 43–45, 55ff; Tambiah, "The Magical Power of Words," pp. 194–97.

155. Brian K. Smith, *Reflections on Resemblance, Ritual and Religion* (New York: Oxford University Press, 1989), pp. 46–49, 69ff.

156. Bourdieu, *Outline of a Theory of Practice,* pp. 114–30, especially pp. 118–19, 125.

157. Bourdieu, *Outline of a Theory of Practice,* pp. 123–25; Lakoff, pp. xiv–xv, 12, 56, 112–13, 154.

158. Bourdieu, *Outline of a Theory of Practice,* pp. 123, 140–42, 148–54.

159. Jacques Derrida, *Writing and Difference,* trans. Alan Bass (Chicago: University of Chicago Press, 1978), especially "Structure, Sign and Play in the Discourse of the Human Sciences," pp. 278–93.

160. Christopher Norris, *Deconstruction: Theory and Practice* (London: Methuen, 1982), pp. 60–64, 70, 74, etc.

161. Michel Foucault, *Language, Counter-Memory, Practice,* trans. Donald F. Bouchard and Sherry Simon (Ithaca, N.Y.: Cornell University Press, 1977), p. 186. In the wake of such critiques it is not surprising to find neo-Marxists like Fredric Jameson and Terry Eagleton attempting to synthesize dialectic and rhetoric. While impressed with the critical stance of the defenders of rhetoric, they are reluctant to forgo the ramifications of the dialectic as a means to ground theory and generate stable "knowledge" (Norris, pp. 74–80).

162. Bourdieu, *Outline of a Theory of Practice*, pp. 87–95, 118–20, 123–24.
163. Bourdieu, *Outline of a Theory of Practice*, p. 91.
164. Dreyfus and Rabinow, p. 187.
165. Ortner, "Theory in Anthropology Since the Sixties," pp. 154–55.
166. Rappaport, p. 217.
167. See Bourdieu, for example, concerning an integral "fuzziness" (*Outline of a Theory of Practice*, pp. 108–9).
168. Lewis, pp. 30–31.
169. Valeri, p. 343.
170. See Part III, pp. 183–84.
171. Bourdieu implies that a subtle strategy of ritualization is the way it fosters a blindness to the real interests people might have in conforming to the ritual (*Outline of a Theory of Practice*, p. 22).
172. Bourdieu, *Outline of a Theory of Practice*, p. 115.
173. Bourdieu, *Outline of a Theory of Practice*, pp. 120, 207 note 75.
174. Lévi-Strauss, *The Naked Man*, pp. 670–72.
175. Tambiah, "The Magical Power of Words," pp. 185 and 188.
176. Rappaport, p. 174.
177. On the unambiguous nature of ritual language, see Rappaport, pp. 190 and 199; and Richard K. Fenn, *Liturgies and Trials: The Secularization of Religious Language* (New York: Pilgrim Press, 1982). On the ambiguous nature of ritual language, see Valeri, pp. 342–45. On the ability of verbal communication to dispense with ritual, see Basil Bernstein, H. L. Elvin, and R. S. Peters, "Ritual in Education," pp. 434, and R. D. Laing, "Ritualization and Abnormal Behavior," pp. 333, both in Huxley.
178. T. Turner compares this approach to that of Van Gennep in that both see ritual as an "iconic embodiment" of social situations, in contrast to Gluckman's approach, which looks at how ritual acts upon its social setting. See Terence S. Turner, "Transformation, Hierarchy and Transcendence: A Reformulation of Van Gennep's Model of the Structure of Rites of Passage," in *Secular Ritual*, ed. Sally F. Moore and Barbara G. Myerhoff (Amsterdam: Van Gorcum, 1977), pp. 59–60.
179. Valeri, p. 344.
180. Tambiah, "The Magical Power of Words," p. 200.
181. Rappaport, pp. 202–4; Valeri, pp. 340–43; and the extreme position of Staal in "The Meaninglessness of Ritual."
182. Bourdieu, *Outline of a Theory of Practice*, pp. 106, 120, 156.
183. Bourdieu, *Outline of a Theory of Practice*, pp. 108–9, 114–24, especially pp. 120 and 123. Bloch also comments that religion and

ritual are the last places to find discursive communication or explanation; see Maurice Bloch, "Symbols, Song, Dance and Features of Articulation: Is Religion an Extreme Form of Traditional Authority?" *Archives Européens de Sociologie* 15 (1974): 68, 71.

184. The linguists Mark Johnson and George Lakoff, among others, present interesting evidence for processes of communication and understanding based on how "nonpropositional schemata" generate meaning without the formulation of propositions. They find that such nonpropositional schemata include three types of structures: basic-level categories, kinesthetic images, and metaphorical projections.

Lakoff focuses on the first two, basic-level categories and kinesthetic images, as preconceptual structures that directly organize bodily experience and indirectly organize conceptual categories. Basic-level categories turn up in the middle of cultural taxonomic systems, specifying what is known as the level of genus, such as cat, dog, tree, and chair, but not Cheshire cat or collie, which descend levels of specification, or "all growing things" or "all furniture," which ascend levels of generalization. He finds that this middle level is basic in two important ways. First, it is the level where people appear most easily to perceive a single holistic gestalt, where distinct objects are most clearly associated with distinct motor movements of the body, and where people most readily learn, remember, and agree on different shapes and activities. Thus, this middle-level of categories is both a psychologically and socially basic level from which people proceed to generalize more encompassing levels of classes and differentiate more narrowly defined classes. It is on this level that researchers find a dramatic consensus across culturally quite different classification systems. For example, in color classification systems, there is cross-cultural consensus at the level of basic colors (black, white, red, etc.), which the eye is equipped to differentiate most immediately, but there is little consensus on the differentiation of nonbasic colors. There is a similar cross-cultural consensus in establishing clearly bounded categories at the level of birds, dogs, cats, trees, and flowers, with similar "prototypical" examples for each, whereas there is little consensus in more refined or generalized levels of classification (Lakoff, pp. 24–30). In Lakoff's second point about middle-level categories, he notes that it is on this level of classification that people appear to experience the maximum sense of "fit" between their inherited folk categories and the world as they experience it. In other words, it is at this level that people's categories are experienced as real, verifiable by experience, and sufficiently socially stable to be the building blocks of shared knowledge systems (Lakoff, pp. 32–37, 46, 200).

The second set of preconceptual structures described by Lakoff are kinesthetic image schemes, which are relatively simple structures that constantly recur in bodily experience. Examples include within–without, front–behind, center–periphery, up–down, part–whole. These schemes form the experiential bases of the third structure explored by Lakoff and Johnson, metaphorical projections of these kinesthetic images to create abstract ideas (Lakoff, pp. 267–68, 272–76).

Lakoff and Johnson's materials can be interpreted as a challenge to those, like Tambiah, who would describe ritual practices as communicating (not through the formulation of propositions) by means of "modeling" an image that can act as a sign. There is a very strong tendency, particularly evident in the work of V. Turner and Valeri, to see the meaning and work of ritual as condensed in such signs/symbols. Lakoff and Johnson suggest, however, that any such process of condensation of categories and relationships into a sign/symbol proceeds from the way in which the body experiences and projects nonpropositional schemes. Hence, the sign/symbol molded by these schemes in the course of the ritual activities is a part of the "environment" produced by ritualization. The sign is misrecognized as impressing itself on and exacting responsiveness from the participants. To focus on the ritually created sign/symbol as the unit or mechanism of ritual is to miss the more fundamental dynamics of ritualization.

V. Turner proposed that such condensed symbols are the basic unit of ritual. While Valeri follows him in noting the effects of the condensed symbol on participants, he also notes how they construct that symbol in the activities of the rite. The data discussed here could lead to a new formulation of the argument, represented by the positions of V. Turner and Lévi-Strauss, on whether ritual creates social categories or social categories create ritual ones.

185. Rappaport, p. 201.
186. Gregory Dix, *The Shape of the Liturgy* (New York: Seabury Press, 1983), originally published in 1945, pp. 12–15.
187. Bloch argues for the intrinsic necessity to ritual (and to ritual authority) of the restricted linguistic codes that attend the formalization of language. However, one can find a number of ritual activities, particularly in the United States today, that involve quite casual language and linguistic flexibility, although formulas of some type are very prevalent. On the other hand, Bloch's argument is concerned with the ritual creation of "traditional authority," not necessarily all ritual activities. See Maurice Bloch, "Why Oratory," in *Political Lan-*

guage and Oratory in Traditional Society (New York: Academic Press, 1975), pp. 1–28.

188. Tambiah "amends" Austin and Searle on performatives by arguing for the importance of context—the cultural conventions for such utterances and social acceptance as legitimate and relevant, both of which are indispensable to the making of a performative utterance (Tambiah, "A Performative Approach to Ritual," p. 127).

189. Said, *The World, the Text, and the Critic,* p. 184. The citation is from Jacques Derrida, *Dissemination,* trans. Barbara Johnson (Chicago: University of Chicago Press, 1981), p. 63.

190. Maurice Bloch, "The Ritual of the Royal Bath in Madagascar," in *Rituals and Royalty: Power and Ceremonial in Traditional Societies,* ed. David Cannadine and Simon Price (Cambridge: Cambridge University Press, 1987), pp. 271–97. On the greater usefulness of asking "how does ritual work" over "what is ritual," see Dreyfus and Rabinow's discussion of Foucault's approach to power (p. 217). I have repeatedly cast the issue as a question of the "efficacy" of ritual, since literature on the "efficacy" of ritual usually concerns how rites are seen to fulfill the expectations of those involved in them, rather than the expectations of theorists as to how they work. On efficacy in general, see Ahern, who reviews various theories of ritual efficacy (pp. 1–17). Meyer Fortes writes of the problem of efficacy as central to the debate over the meaning and function of ritual in his preface to M. F. C. Bourdillon and Meyer Fortes, eds., *Sacrifice* (New York: Academic Press, 1980), p. xviii. Also see Valeri on the efficacy of rites (p. 74).

191. Bloch, *Political Language and Oratory,* p. 57.

192. Bloch, "The Ritual of the Royal Bath in Madagascar," pp. 271–97.

193. Formalization is also intrinsic to S. F. Nadel's treatment of ritual action; see the discussion of Nadel in Jacquetta Hill Burnett, "Ceremony, Rites, and Economy in the Student System of an American High School," *Human Organization* 28 (1969): 1–2.

194. Douglas, *Natural Symbols,* p. 21.

Chapter 6

195. J. C. Heesterman, *The Inner Conflict of Tradition* (Chicago: University of Chicago Press, 1985), pp. 1–2, 10–15.

196. Hobsbawn and Ranger, pp. 2–3ff, 247–51.

197. Jack Goody and Ian Watt, "The Consequences of Literacy," in *Lit-*

eracy in Traditional Societies, ed. Jack R. Goody (Cambridge: Cambridge University Press, 1968), p. 24.

198. Goody, *The Logic of Writing,* pp. 7, 9, 129–31. There is a concomitant notion that literacy, especially the wide-scale literacy afforded by printing, has a negative effect on the vitality of ritual in a culture. John Bossy challenges this idea in *Christianity in the West, 1400–1700* (Oxford: Oxford University Press, 1985). On this general topic, and citing Bossy, see Andrew E. Barnes, "Review Essay: Religious Reform and the War Against Ritual," *Journal of Ritual Studies* 4, no. 1 (1990): 127–33.

199. Rappaport, pp. 179–82ff. An interesting example that challenges the arguments of Rappaport and Hobsbawn and Ranger is provided by Walter Pitts's study of how an oral "tradition," particularly a style of preaching, is maintained in a contemporary American Afro-Baptist church. This style of preaching involves the transition from one dialect to another in order to signal the important spiritual shift that "makes the ritual work." See Walter Pitts, "Keep the Fire Burnin': Language and Ritual in the Afro-Baptist Church," *Journal of the American Academy of Religion* 56, no. 1 (1988): 77–97.

200. Valeri, p. 342.

201. Hobsbawn and Ranger, p. 1.

202. P. Steven Sangren, *History and Magical Power in a Chinese Community* (Stanford: Stanford University Press, 1987), pp. 207–15.

203. Bloch, *Political Language and Oratory,* pp. 1–28.

204. Bloch, *Political Language and Oratory,* pp. 3–4, 9.

205. Bloch, *Political Language and Oratory,* pp. 12, 16, and 22ff.

206. In her study of the Tshidi, which I will discuss further in Part III, Comaroff gives evidence, from the history of this one African people, for two very different sets of ritual strategies—one for producing a sense of how traditional authority and social life participate in the structure of the order of the cosmos, and another, focused on fragmentation, exorcism, and healing, that provides both compliance with and resistance to colonial domination (pp. 78–120, 194–251).

207. Frits Staal, "The Sound of Religion: I–III," *Numen* 33, no. 1 (1986): 57–58.

208. Hobsbawn, "Mass-Producing Traditions," p. 279.

209. Hobsbawn, "Mass-Producing Traditions," p. 280.

210. Moore and Myerhoff, p. 8.

211. Jonathan Z. Smith in "The Bare Facts of Ritual," in *Imagining Religion: From Babylon to Jonestown* (Chicago: University of Chicago Press, 1982), p. 53.

212. Bell, "Ritual, Change and Changing Rituals," pp. 31–41.

213. See Bourdieu, *Outline of a Theory of Practice*, pp. 97–98. A synchronic view of ritual, Bourdieu warns, demands the simultaneous mobilization of all levels of the hierarchical system, demonstrating only the relations of domination and dependence. For Bourdieu, this sort of theoretical codification of a ritual calendar, which essentially reduces temporal relationships to synchronic ones, will inevitably fail to see how the activities of ritualization can do what they do when they are played out step by step in time. Such codification at the hands of either foreign *or* indigenous "experts" always creates a false, lacuna-free whole, intrinsic to the demonstration of their expertise.

214. Valeri, pp. 109–29, 172–88.

215. Sangren, pp. 1, 13–16, 105–26.

216. James J. Fox, "The Ceremonial System of Savu," in *The Implication of Reality: Essays in Southeast Asian Coherence Systems*, ed. A. L. Becker and Aram A. Yengoyan (Norwood, N.J.: Ablex, 1979), pp. 152–56.

217. Fox, p. 158.

218. Rappaport, p. 40.

219. Rappaport, p. 41.

220. Rappaport, p. 41.

221. Rappaport, pp. 101ff, 116, 121.

222. Bourdieu, *Outline of a Theory of Practice*, pp. 194–95.

223. Valeri, pp. 109–29, 172–88, and p. 134 in particular.

224. Sangren, p. 91.

225. Sangren, pp. 91 and 122.

226. Charles F. Keyes, "Buddhist Pilgrimage Centers and the Twelve-Year Cycle: Northern Thai Moral Order in Space and Time," *History of Religions* 15, no. 1 (1975): 71–89.

227. Bloch, "The Ritual of the Royal Bath," pp. 296–97.

228. Bloch, *Political Language and Oratory*, p. 9.

229. David McMullen, "Bureaucrats and Cosmology: The Ritual Code of T'ang China," in *Rituals of Royalty: Power and Ceremonial in Traditional Societies*, ed. David Cannadine and Simon Price (Cambridge: Cambridge University Press, 1987), pp. 181–236.

230. McMullen, p. 198, with other examples on pp. 194–95.

231. McMullen, pp. 198–99. McMullen does not develop the reverse argument, easily done in the Chinese case, concerning the elaboration of imperial ritual from local practice.

232. Sangren, pp. 91–92.

233. Sangren, pp. 215–25. Also see James L. Watson, "Standardizing the Gods: The Promotion of T'ien Hou ('Empress of Heaven') Along the South China Coast, 960–1960," in *Popular Culture in Late Imperial*

China, ed. David Johnson, Andrew J. Nathan, and Evelyn S. Rawski (Berkeley: University of California Press, 1985), pp. 292–324. Watson notes that "the Chinese state intervened in local cults in subtle ways to impose a kind of unity on regional and local-level cults," which resulted in "a surprisingly high degree of uniformity" (p. 293). Indeed, the promotion of state-approved cults was so successful in places that it effectively drove out the worship of local gods. Watson specifically explores the cult of the goddess T'ien Hou, the official title conferred on the goddess whom Sangren studied under her original name, Matsu. He describes how the state decided that it was "expedient" to adopt and endorse her to assist in the pacification of the southern coastal regions in the twelfth century. As a result she became the focus of most of the religious worship in that region. Thus, he tracks the "up and down" flow of ideas by which "a minor deity...was adopted by the state, transformed in important ways, and then reimposed on local communities as an officially recognized goddess" (p. 294). Yet Watson does not simply interpret the extended T'ien Hou cult in terms of the integrative functions formulated by Durkheim. He also finds represented in the goddess's cults a hierarchy of understanding and power: she came to mean something different to different groups of people according to their place in this hierarchy. Thus, among local elites, building temples for the goddess signaled their willingness "to join the mainstream of Chinese culture." However, among semiliterate landowning lineages, and in direct contrast to the role of her cult in Taiwan, the goddess is seen as "jealous and vindictive," closely associated with bitter territorial distinctions and loyalties. Thus, in this context, she is not a motherly figure who promotes the transcendence of local affiliations through pilgrimage and festivals (pp. 312–13, 318–19). In terms of cultural integration, Watson's study also suggests that a hierarchy of power may be intrinsically necessary to the dynamics of cultural integration.

234. Sangren, p. 124. Watson's emphasis on form over content and Sangren's on a principle of pure hierarchy are somewhat awkward in their current formulations, but both men are pointing to how strategies of ritualization (particularly hierarchization, homologization, and privileged opposition), variously deployed in many different situations, generate a differentiated and integrated social system.

235. Joachim Wach, *Sociology of Religion* (Chicago: University of Chicago Press, 1971), originally published in 1944, pp. 214–18.

236. Douglas, *Natural Symbols,* pp. 86–87.

237. Lane, p. 14. For a good account of the social and historical context in which a completely new corpus of rites is designed and imple-

mented, see Steven M. Gelber and Martin L. Cook, *Saving the Earth: The History of a Middle-Class Millenarian Movement* (Berkeley: University of California Press, 1990).

238. Max Weber, *The Sociology of Religion*, trans. Ephraim Fischoff (New York: Beacon Press, 1963), originally published in 1922.

239. See Reinhard Bendix, *Max Weber: An Intellectual Portrait* (Berkeley: University of California Press, 1977), originally published in 1960, pp. 88–89.

240. Dowling, pp. 26–27, and Jameson, *The Political Unconscious*, pp. 62ff.

241. Bourdieu, *Outline of a Theory of Practice*, pp. 21, 165, 170–71, 184–89, 194. His interest in and analysis of education are presented more fully in Pierre Bourdieu and Jean-Claude Passeron, *Reproduction in Education, Society and Culture*, trans. Richard Nice (Beverly Hills, Calif.: Sage Publications, 1977).

242. Bourdieu, *Outline of a Theory of Practice*, p. 184.

243. Bourdieu, *Outline of a Theory of Practice*, pp. 40–41. Also see Alvin W. Gouldner, *The Function of Intellectuals and the Rise of the New Class* (New York: Seabury Press, 1979). Gouldner echoes Bourdieu's discussion of how a social class and a particular mode of social discourse mutually constitute each other, and how processes like "credentialing" redefine labor as valuable only when it conforms to cultural norms objectified by the new class of credentialed experts (pp. 21–29; Bourdieu, p. 170). Gouldner suggests that the ideology of discourse accompanying the rise of an expert class bases itself on a belief in the autonomy of speech and action, autonomous because they are seen as rule-oriented rather than controlled by external forces (p. 34).

244. Goody, *The Logic of Writing*, pp. 11–12, 15–16, 27. On the social effects of literacy, also see Brian Stock, *The Implications of Literacy* (Princeton: Princeton University Press, 1983). The influence of literacy is also linked to the spread of printing; see Lucien Febvre and Henri-Jean Martin, *The Coming of the Book: The Impact of Printing 1450–1800*, trans. David Gerard (London: NLB, 1976), originally published in 1958; and Elizabeth Eisenstein, *The Printing Press as an Agent of Change* (Cambridge: Cambridge University Press, 1979).

245. Douglas, *Natural Symbols*, pp. 22, 58, 70–71.

246. Goody, *The Logic of Writing*, p. 16. As for religious specialists in oral cultures, Douglas discusses the Dinka spear-master and cites E. E. Evans-Pritchard's contrast (*Nuer Religion* [Oxford: Oxford University Press, 1956], pp. 292–93) of the Nuer priest (functionary)

164 *Notes*

and the Nuer prophet (charismatic healer) (*Natural Symbols*, p. 124). Morris also discusses Evans-Pritchard's 1940 analysis (*The Nuer* [Oxford: Oxford University Press, 1940]), which linked the rise of the Nuer prophet with social changes under colonialism (p. 201). Goody (*The Logic of Writing*, p. 118) does argue that religion is one of the first areas of social life to register the forces of social stratification and specialization.

247. Valeri, pp. 135–37.
248. Valeri, pp. 137–38.
249. Valeri, p. 139.
250. Peter Brown (*The Making of Late Antiquity* [Cambridge, Mass.: Harvard University Press, 1978], pp. 12, 19), for example, has described how the nature and "locus" of divine power shifted in the late antique world to mean something from "outside the human community" that could be represented on earth by specially empowered agents whose relationship with the supernatural was stable, irreversible, and clearly distinct from that of the sorcerer. A similar situation attended the emergence of a Taoist priesthood; see Catherine Bell, "Ritualization of Texts and Textualization of Ritual in the Codification of Taoist Liturgy," *History of Religions* 27, no. 4 (1988): 366–92.
251. Ahern draws this distinction in terms of illocutionary power. She argues that specialists are needed for rituals in which "strong" illocutionary acts are made, namely, formal requests which are thought to affect the immediate environment automatically. On the other hand, private rituals are then primarily a matter of "weak" illocutionary acts, in which one expresses wishes, not demands, which may or may not be fulfilled. See Ahern, pp. 13–14.
252. The circularity of this is captured neatly in the following statement: "The authority of the Brahmin is dependent on the authority of the Veda, and the Veda exists only because of the traditional function the Brahmin has assumed for its preservation." B. K. Smith, *Reflections on Resemblance, Ritual and Religion*, p. 13.
253. B. K. Smith, *Reflections on Resemblance, Ritual and Religion*, p. 143.
254. B. K. Smith, *Reflections on Resemblance, Ritual and Religion*, p. 144.
255. B. K. Smith, *Reflections on Resemblance, Ritual and Religion*, p. 148.
256. B. K. Smith, *Reflections on Resemblance, Ritual and Religion*, p. 151.
257. B. K. Smith develops this idea in connection with the fact that as the Vedic ritual system declined, domestic rites became very important in the subsequent development of Hinduism. The principle of identity appears to be a later development of something very latent in the hierarchization of rituals under brahmin domination, serving as a

point of contrast between Hinduism and Vedism (*Reflections on Resemblance, Ritual and Religion*).

258. The brahmin's ritual expertise ultimately comes to depend on four factors: caste, which inscribes social distinctions and hierarchy into the very structure of the cosmos; initiation into study of the Vedas as a "twice-born" male through the *upanayana* ritual; training in recitation of the Vedas, a feat requiring careful pedagogy, memorization, and leisure time that dramatically reduces accessibility; and the performance of successively powerful rituals, the more impressive of which can be undertaken only by someone who has performed others in a series. Staal describes the importance of the chants in the construction of the fire altar: "Under duress, ritual acts may be neglected, glossed over, or changed, but recitations must be maintained at all cost, and without modification. . . . The construction of the fire altar involves the deposition of more than a thousand bricks, of specific sizes and shapes, and in a complicated pattern. However, the physical deposition of the bricks is unimportant, what counts in their consecration by mantras. This is obvious from the fact that, though the order of bricks is ritually prescribed, the bricks are actually put down in any order, and not at the proper time. When they are consecrated, however, the prescribed order is adhered to and the correct time is observed. . . . That this emphasis on mantras has been the same for at least 2500 years is demonstrated by a statement in the Satapatha Brahmana (9.1.2.17): 'This fire altar is language, for it is constructed with language.'" (Frits Staal, *Agni: The Vedic Ritual of the Fire Altar*, 2 vols. [Berkeley, Calif.: Asian Humanities Press, 1983], vol. 1, p. 18). The language is the exclusive property of each brahmin tradition, transmitted only from master to student, and except for the names of deities, generally unintelligible even to the brahmin.

259. Valeri notes the openness of the pantheon at the bottom level, where the spontaneous generation of deities frequently occurs (p. 36).

260. There are many examples of ritual codifications granting a central place to those rites that legitimate the ruler while simultaneously linking those rites to traditional practices present throughout the social hierarchy. See Averil Cameron, "The Construction of Court Ritual: The Byzantine *Book of Ceremonies*," in *Rituals of Royalty: Power and Ceremonial in Traditional Societies*, ed. David Cannadine and Simon Price (Cambridge: Cambridge University Press, 1987), pp. 106–36.

261. Goody, *The Logic of Writing*, pp. 16–18.

262. Goody, *The Logic of Writing*, p. 9.

263. Goody, *The Logic of Writing*, p. 30.

264. For good examples of this form of Chinese casuistry, see McMullen, pp. 220–21.
265. Bruce Lincoln raises the interesting case of the Swazi Ncwala rite, originally recorded by Hilda Kuper (and studied by Gluckman and Beidelman), who was unaware of the very particular political forces shaping the version of the Ncwala she observed. See Bruce Lincoln, *Discourse and the Construction of Society* (New York: Oxford University Press, 1989), pp. 53–74.
266. McMullen, pp. 201–2. Heesterman raises the issue of what happens if this gap gets too big (p. 3).
267. Goody, *The Logic of Writing*, pp. 14 and 44. Heesterman also describes the "interiorization" of the Vedic sacrifice in later Indian religions when "ritualism" had advanced to its logical conclusion (cited in B. K. Smith, *Reflections on Resemblance, Ritual and Religion*, pp. 194, 211–12; also see Heesterman, p. 4). It has long been an assumption of modernization theory that individualism, universal values, and moral/ethical concerns bring about a decreased reliance on ritual. Some historians of literacy and its cultural impact also make this connection (Stock, p. 50). Douglas's typologies, of course, also suggest that ritual is less dense and important in societies with these features. Yet there is really very little evidence to suggest that ritual in general declines per se. It may be more accurate to say that it shifts. For example, as the scale of the community grows, as in the emergence of a "national" community, the density of ritual is rearranged, as certain social ties diminish in importance within the new hierarchy or become more critical for the constitution of community. National rituals may emerge as local village life breaks down, or voluntary organizations that cut across older relations of kin and village may emerge as centers or purveyors of ritual activities.
268. Goody, *The Logic of Writing*, p. 32
269. B. K. Smith, *Reflections on Resemblance, Ritual and Religion*, pp. 202–4, 215–18.
270. Goody has strongly argued for the role of writing and standardization in promoting universal values over particular or local values. Whereas oral transmissions would be modified as they traveled, written texts can be transmitted intact to groups with different cultural assumptions. At the same time, rewriting, as in translation, tends to eliminate cultural obstacles in favor of more general features and values. Indeed, things are often written down primarily to enable them to travel beyond the confines of a particular group. Goody uses this argument to explain how "religions of the book"—such as Christianity, Judaism, Islam, Buddhism, and Hinduism—were able to become world

religions. A good example of this process is provided by Glen Dudbridge in his close study of successive versions of an Indian Buddhist
tale as it came to be transmitted in China (*The Legend of Miao-shan*
[London: Ithaca Press, 1978]). Watson provides a more ethnographic
but equally effective example in his study of another, not unrelated,
goddess ("Standardizing the Gods").

It has been argued that literacy causes the unarticulated *doxa* of
a community to give way to the formulation and authority of orthodoxy. Some scholars suggest that orthodoxy emerges primarily in
the context of a challenge and the ensuing struggle among contending
sets of ideas (John G. Gager, *Kingdom and Community: The Social
World of Early Christianity* [Englewood Cliffs, N.J.: Prentice-Hall,
1975], pp. 76–88). But Goody points out that such a struggle can
develop only when doctrinal points come to be sufficiently fixed and
explicit. In other words, he implies, written materials both make
disagreement possible and make it more than just a very local affair.
The social stratification and the universalization of values that allows
pluralism result, Goody suggests, in the breakdown of the type of
homogeneous "worldview" associated with tribal cultures and open
the way to the development of "ideologies" as the interests of particular groups or classes in the society (Goody, *The Logic of Writing*,
p. 22).

Evidence also suggests that the demand for orthodoxy will prevail
over a demand for orthopraxy when systems of ideas and practices
spread across ethnically and culturally distinct communities. Local
communities tend to be more attached to traditional communal practices than to abstract ideas. Since interpretations change more easily,
the old practices tend to be reinterpreted. Thus, early Christianity
had to decide whether converted Gentiles should take on the practices
of orthodox Judaism. In the process of formulating what should be
"brought to the Gentiles," an expedient emphasis was placed on
"belief" in Jesus Christ, rather than the dietary and initiatory customs
associated with Hebrew communities quite alien to the Gentiles.
Orthodoxy not only may emerge in a struggle over beliefs; it may
also emerge when an emphasis on belief can effectively unite a larger
community embracing many local traditions of praxis. According to
this reasoning, Christianity sought to evangelize without necessarily
destroying local community, which was a pattern in the spread of
Buddhism as well. The issue of local rites is a very interesting one in
the history of the spread of Christianity, and for the most part the
spirit was one of accommodation. A notable exception was the controversy over ancestor rites in China and Africa.

271. Kristofer Schipper, "Vernacular and Classical Ritual in Taoism," *Journal of Asian Studies* 45, no. 1 (1985): 34–35, 46.

272. James L. Watson, "Funeral Specialists in Cantonese Society: Pollution, Performances, and Social Hierarchy," in *Death Ritual in Late Imperial and Modern China,* ed. James L. Watson and Evelyn S. Rawski (Berkeley: University of California Press, 1988), p. 119.

273. James Hayes, "Specialists and Written Materials in the Village World," in *Popular Culture in Late Imperial China,* ed. David Johnson, Andrew J. Nathan, and Evelyn S. Rawski, (Berkeley: University of California Press, 1985), pp. 75–111.

274. Watson, "Funeral Specialists in Cantonese Society," pp. 132–33; and Susan Naquin, "Funeral in North China: Uniformity and Variations," in *Death Ritual in Late Imperial and Modern China,* ed. James L. Watson and Evelyn S. Rawski (Berkeley: University of California Press, 1988), p. 61.

275. Staal, *Agni,* vol. 1, p. 2.

III
RITUAL AND POWER

Part I addressed the basic question, What is ritual? Part II, How does ritual do what we say it does? This third part engages yet another fundamental query: When and why do the strategies of ritualization appear to be the appropriate or effective thing to do? The standard approach to the issue implied by 'when and why ritual?' has tended to look at how ritual functions as an instrument of social control. The type of social control thought to be wielded by ritual has been envisaged in a variety of ways. For some it is a matter of mental indoctrination or behavioral conditioning, either through repetitive drills or the effective states induced by group enthusiasm.[1] Others have emphasized the cognitive influence of the 'modeled' and 'idealized' relations by which ritual defines what is or should be.[2] Hence, the emphasis is sometimes on the effect of communal ritual on individual psychology, at other times on ritual's role in structuring interactive relationships. These theoretical descriptions of how ritual constitutes a form of social control frequently overlap with other theories concerning the role of ritual in effecting social change or social conformity. One recent study of political rituals points out that ritual attends conservative politics of 'reaction' as well as the potentially transformative politics of 'revolution.'[3] How ritual practices can serve both social control and social change is a fitting conundrum with which to launch the discussion here.

Paralleling the arguments of the previous two parts, I will first analyze some of the impetus for approaching ritual as a mechanism of social control and suggest how the discourse that emerges comes to be unduly constrained and closed. Second, using the approach to ritualization developed in Part II, I will build upon some alternative understandings of social dynamics to delineate a relationship between the strategies of ritualization and the construction of particular types of power relations. In brief, it is my general thesis here that ritualization, as a strategic mode of action effective within certain social orders, does not, in any useful understanding of the words, 'control' individuals or society. Yet ritualization *is* very much concerned with power. Closely involved with the objectification and legitimation of an ordering of power as an assumption of the way things really are, ritualization is a strategic arena for the embodiment of power relations. Hence, the relationship of ritualization and social control may be better approached in terms of how ritual activities constitute a specific embodiment and exercise of power.

7

Ritual Control

Durkheim's model of ritual underlies four influential theses concerning ritual as a means of social control: the social solidarity thesis, the channeling of conflict thesis, the repression thesis, and the definition of reality thesis. Durkheim saw ritual as dramatizing collective representations and endowing them with a mystical ethos that in the course of the communal experience did not merely promote acceptance of those representations but also inculcated deep-seated affective responses to them. The simplest form of his model, the social solidarity thesis, suggests that ritual exercises control through its promotion of consensus and the psychological and cognitive ramifications of such consensus. In their own ways, Robertson Smith, Evans-Pritchard, Fortes, and Munn all appealed to this basic feature of ritual in describing its role in socialization. They are representative of the tendency, as David Kertzer puts it, to see social solidarity as "a requirement of society" and ritual as "an indispensable element in the creation of that solidarity."[4]

Stephen Lukes, among others, has critiqued this social solidarity approach to the analysis of modern political rituals, particularly as it is enshrined in such classic studies as the Shils and Young interpretation of the British coronation ceremony, W. Lloyd Warner's work on American rituals, Robert N. Bellah on civil religion, and Sidney Verba on the media events surrounding the assassination of John F. Kennedy.[5] Lukes argues that the Durkheimian notion of social integration and value consensus effected by means of "collective effervescences" is too simple to deal adequately with the complexity and range of political rituals. Lukes goes on to demonstrate that collective effervescences do not so much unite the community as strengthen the socially more dominant group through a "mobilization of bias."[6] In this way, Lukes emphasizes the politics of dominance and inequality underlying the group consciousness forged by ritual, but he does not deny that ritual is uniquely geared to generate this revised form of solidarity.

Although Gluckman and V. Turner both came out of the Durkheimian tradition, they significantly altered the thrust of its approach to the issue of social control by addressing the ways in which ritual deals with conflicts. Their work, which suggests that ritual controls by forestalling overt rebellion or other threats to social unity, has given rise to the 'channeling of conflict theory.' Gluckman's studies of "rites of rebellion" present ritual as a type of safety valve that formally arranges the diffusion of social tensions and personal emotions generated by social conflict.[7] "Tribal rituals entail dramatization of the moral relations of the group," writes Gluckman, " . . . [and] ritual is effective because it exhibits all the tensions and strife inherent in social life itself."[8] Lane echoes this position in her study of Soviet ritual as a "tool of cultural management" and a strategy for maintaining social control.[9] In an extension of this approach, Edelman describes ritualization as a means of preserving strained social relations by simultaneously escalating and orchestrating conflict in such a way that it has to be and can be resolved.[10]

V. Turner worked out a detailed description of the way in which ritual concurrently affords the formal structuring that maintains the ordered value system of a group as well as a cathartic experience of *communitas,* or antistructure. As a dialectic of structure and antistructure, ritual works as a "mechanism that periodically converts the obligatory into the desirable." In other words, "norms and values, on the one hand, become saturated with emotion, while the gross and basic emotions become ennobled through contact with social values. The irksomeness of moral constraint is transformed into the 'love of virtue.' "[11] As with Gluckman's formulation, the result is conflict resolution and social equilibrium.

Although both Gluckman and V. Turner addressed social and structural conflicts rather than psychological conflict within individuals, their general approach has tended to direct attention to the individual as an entity controlled by group processes. Indeed, their language often parallels that used to describe the phenomenon of repression or sublimation in psychological studies.[12] Ultimately, the struggle between the individual psyche and society is never seen as simply out there in the social arena, but within each person as well. For Durkheim, as we saw in Part I, the person is ultimately seen as two people, "the material and the spiritual beings who coexist within us."[13] Tapping this psychological dimension, students of Gluckman and Turner are concerned to show how ritual integrates the social and the individual both externally and internally. They are not particularly concerned with Lukes's insight into how ritual forces people to coexist in some relation of domination and subordination. Although these theorists all have some sympathy for more Marxist approaches to social tension, it is the psychosocial dimension in Durkheimian studies of ritual as conflict management that keeps the Gluckman–Turner approach quite distinct from that of Lukes.

The psychological overtones accompanying studies of ritual as social control in the Durkheim–Gluckman–V. Turner lineage have also been developed quite explicitly and independently of the constraints of a social theory, notably in the work of René Girard and Walter Burkert, among others. Girard and Burkert focus, for example, on ritual sacrifice as controlling, channelling, and finally repressing human violence so as to allow for ordered social life.[14] Using Freudian notions of desire, guilt, and an original murder at the hands of the group, Girard's *La Violence et le sacré* presents a theory of ritual sacrifice as the central act of a cultural system generated by primal violence. Sacrifice, as the ritualized killing of substitutes, is itself a substitute for the violence that continually threatens to consume society.[15] Burkert's *Homo Necans* similarly argues that the irrational activities of sacrifice that are preserved at the core of Greek religion and civilization derive from the ritualization of the hunt in pre-Greek society. His theory of the ritualized hunt also accounts for the subsequent emergence of myth, religion, and civilization.[16]

Drawing on ethological as well as psychological models, Girard and Burkert both conclude that ritualization is the controlled displacement of chaotic and aggressive impulses. Hence, ritualization is central to culture as the means to dominate nature and the natural violence within human beings. Although ritual (= culture) is the necessary repression of this violence (= nature), culture still remains dependent upon the energy of aggression as well as its restraint.[17] This perspective is taken further in Heesterman's study of Vedic ritual, *The Inner Conflict of Tradition*. Heesterman argues that in a preclassical age in ancient India, there was a sacrificial cycle of raids, contests, and battles marked not only by its violence but also by a sense of the paradox of killing for the sake of giving life. Then, in a type of cultural breakthrough comparable to Burkert's ritualization of the kill, the chaos of the sacrificial cycle was transformed into the transcendent, static, and absolute order of Vedic ritual.[18] The result, as B. K. Smith points out, is a contrast between the sanitized, perfected world of ritual and the risk, violence, and disorder of sacrifice—the virtual differentiation of the violence of sacrifice from the cultural control of ritual.[19] In the end, for Heesterman, ritual structure is totally repressive: instead of channeling violence, the order of ritual completely denies it.

Valeri points to the traditional gulf between anthropology and psychology in a brief critique of Girard's assumption that violence is a 'pure' psychological process independent of culture but still generative of and controlled by cultural activities like ritual.[20] In their concern to track the rise of human culture from its roots in nature, understood simply as barbaric, violent, and generally anticultural and antihuman, such psychological approaches end up positing metacultural forces that nonetheless direct and shape culture. Valeri's anthropological approach, of course, recognizes nothing outside of or before culture. Yet even ethological studies would take issue with such a Freudian interpretation of the emergence of social behaviors. In a discussion of successive theories of ritual among phenomenologists and historians of religions Burton Mack unwittingly chronicles just how slow a process it has been for these scholars to come to see ritual in any truly social or cultural context.[21] While Girard's and Burkert's theories have their sympathizers, in actual fact few theorists of ritual pursue the 'repression thesis' approach any longer. Those attracted to the scientific aspects of psychology are now more likely to embrace the 'scientism' of ethological and ecological frameworks, where Burkert also gravitates. Yet those interested in discussing the issues raised by theologians in terms other than those of theology still find psychological language useful. For example, in an introduction to a volume of papers on sacrifice from both anthropologists and theologians, Fortes resorts to such psychological theories in an attempt to redress the " 'embarrassed silence' of anthropologists on 'the relationship between the effects of rituals and what participants expect to achieve through them.' " He suggests that the "universal infantile experience of helpless dependency" gives rise to "rituals of defense" against "the inescapable vulnerability of humanity."[22] As Valeri's critique goes on to imply, however, it is contradictory to see individual psychological processes as the source of social institutions that reflect and control these psychological experiences but are never able to ameliorate them. To approach cultural rituals as rooted in purely psychological conflicts—as opposed to the Gluckman– V. Turner approach to social rites and social conflicts—is to see ritual as an oppression inherently necessary to society, which is defined in turn as the repression of the individual.

Whereas the repression thesis emphasizes how ritual exercises control over the individual's affective state, the fourth approach, the definition of reality thesis, focuses on how ritual models ideal relations and structures of values. Examples of this approach include the work of Geertz, T. Turner, Douglas, and Lukes. They tend to see ritual as a symbolic modeling of the social order, with this imaging or iconic quality as the basis of its efficacy.[23] It is significant, however, that these theorists do not explicitly address how ritual 'controls' but how it 'defines' social norms and presents them for internalization. Lukes, for example, urges that more attention be given to the cognitive over the affective dimensions of ritual, and to the type of power that ritual exercises in this way. Ritual, he argues, "helps to define as authoritative certain ways of seeing society: it serves to specify what in society is of special significance, it draws people's attention to certain forms of relationships and activity—and at the same time, therefore, it deflects their attention from other forms, since every way of seeing is also a way of not seeing."[24]

Geertz explores this more cognitive direction particularly in his study of Balinese kingship where ritual is no longer seen in the direct service of social solidarity but in the service of 'reality.'[25] He suggests that the ability to define an order as 'the real' in both its internal structure and its limits is a form of control that is not experienced as such by the people involved. That is, culture uses ritual to control by means of sets of assumptions about the way things are and should be.[26] The invisibility of ritual in naturalizing assumptions about the nature of reality denotes in part the basis of its effectiveness. Others, however, call attention to the fact that ritual activities are not the preeminent or only forms of invisible control. Similarly imperceptible control is exercised by such simple and conventional admonishments as "be respectful to elders."[27] For Bourdieu, as we noted earlier, a whole cosmology is communicated in the injunction to "stand up straight!" The trick of such social pedagogy lies in how "it extorts the essential while seeming to demand the insignificant."[28]

In the main, proponents of the definition of reality thesis seek to find in ritual a single central mechanism for the communication of culture, the internalization of values, and the individual's cognitive perception of a universe that generally fits with these values. Those who diverge from the more mechanistic aspects of this approach, like Bloch and Bourdieu, tend to treat ritual as a particular instance of a larger category of strategic practices characterized by formalization. While the definition of reality thesis improves on the preceding three models by reworking them in terms of a more subtle understanding of social control, it continues the tendency to see rite as a nearly magical mechanism of social alchemy by which the irksomeness of human experience is transformed into the desirable, the unmentionable, or the really real.[29] This type of focus on ritual obscures a very basic issue, namely, the particular types of social arrangements in which ritual activities are an effective way of defining reality. No matter which definition of ritual is used, it is obvious that not every society or subgroup appeals to ritual activities in the same way and to the same degree. Hence, any theory of ritual as social control must also specify what type of society or community is likely to depend heavily on this form of control and why.

Proponents of the first three theses—the solidarity thesis, the channeling of conflict theory, and the repression thesis—are likely to respond to this issue by equating ritual modes of control with homogeneous tribal societies and so-called legal modes with technologically developed and socially diverse societies. At the same time, they are very responsive to the presence of ritual forms of control in special areas of technological societies, as various studies by V. Turner, Lukes, and Douglas among others readily demonstrate. In contrast, proponents of the definition of reality thesis tend to back away from any polarization of traditional and modern societies. Concerned with delineating a specifically cultural level of analysis, they are reluctant to appear too dependent upon a level of sociological analysis. Nonetheless, they have failed to find an alternative way of appreciating the problem of ritual context.

Typologies and Hierarchies

Various attempts have been made to see how a dependence on ritualized activities for social cohesion and control correlates with modes of social organization. Bourdieu, for example, notes that ritual assumes a fair degree of consensus, whereas legalistic rules of law and order assume much less. Yet he adds, somewhat contradictorily, that increased ritualization accompanies increased distance between groups that would appear to have little basis for consensus.[30] Gluckman, in much more detail, describes ritualization as a feature only of high-consensus small-scale societies where, in the context of relatively undifferentiated social relations, conflicts developed among overlapping groups and organizations. "Persons are intricately involved with the same sets of fellows in varied systems of purposive activity," he writes. "Cross-cutting allegiances and processes of internal development within sets of relations establish ambivalence and conflict within each group. Ritual cloaks the fundamental disharmonies of social structure by affirming major loyalties to be beyond question."[31] Gluckman finds that ritualization is not important in highly differentiated societies since such societies not only segregate roles but also segregate conflicts.[32] In differentiated societies other "mechanisms of redress" operate as alternatives to the ritual mechanisms used in tribal societies.[33] He does not develop this line of reasoning, however, and many studies of modern ritual in industrial societies appear to apply Gluckman's tribal-based theory of ritual without worrying about these distinctions.[34]

Douglas has advanced a very systematic framework for understanding both the degree and the style of ritual in various types of societies. She suggests that ritualization correlates with and contributes to the restraining effect of closed and highly structured societies.[35] Using Basil Bernstein's work on linguistic codes, Douglas argues that particular ritual patterns or styles encode and thereby promote particular social patterns. In other words, symbolic systems such as ritual both realize and regulate the structure of social relations. Like forms of speech, forms of ritual are "transmitters of culture, which are generated in social relations and which, by their selections and emphases, exercise a constraining effect on social behavior."[36] Within this framework, Douglas goes on to indicate the relationship of highly elaborate ritual systems on the one hand, or highly secularized antiritual activities on the other, to particular forms of social structure. As she notes, this framework makes a radical break from the reasoning that connects secularism with modernity and ritualization with tribal society. Hence, Douglas approaches secularization as the loosening of social ties, and she finds it among industrialized nations as well as the Ituri pygmies, the Basseri nomads, and the Nuer and Dinka of the Sudan.[37] She concludes, therefore, that ritual is important in societies that are (1) closed social groups with (2) restricted codes of linguistic and symbolic communication, in which (3) there is great emphasis on hierarchical position as opposed to personal identity and (4) yet a general social consensus still upholds the system. Her charting of these characteristics as degrees of grid and group to create four typical societies is well known.[38]

Based on Douglas's analysis, then, ritual is an important and effective means of social control in only certain types of societies, namely, closed and hierarchical ones. Such societies must have a marked hierarchical structure of differentiated positions as well as a strong sense of corporate identity, both evidenced in an assumption that interpersonal relations should be subordinated to the ordering of roles or positions. The group is simultaneously both highly differentiated *and* exalted as a corporate unity above the interests of the self.[39] The centrality of a marked social hierarchy to ritual practice, as we saw in Part II, has been suggested by a number of writers. Leach argues that ritual is customary behavior, almost a form of speech, which makes statements about the hierarchical relations among people.[40] Bloch suggests that ritual, as formalization, is an effective form of power in those societies in which traditional authority, in the Weberian sense, dominates. Such societies, he adds, tend to be "oppressively hierarchical."[41] Valeri suggests that it is hierarchy, as the structuring of people, gods, and rites, that is the fundamental criterion for the efficacy of any sacrifice. He sees hierarchy itself as the essential and immediate context of ritual.[42]

Despite this form of support, Douglas's system has also been subject to some criticism. John Comaroff raised the problem of typologies in general—that they merely promote simple exercises in classification. They are of little value, he maintains, unless used to explore the ongoing utilization and control of both restricted and elaborated codes *in relation to each other.*[43] A more immediately pertinent problem arises in Douglas's description of exactly *how* ritual encodes, realizes, promotes, and regulates social relationships. She uses the imagery of a ritual juxtaposition of two bodies, the social body and the physical body. Attitudes to the body are a key to the system of ordering that pervades every aspect of a society, she argues, and are immediately reflected in the styles of ritual and cosmological formulations. On the one hand, "the social body constrains the way the physical body is perceived." On the other hand, "the physical experience of the body, always modified by the social categories through which it is known, sustains a particular view of society." Hence, "there is a continual exchange of meanings" between these two bodies "so that each reinforces the categories of the other."[44] Ultimately, however, and very much in the spirit of Durkheim, Douglas does not see these two bodies as fully integrated. She merely concludes that "sometimes they are so near as to be almost merged; sometimes they are far apart. The tension between them allows the elaboration of meanings."[45]

While Douglas provides a brilliant exploration of the way in which natural symbols and rituals play upon an isomorphism of the personal body and its larger (macrocosmic) contextual spheres, she also reduces these dynamics to the operation of a simple Durkheimian tension between self and society. Elsewhere Douglas alludes to a more complex dynamic, one that seeks the systemic correlation of levels of meaning among the body, society, and the cosmos.[46] Yet in the end Douglas's notion of the social body is one of the ways in which her social functionalism grants priority to society and a sociological level of analysis. V. Turner, in contrast, attempted to break out of this functionalism by arguing the opposite: that the body is primary, the *fons et origo* of all social classification.[47] However, the main point is not which is primary in some absolute sense, but rather whether the supposed primacy of one or the other, or simply their strategic correlation, is important to ritualization.

Douglas makes several points that are worth underscoring here. First, ritualization, as a particularly effective strategy of social action, is correlated with closed and hierarchical societies. Second, the efficacy of ritualization is seen to operate at least in part through the physical interaction (projection and embodiment) of the personal body with symbolically structured social schemes, which could be the social body for Durkheim or the projected 'environment' discussed in Part II. This interaction collapses, orders, and nuances social and cosmic relations. Where Durkheim saw two bodies juxtaposed, Douglas sees two involved in the mutual constitution of each other. As I suggested earlier, it is the unrecognized primacy of the body in a ritualized environment that distinguishes ritualization from other social strategies. Third, Douglas also demonstrates that despite its importance in particular types of societies, ritual has no intrinsic priority as a social strategy in establishing and maintaining such a society. Rather it works in concert with many other forms of activity and types of attitudes. Hence, ritualization is not a single-handed method or mechanism of social control; it is one of several ways of reproducing and manipulating the basic cultural order of a society as it is experienced by, embodied in, and reproduced by persons.

Although Douglas's functionalism, which privileges the molding effect of the social body upon the personal body, sometimes appears a bit doctrinaire, it is a useful contrast to the intellectualism of Valeri's approach to how ritual defines reality. He argues that "the reproduction of Hawaiian society requires the reproduction of the *concept* of man on which this society is based."[48] This concept, which "is embodied by the totality of the gods that appear in ritual," is particularly condensed in the *Haku 'ohi'a*, a piece of wood carved into human form and transformed into the god Ku. This image is "the most encompassing ritual symbol created by the Hawaiians" and its reproduction in ritual "has, or should have, the effect of reproducing the concept that the image represents." That is, as an objectification of the society's concept of human beings, the image both symbolizes society and "reconstitutes" it.[49] Valeri goes on to explain that the ritual communication of such a concept differs from linguistic communication since the former plays on ambiguity to produce "model experiences" whose underlying codes are inferred and mastered. Ritual, he argues, is a matter of "programmed learning through activities that involve the apperception of codes, principles, concepts and their reproduction in practice, in action."[50]

From their different starting points, Douglas and Valeri converge with an implicit recognition that the social control wielded by ritual is a more complex phenomenon than the manipulation of affective states or cognitive categories. One needs to ask, first, how ritual effects the embodiment of principles for an ordering of reality and, second, how this embodiment works within and is generative of hierarchical and/or closed societies. Yet the more complex phenomenon suggested by these questions also implies the limits of the notion of social control per se. In the sections that follow I will work out an alternative interpretation of the social functions of ritual, namely, how the strategies of ordering and reproduction embodied through ritualization relate to the larger question of the organization of power relations in a society. Hence, I will attempt to demonstrate that ritual does not control; rather, it constitutes a particular dynamic of social empowerment. To generate and establish this interpretive framework, I need to engage several other issues basic to how we have conceived ritual, namely, belief, ideology, and legitimation. Reconceiving the dynamics at stake in these forms of social phenomena makes it possible to reconceive ritualization.

8

Ritual, Belief, and Ideology

The study of ritual has always assumed the close association of rite with belief. As we have seen, ritual has generally been thought to express beliefs in symbolic ways for the purposes of their continual reaffirmation and inculcation. This relationship is particularly prominent in theories of ritual as a form of social control. Hence, any attempt to leave behind the notion of ritual as an ideologizing mechanism for transforming ideas into sentiments and sentiments into significance, to paraphrase V. Turner and Geertz, will require a new analysis of the nature of belief and its relationship to ritualization. In the following sections I will argue that the projection and embodiment of schemes in ritualization is more effectively viewed as a 'mastering' of relationships of power relations within an arena that affords a negotiated appropriation of the dominant values embedded in the symbolic schemes. To analyze the relationship of ritualization to belief, therefore, I will focus on the tension and struggle involved in this negotiated appropriation, rather than on the production of doctrines neatly internalized as assumptions about reality.

Ambiguous Symbols and Unstable Beliefs

Religious beliefs have been understood in a variety of ways—as pseudoscientific explanations, rationalizations of customary behavior, personal or communal ideologies, or highly structured doctrinal formulations whose content has little import on behavior. When defined in terms of the mental states of individuals, belief has been deemed beyond the reach of social analysis.[51] Yet belief has also been described as irreducibly social in nature, a matter of collectively significant activities rather than personally held concepts or attitudes.[52] More frequently, belief systems are understood to be a matter of cultural worldviews or communally constructed ideological systems, quite beyond what a particular person may or may not hold to be true.[53] Martin Southwold combines these last two positions by distinguishing between those religious tenets that are subject to question or doubt and those that are not. The latter group, he suggests, are empirically indeterminant, axiomatic, symbolic, and collective by necessity.[54] They are simultaneously symbolic actions that define reality and a mode of discourse that interprets experiences of reality.[55] "Contrary to the conventional wisdom concerning our own religious history," he remarks, "a religion comes to be rejected not as simply false but rather as inappropriate or unfitting."[56]

The traditional association of belief and ritual is also challenged by growing evidence that most symbolic action, even the basic symbols of a community's ritual life, can be very unclear to participants or interpreted by them in very dissimilar ways. Fernandez's work on the Fang cult is the most well-known example of the different ways in which ritual symbols can be understood by participants. Yet he argues that despite the different "cultural" interpretations attached to them, such symbols still promote "social" solidarity.[57] This suggests that some level or degree of social consensus does not depend upon shared information or beliefs, and ritual need not be seen as a simple medium of communicating such information or beliefs.[58] Indeed, for Fernandez, ritual forms of solidarity are usefully promoted *because* they rarely make any interpretation explicit; that is, they focus on common symbols, not on statements of belief. Although this distinction between what is cultural (interpretations, beliefs) and what is social (activity, ritual) remains problematic, Fernandez's conclusion that ritual does not appear to communicate common understandings of its central symbols is very significant.[59]

Evidence for the diversity of interpretations and beliefs among members of small ritual communities is also supported by the findings of Jordan in a Taiwanese village and Peter Stromberg in a small

Swedish church.[60] Another study of Taiwanese sectarian groups by Jordan and Daniel Overmyer goes even further in challenging the notion of a social consensus effected by ritual. Like Fernandez, the authors found that most members of the sectarian communities were "simultaneously both believers and skeptics"; unlike Fernandez, they suggest that this very ambivalence has a positive effect on the constitution of the religious community.[61] In his study of the forms of the cult of the Taiwanese goddess Matsu, Watson concludes that the genius of Chinese policies for national unity lay in their imposition of ritual structures (form), not dogmatic beliefs (content). Like Jordan and Overmyer, he points to the importance of ambiguity in ordering and unifying diverse groups.[62] This evidence suggests that symbols and symbolic action not only fail to communicate clear and shared understandings, but the obvious ambiguity or overdetermination of much religious symbolism may even be integral to its efficacy.[63]

As with ritual, most attempts to analyze how symbols do what they do also assume that the purpose of symbolism is sociocultural solidarity by means of the naturalization of political and ideological values. In a pattern that will be familiar to the reader by now, these theoretical descriptions first distinguish categories of experience in order subsequently to show how symbols collapse these categories to afford an experience of participation or integration. For example, when Abner Cohen addresses the ambiguity of symbols, he finds their "multidimensionality" to be essentially a bivocal structure addressing existential ends on the one hand and political ends on the other.[64] Also with regard to the ambiguity of symbols, V. Turner identified the symbol as the smallest unit of ritual and, therefore, the smallest 'mechanism' of the transformation and integration effected in ritual. Similar to Cohen's distinction between the existential and political dimensions of symbols, Turner distinguished sensory and ideological poles. Then, in regard to the transformative effect of ritual, he described an interchange between these poles by which one experiences (or senses) the ideological as the real.[65] Although these analyses succumb to the pattern of ritual theory critiqued in Part I, they attempt to identify the ambiguity of ritual symbolism and deem such ambiguity to be essential to ritual.

In addition to the evidence for the fundamental ambiguity of symbols, there is also evidence that religious beliefs are relatively unstable and unsystematic for most people. Instead of well-formulated beliefs, most religions are little more than "collections of notions."[66] Philip Converse demonstrated this point quite graphically in a study of belief systems among elites in contrast to such systems among the mass public.[67] With regard to political beliefs, he found that systems of ideas, beliefs, or ideological attitudes do not filter down much beyond the class of professionals who deal with them on a regular basis.[68] Among the public at large, beliefs and opinions become increasingly incoherent with each other as the level of sophistication and education decreases. That is to say, beliefs or attitudes are increasingly less constrained by logic on the one hand while becoming more affected by local group interests on the other. The dissociation of logically related ideas proceeds down the social ranks to such an extent that it is impossible to find any significant public participation in the belief systems found among elites.[69] In addition, nonsystematic clusters of ideas, so much more prevalent than wide-ranging systems of beliefs, show great instability over even short periods of time. Converse concluded that the factors affecting the juxtaposition of beliefs were most likely to be social (group affiliations), then psychological (expressive of individual idiosyncratic orientations); the logical coherence of beliefs was the least likely factor to affect which beliefs were juxtaposed.[70]

In contrast to the evidence on beliefs, however, Converse found that even poorly educated adherents of different creeds, people who had little in the way of a coherent belief system and no grasp of theological conceptions, still tended to have a "fairly accurate knowledge of concrete matters of ritual and mundane taboos."[71] This point may supply the more appropriate framework for assessing the experiences, noted in Part I, that Singer had with the brahmins of Madras. The fact that they responded to his abstract generalizations about Hinduism with an invitation to view a particular ceremony should not be taken as evidence of the fact that such a ceremony contains and expresses the essential whole of Hinduism. Rather, 'Hinduism' existed for those brahmins only in terms of such activities. Hinduism for Hindus is not a coherent belief system but, first and foremost, a collection of practices. It is the collection of practices as such that needs to be explored further in order to understand their sense of religious action. Converse's conclusion about formal beliefs in comparison to particular practices also recalls the story of one exasperated foreign missionary in China. He could successfully convince the Chinese that they were foolish to bow to statues, he asserted, only to have them giggle shyly and admit that they would continue to do it anyway.[72]

Converse's findings support some of the conclusions reached by Goody and Watt's exploration of the ramifications of literacy. Goody and Watt correlate the systematic formulation of beliefs not with social cohesion or ritual forms of social control but with the stratification of a society and the increasingly more abstract organizations of people within it (e.g., as a 'nation' as opposed to a village). Accompanying the logical and systematic formulation of beliefs is a process of universalization, which can render beliefs much less able to explain the local and particular in an effective way.[73] Hence, coherent and shared systems of beliefs will occur among a relatively small class who specialize in them and will not readily drift down to be shared by the society as a whole.

These studies give evidence for the ambiguity and instability of beliefs and symbols as well as the inability of ritual to control by virtue of any consensus based on shared beliefs. They also suggest that ritualized activities specifically do *not* promote belief or conviction. On the contrary, ritualized practices afford a great diversity of interpretation in exchange for little more than consent to the form of the activities.[74] This minimal consent actually contrasts with the degree of conviction frequently required in more day-to-day activities as, for example, the spontaneous sincerity that must be conveyed in many forms of conversation. Curiously, Rappaport makes this type of argument for myth, not ritual. Whereas a ritual specifies a performer's relationship to what is being performed, he notes, myth does not: one can recite a myth without necessarily believing it, but one cannot participate in a ritual without believing it or being perceived as committed to it.[75] However, the foregoing arguments suggest that it is exactly this sort of formal and thereby noncommittal participation that ritualized practices do allow.

Despite the evidence for the ambiguous, unstable, and inconsistent nature of belief systems, recent literature persists in the view that ritual has an important social function with regard to inculcating belief. "By repetitively employing a limited pool of powerful symbols, often associated with emotional fervor," writes Kertzer, "rituals are an important molder of political beliefs."[76] He argues that the shared activities of ritual effect this molding of belief, while public identification with a group reinforces the individual's attachment to the group.[77] Although Kertzer regards ritual as a relatively straightforward mechanism for social solidarity, that solidarity is seen to derive not from the formulation and communication of coherent beliefs held in common by participants but from the *activities* of ritual per se. Despite this useful shift of emphasis, however, Kertzer's analysis still relies on Durkheim's cultic chemistry of public avowals and emotional reinforcement.

Ideology

According to the preceding arguments, ritual does not necessarily cultivate or inculcate shared beliefs for the sake of solidarity and social control, although this is a common understanding of ritual. Even without invoking the issue of specific beliefs or beliefs systems, many have seen the activities and effects of ritual in terms of some type of ideological conditioning. This perspective is based, of course, on a fairly simplistic understanding of ideology (as was the case with belief) and the persistent notion that social solidarity is the goal of any and all ritual mechanisms. Undoubtedly, however, this perspective reflects other forces in scholarship as well, including, perhaps, a distrust of organized religion and the general antiritualism of our culture, both features correlating with the grid/group characteristics of American society. Indeed, religion and religious beliefs have been a historically consistent starting point for the study of ideology.[78] Well before Marx critiqued religion as the ideological opiate of the people, religion had been used as an important forerunner of the critical notion of ideology.[79] Given its background in relation to ritual and to religion, it is worth reviewing and reassessing the notion of ideology.

While Marxist uses of the term have varied significantly and been subject to continual redefinition, basic orientations toward the notion of ideology are similar to those I previously reviewed for belief.[80] On the one hand, ideology has been seen in terms of the neutral perspective of a cultural worldview, the body of ideas, values, and assumptions fundamental to a society and shared by all members. On the other hand, ideology has also been cast in a more critical perspective as sets of doctrines promoted by the dominant social group because those doctrines support their interests over the interests of other groups in the society. In the former view, ideology-as-worldview, the tendency is to envision ideology as a single, relatively unarticulated system common to all and indispensable to social solidarity.[81] In the latter view, that of ideology-of-the-dominant-class, however, the emphasis is on a more limited set of ideas that reflects the divisions of society, serving solidarity insofar as it stabilizes the domination of one group over another.

When used to describe a single embracing and unarticulated worldview, the term 'ideology' has been effective in highlighting three processes: first, the cultural construction of reality as intrinsic to social integration and cohesion; second, socialization (either through inarticulate forms or fully objectified institutions) as the means by which values and norms are assumed without question; and third, the "structuring" processes of cultural reproduction displayed in the realm of ideas, beliefs, and values as well as the realms of economics or politics. Thus, ideology-as-worldview has nuanced the notion of 'culture' to suggest something less benign, passive, or epiphenomenal.[82]

Criticism of the ideology-as-worldview perspective focuses primarily on its 'totalistic fallacy,' the assumption that a group is dominated by a single, holistic set of ideas, which acts as the cement for the society. For both Durkheimian functionalists and structural Marxists, ideology has been conceived as a universal dimension of social life and central to social cohesion.[83] Yet the desire to account for social cohesion and the reproduction of society has promoted the notion of a single dominant ideology that ensures unified social reproduction even through various means of mystification.[84] Recently, however, it is being more widely argued that ideology is not a single dominant set of ideas and values, and ideologies do not operate through single ideas or symbols.[85]

The second understanding of ideology, as dominant class interests, is also problematic. It simultaneously casts ideology as self-conscious and articulate, but also 'false' and able to dominate through mystification. Although he does not allude to Converse's findings, J. G. Merquior similarly suggests that functionalists and Marxists alike have exaggerated the degree to which various social mechanisms can imprint specific attitudes upon the minds of the subordinate classes. He takes Althusser to task for his notion of a one-way process by which the elites ideologize to control the masses and he challenges the "crystallization bias" that assumes an ideology to be fully articulated and self-conscious.[86] Others have argued that a single, holistic ideology reflecting the interests of just one class completely exaggerates the coherence and consensus of ideological discourse. Moreover, an ideology can scarcely be considered a matter of false images since as a discourse it operates through language, a medium of social action and constitutive of what is real.[87] Ultimately, the dominant-class perspective on ideology has been challenged by the familiar question "Exactly how does ideology do what we say it does, make people internalize values that do not benefit them?"[88]

For Merquior this question is unanswerable because of the assumptions on which it is based. First, dominated classes rarely internalize the values of the dominant class in any simple way. At best, they accept or consent to the values of the dominant class, which is quite different from belief in the legitimacy of those values.[89] John B. Thompson makes a similar point: consent may be given to a coherent dominant value system until a coherent alternative view is worked out, but such consent is *not* an internalization of these values or even the acceptance of them as legitimate.[90] He questions whether social reproduction really requires consensus concerning dominant values, suggesting that it does not. Social stability and reproduction may just as plausibly depend upon "pervasive fragmentation of the social order and proliferation of divisions among its members." For example, reproduction of the social order may depend less upon a consensus "than a lack of consensus at the very point where oppositional attitudes could be translated into political action."[91]

Having critiqued the ideology-as-worldview perspective for its false assumption of a "holism," Merquior finds the same assumption to underlie the ideology-of-the-dominant-class perspective. Both imply a holism in their notions of a set of dominant values promoted among the subordinate classes or a set of values for the whole society. Ideologies, even more or less coherent ideas associated with a more or less coherent social class, are never holistic, he argues. Nor, one might also argue, do they dominate by exercising coerced internalization. Ideologies are always factional and as such reduce the scope of any core values.[92] In effect, Merquior attempts to free the notion of ideology from every vestige of 'belief' as a matter of personal conviction.[93] Not only is ideology *not* a matter of belief; in actuality it rarely demands belief. Ideologies function as such by not requiring complete faith in each tenet or idea; all that is required is consent.

In opposition to the language of belief and internalization, Merquior is building on Gramsci's notions of consent and negotiation. For Gramsci, hegemonic discourse is dialogic not monolithic, defined by opposition even when the antagonistic voices are suppressed into silence.[94] Subordinated classes consent to a "negotiated" version of the dominant values when there are no articulated alternatives. Thus, outside of the dominant class, an ideology tends to consist of unexamined assumptions which amount to a "manipulation of bias" in favor of the dominant group.[95] As a consequence, ideologies are not primarily for the consumption of the exploited classes, but for the internal self-understanding of the class producing the ideology. In this way, Merquior argues, ideology is a veil that hides a group from itself, not a mask that threatens and dupes a subordinate group.[96] It is necessary to stop seeing ideology "as a vehicle of unanimous legitimacy beliefs" and begin to "see it as the instrument of an appropriation of a rhetoric of legitimacy by power-holding or power-seeking groups."[97] As a self-deluding and unconscious veiling, ideology connotes power without denoting it; it distorts the image of social reality within a class and sublimates the class's bias.[98]

Bourdieu draws attention to the "complicity" of the subordinated classes, a complicity necessary to the symbolic domination of ideology. This complicity with dominant-class values is neither passive submission on the one hand nor free adoption on the other. It is fundamentally an act of misrecognition by which the dominated class accepts the legitimacy of the values of the dominant class and applies the criteria of these values to its own practices, even when doing so is not favorable to it.[99] Bourdieu implies, however, that this act of misrecognition is essentially a strategic engagement in a struggle over symbols, a struggle in which contending factions seek "to impose the definition of the social world most in conformity with their interests."[100] Misrecognition is, therefore, not a matter of being duped, but a strategy for appropriating symbols, despite how structured and structuring the symbols may prove to be in practice. Indeed, for Bourdieu, it is only in this process of struggling to appropriate symbols that symbols become the prime instrument of social integration and consensus.[101] There may be no agreement on the symbol and a dramatic degree of variation when any interpretation is attempted, as Fernandez found, but still the same symbols are a common focus of engagement, a negotiated conflict.

Complicity, struggle, negotiation—these terms all aim to rethink ideology as a lived and practical consciousness, as a partial and oppositional process actively constructed by all involved and taking place in the very organization of everyday life.[102] Hence, ideology is *not* a coherent set of ideas, statements, or attitudes imposed on people who dutifully internalize them. Nor are societies themselves a matter of unitary social systems or totalities that act as one.[103] Any ideology is always in dialogue with, and thus shaped and constrained by, the voices it is suppressing, manipulating, echoing.[104] In other words, ideologies exist only in concrete historical forms and in specific relations to other ideologies.[105] Similarly, people do not simply acquire beliefs or attitudes imposed on them by others. If the manipulation of bias is a matter of unarticulated dispositions (e.g., "Stand up straight!"), then these dispositions must be embodied and reproduced in many activities that actively support them without much contradiction. If the manipulation of bias is a matter of clear and articulated statements ("God, guts, and guns made America great!"), then people have culturally basic 'epistemic principles' with which to evaluate and reflect upon ideas.[106] When they agree, they do not passively follow or obey; they appropriate, negotiate, qualify. Evidence suggests a rich variety of ways in which people can consent, resist, or manipulate aspects of dominant ideologies. Subcultures, according to Hebdige and others, are forms of resistance "obliquely represented in style" to be sure, but certainly not the passive obedience of people completely duped.[107] In this vein, others have proposed that ideology has nothing to do with a state of mind, but rather should be seen as a set of practices that "foreclose" the potentially infinite meaning of various cultural elements and relations in determinate ways.[108]

This counter approach to ideology has various ramifications. First, it affects our image of the actor–subject–agent who is both embedded in and generative of ideology. The actor emerges as divided, decentered, overdetermined, but quite active. He or she is constituted by structured and structuring dispositions, in Bourdieu's terms, which yield a variety of strategies, more or less effective in turn at appropriating a redemptive misrecognition of the hegemonic order.[109] This approach has other implications as well. Complicity, struggle, and negotiation all suggest that ideological discourse, no matter how fractured and plural, does have limits, assumptions, and shared interests. Indeed, as a strategy for *not* using coercive physical force, ideology assumes that it will not be met by physical force in return. People will recognize their own self-interest in some aspects of its dynamics.[110] Ideological strategies are particular forms of power struggling, effective when sheer violence would dissolve the society, when people are open to the rhetoric of collectivity and unity because it is in their own interests to be so united, or when reality testing of the values and ramifications of the ideology can remain nonempirical and unaware of the limits within which they are operating. Utopian in their very nature, Jameson argues, all ideologies possess their own kind of truth, a kind of comprehensibility within the limits that the ideology defines.[111]

Bourdieu denotes this limited sphere of comprehensibility as *doxa*, that which is neither questioned nor known to be known.[112] "Every established order," he writes, "tends to produce ... the naturalization of its own arbitrariness" by means of a "play of assumptions" and the sense of limits which constitute the social sense of reality.[113] Is this sense of reality the result of the exercise of social control? Hardly. It is certainly in the interests of people to have some sense of reality by virtue of which they can live in communication with others. Indeed, it may well be the constraints of community as much as the interests of particular groups that hold ideas together for the sake of a flexibly unformulated but practically coherent worldview, even when that worldview limits, ranks, marginalizes, or frustrates.[114]

Although each pursues independent analyses, Merquior, J. B. Thompson, and Bourdieu similarly conclude that ideology is best understood as a strategy of power, a process whereby certain social practices or institutions are depicted to be 'natural' and 'right.' While such a strategy implies the existence of a group or groups whose members stand to gain in some way by an acceptance of these practices, it also implies the existence of some form of opposition. Thus, ideologization may imply an unequal distribution of power, but it also indicates a greater distribution of power than would exist in relationships defined by sheer force. It is a strategy intimately connected with legitimation, discourse, and fairly high degrees of social complicity and maneuverability.[115]

Legitimation

Since Frazer and A. M. Hocart addressed the nature of sacred kingship at the beginning of this century, historians, sociologists, and anthropologists have found the notions of ritual, political power, and the legitimation of that power to be closely interdependent.[116] It is appropriate, therefore, that several recent analyses of sacred kingship have begun to challenge this interdependence. Geertz's study of Balinese kingship, for example, specifically attacks the traditional perspective that ritual functions to legitimate the exercise of political power. He argues that such a view casts ritual as mere "artifice" designed to disguise the brute exercise of "real" power.[117] His attempt to break down the distinction between ritual and politics suggests a provocative challenge to the notions of legitimation and power.

Two stories from Chinese history, retold in Howard Wechsler's study of ritual legitimation in China, illustrate a fundamental dilemma in understanding the relationship of ritual and political power. The first story tells how the founder of the Han dynasty (206 B.C.E.–221 C.E.) protested when advised that the time had come to consult the books on Confucian ethics and ritual. "All I possess I have won on horseback," he exclaimed. "Why should I now bother with those musty old texts?" "Your Majesty may have won it on horseback," retorted his chief counselor, "but can you rule it on horseback?"[118] In a second story from the T'ang dynasty the perspective shifts and it is not sufficient simply to consult the old books and reenact the ancient rites. Based on his study of the stars and portents, the Grand Astrologer alerted the T'ang emperor to the need to fashion his own distinctive ceremonial. He should at least change the calendar, the colors of court dress, and the names of the government offices so that the people could see the distinct virtue of his rule.[119] An appeal to traditional ritual is necessary to legitimate the first ruler but insufficient for the second ruler, who needed to take tradition in hand and put his stamp on it. Most simply, these stories illustrate that the invocation of tradition for the sake of legitimation is not standardized. They also represent another point. Based on the testimony of historical records, there are probably few peoples more overt and self-conscious than the Chinese in their manipulation of ritual for political ends; at the same time there is no culture where it would be less appropriate to regard ritual as mere artifice to mask the origins and exercise of power.

In addressing these paradoxes, Geertz describes how we cling to the simplistic misconception that power is the imposition of one person's or group's will on others through a threat of violence.[120] Because of this misconception, we rarely escape the associated assumption that ritual, as artifice, is there simply to disguise the crude instruments of power. In opposing the symbolic to the real, he argues, we see power as only external to its workings.[121] Several subsequent studies, particularly those by Cannadine and Bloch, have challenged and extended this analysis with a series of useful questions.[122] If ritual is not merely a mask for power, if it is itself a form of power, then exactly what form of power is it?[123] And again, how does ritual do what we keep saying it does: How does it actually inculcate cultural or political values, converting beliefs about another world into facts about this one and vice versa, and "inventing" traditions even as it purports to be transmitting them?[124]

These questions reflect a concern to analyze symbols and rites as real, effective, and powerful, not as simply secondary and expressive or as mere ideological tools that brainwash by dint of redundant assertions and group enthusiasm. Answers to these questions would impinge upon any approach to the notion of legitimation. Although the common use of the term "legitimation" implies a simple opposition of force to artifice or the real to the symbolic, it is generally well understood that legitimation is one of the powerful things that ritual does. When Reinhard Bendix writes that "legitimation achieves what power alone cannot," he means that rite commands more surely than brute physical force.[125] Others have explained legitimacy as the foundation of any and all political power, since physical coercion can become authority only when 'clothed' (however artificially) in legitimacy.[126] Ultimately, concludes one scholar of Chinese history, the social order is maintained not by law at all, but by ritual.[127] Certainly, it is in discussing legitimacy as a form of power eclipsing brute force that ritual comes to have great significance for political analysis.[128]

Three points underlie the attempts by Geertz, Cannadine, and Bloch to explain how rituals, especially so-called rituals of legitimation, do what they do. First, effective political ritual evokes a complex cluster of traditional symbols and postures of appropriate moral leadership, but it orchestrates them to differentiate itself, this particular political authority, from what has gone before. Thus, ritual is built out of widely accepted blocks of tradition, generating a sense of cultural continuity even when the juxtaposition of these blocks defines a unique ritual ethos.[129] Second, rather than affirming clear and dogmatic values to impress them directly into the minds of participants, ritual actually constructs an argument, a set of tensions.[130] According to Geertz, the Balinese state cult was *not* a cult of the state: "It was an argument made over and over again in the insistent vocabulary of ritual" that status in this world is based on the inherent hierarchical order of the cosmos itself, and therefore "the arrangements of human life are but approximations, more close or less, to those of the divine."[131] Third, ritual does not disguise the exercise of power, nor does it refer, express, or symbolize anything outside itself. In other words, political rituals do not refer to politics, as Geertz has strained to express, they *are* politics. Ritual is the thing itself. It *is* power; it acts and it actuates.[132] Geertz argues that to see the power in the political performances of the Balinese state we must put aside the opposition of symbolic to real, the aesthetic to the practice; we must see power as not external to its workings.[133] For Cannadine as well, "Ritual is not the mask of force, but is itself a type of power."[134]

The perspectives of Geertz and Cannadine are in contrast to Cohen's formulation that "power relations are objectified, developed, maintained, expressed, or camouflaged by means of symbolic forms and patterns of action."[135] While Cohen backs off from maintaining that power is external to these forms and actions, he allows at least a semantic capitulation to the theoretical primacy or priority of power by treating symbolic forms and actions as its vehicles, however indispensable.[136] Geertz and Cannadine push instead for a recognition of ritual as a strategic form of cultural practice.

In sum, it is a major reversal of traditional theory to hypothesize that ritual activity is not the 'instrument' of more basic purposes, such as power, politics, or social control, which are usually seen as existing before or outside the activities of the rite. It puts interpretive analysis on a new footing to suggest that ritual practices are themselves the very production and negotiation of power relations. In the following chapter I will attempt to demonstrate this alternative position more fully by showing how ritualization as a strategic mode of practice produces nuanced relationships of power, relationships characterized by acceptance and resistance, negotiated appropriation, and redemptive reinterpretation of the hegemonic order.

9

The Power of Ritualization

The argument of this chapter is essentially a simple one: ritualization is first and foremost a strategy for the construction of certain types of power relationships effective within particular social organizations. I will attempt to develop a fuller description of the strategy of ritualization in order to return to the question with which Part III began, Why and when is ritualization an appropriate and effective way of acting? This question and its answer should be understood as an alternative to the view that ritual is a functional mechanism or expressive medium in the service of social solidarity and control. A focus on activity itself as the framework within which to understand ritual activity illuminates the complex nature of power relations.

Theories of Power

As with 'ritual,' 'belief,' and 'ideology,' the term 'power' has been variously constituted for different projects. Fairly standard understandings involve the positive notion of 'influence' on the one hand and the negative notion of 'force' on the other.[137] Whereas influence is understood as inherent, nonspecific, and controlling, force is considered intentional, specific, and threatening.[138] Distinctions between power as implicit social control and power as explicit acts of political coercion frequently generate an opposition between so-called symbolic power, associated with ritual and ideology, and so-called secular power, associated with agencies and institutions of force.[139] Yet, whether it is formulated as influence or coercion, symbols or weapons, power has consistently been seen as something one possesses or not, and something that gives one some form of control over others (to the benefit of one party and the detriment of another). This view of power correlates with the tendency to see ideology as a totalistic worldview or a tool of the dominant classes. It also correlates with such traditional notions of religious power as the Weberian concept of charisma as a personal quality rather than a social relationship.[140] However, good arguments have also been advanced to support revision of our notion of power to reflect more accurately how power is constituted by social relationships and practices.

In a coherent tradition of thinking about power that can be traced from Thomas Hobbes's *Leviathan* through Lukes's *Power: A Radical View,* power has been understood on the model of sovereignty: "Power as a locus of will, as a supreme agency to which other wills would bend, as prohibitory; the classic conception of power as zero-sum; in short, power as negation of the power of others." In its more subtle and Marxist forms, this approach sees the "most insidious" exercise of sovereignlike power extend into dominion over individual subjectivity, giving rise to false consciousness and the unrecognized loss of an autonomous will.[141]

Lukes, for example, has organized some of the more significant theories of power formulated since Weber and Talcott Parsons in terms of various "dimensions."[142] The first dimension is represented by Robert Dahl's description of power as decision making, person to person in its exercise (as opposed to the 'possession' of power), having mechanical features (as a type of physical coercion), and identified with situations of overt conflict.[143] Peter Bachrach and Morton S. Baratz, representing a second dimension in Lukes's analysis, critiqued Dahl and proposed a broader, four-part typology: power as coercion, as authority, as influence, and as force. Considering both unconscious acts and the failure to act as involving the exercise of power, they paid more attention to situations of covert conflict.[144] Lukes's own "third dimension" of power attempted to encompass these earlier theories while going beyond them to address more subtle dynamics of power, such as ideology. Lukes attempted to shift the focus from an emphasis on individual behavior and observable conflict to a focus on relationships and structures that control agendas affecting potential issues and latent conflict.[145] Roderick Martin formulated a similar notion of power as fully embedded in the structure of human interactions or social relations, not within individual actors or necessarily in situations of conflict.[146]

These third-dimension approaches have facilitated the elaboration of 'symbolic power.' Broadly defined, symbolic power is "the power to constitute the given by stating it, to create appearances and belief, to confirm or transform the vision of the world and thereby action in the world, and therefore the world itself."[147] Based on this type of understanding of the order of power in symbolic activities, Cohen explicitly identifies ideology as a particular strategy of power.[148] Bourdieu similarly locates power in the boundaries of what can be said and thought, a people's sense of reality, by which every social order naturalizes its own arbitrariness.[149]

An alternative understanding of power, which some analysts have traced back to Machiavelli, appears in the work of Foucault and those influenced by him.[150] For Foucault, power is contingent, local, imprecise, relational, and organizational. In particular, he breaks with the longstanding premise that "power, whether localised or invested in a monarch, a community of citizens or a class dictatorship, consists in some substantive instance or agency of sovereignty."[151] He also rejects the notion of a dominant ideology perpetrated by the ruling class to serve its real interests, a view supported by the sovereignty model. For Foucault, power does not exist as a substantive entity that can be possessed or wielded, nor is it some 'thing' that exists in historical forms and causal effects. Since these qualities are all implied in a 'theory' of power, Foucault is determined to avoid theories in favor of an "analytics of power."[152] Only by staying free of the substantive approach, he implies, can one truly analyze power in terms of human relations.[153] He chooses a different language to interpret power as a matter of techniques and discursive practices that comprise the micropolitics of everyday life.

Foucault defines a relationship of power as a mode of action that does not intend to act directly on persons or things, which is what violence does, but indirectly on actions. The exercise of power is "always a way of acting upon an acting subject or acting subjects by virtue of their acting or being capable of action." It is a matter, therefore, of directing the activity of others, "guiding the possibility of conduct and putting in order the possible outcome." To govern, as an example of the exercise of power, is "to structure the possible field of action of others."[154] As a whole structure of actions brought to bear on other actions, power is constituted by a cluster of relations and it simultaneously produces in turn "a more-or-less-organised, hierarchical, co-ordinated cluster of relations."[155] As such, power relations are deeply embedded in the network of social relations and basic, therefore, to any society.[156] Or, as Geertz would put it, power is not something external to its social workings. Analogous as well to Bloch's revision of Geertz's "poetics of power," Foucault also sees the strategies of power used by kings and governments as embedded in and dependent upon the level of "microrelations" of power, the local interactions and petty calculations of daily life.[157]

At the same time, Foucault argues that relations of power are not simply engendered from the top down, but from the bottom up as well. On both micro and macro levels, there are always "movements in the opposite direction, whereby strategies which co-ordinate relations of power produce new effects and advance into hitherto unaffected domains."[158] Although there are tops and bottoms, since micropower relations are always unequal, there can be no movement down from the top without a conduit from below. For example, the establishment and maintenance of the power of kings or the power of capitalism has to be rooted in preexisting forms of behavior, socialized bodies, and local relations of power, which could not be mere projections of the central power and still effectively maintain and legitimate that power.[159]

In this way, power is neither an entity external to how and where it works, nor is it an effect of the confrontation between two opposed adversaries or a simple dominant–dominated relationship. Indeed, Foucault argues, power is exercised over "free subjects, and only insofar as they are free," that is, with the option of acting differently. If various conditions do away with all options, then it would no longer be a relationship of power per se.[160] Power and freedom do not come to a "face-to-face confrontation" as mutually exclusive states. Their relationship is much more complicated for Foucault. Freedom is the condition, as well as the precondition, for the exercise of power. Freedom is power's "permanent support, since without the possibility of recalcitrance, power would be equivalent to a physical determination."[161] In other words, the existence of freedom (in the sense of accessible options) is necessary to the exercise of power or else what might be thought to be power is really something much more like the force of necessity. Power must be grasped as quite different from the forces of violence or coercion.

The necessity of freedom to the exercise of power gives rise to Foucault's understanding of resistance. At the heart of power relationships lies an insubordination or resistance, an "essential obstinacy on the part of the principles of freedom," which means that there can be "no relationship of power without the means of escape or possible flight."[162] Hence, to explore power is to explore a necessary and simultaneous resistance to power that continues to provoke and legitimize its exercise. "Every power relationship implies, at least *in potentia*," he writes, "a strategy of struggle, in which the two forces are not superimposed, do not lose their specific nature, or do not finally become confused. Each constitutes for the other a kind of permanent limit, a point of possible reversal."[163] Every power relationship implies the potential for struggle or confrontation, a confrontation that participants in the relationship mistakenly think they may win, even though they cannot win *and* remain (as a winner) within a power relationship. Indeed, every confrontation potentially aims at the stabilization of the power relation. A power relationship undoes itself when, pushing to quell completely the insubordination necessary to it, it succeeds in reducing the other to total subservience or in transforming the other into an overt adversary.[164] For Foucault, therefore, the exercise of power is a strategic choice from among ways of interacting and it depends upon a variety of practices chosen by the parties involved to maintain the relationship as one of power.

In attempting to depict how this type of power is exercised, Foucault consistently chooses the nomenclature of 'ritual' to evoke the mechanisms and dynamics of power. He is not, however, concerned to analyze ritual per se or even to generate a description of ritual as an autonomous phenomenon. 'Ritual' is one of several words he uses to indicate formalized, routinized, and often supervised practices that mold the body. He repeatedly refers to "meticulous rituals of power," "liturgies of punishment," "legal" and "penal ceremonies," and so on.[165] In each of his distinct analyses of organized relationships of power (his studies of madness, the clinic, punishment, sexuality, etc.), the notion of ritual techniques is used "to specify how power works, what it does and how it does it."[166] These discussions provide interesting support for the framework for understanding ritual activities laid out so far, as well as interesting evidence of the assumptions about ritualized behavior that lead one to link discipline and pagentry, the meticulous and the routinized. Most significantly, however, Foucault's discussion helps clarify the purposes of ritualization as an effective way of acting, namely, how the production of ritualized agents is a strategy for the construction of particular relationships of power effective in particular social situations. His contribution in this regard hinges on his appreciation of the centrality of the body.

For Foucault, the body is "the place where the most minute and local social practices are linked up with the large scale organization of power."[167] The body is a political field: "Power relations have an immediate hold upon it; they invest it, mark it, train it, torture it, force it to carry out tasks, to perform ceremonies, to emit signs."[168] The body is the most basic and fundamental level of power relations, the "microphysics" of the micropolitics of power.[169] Ritualization, Foucault appears to imply, is a central way that power operates; it constitutes a political technology of the body.

Ritual is basic to Foucault's notion of the constitution and exercise of power simply because of the way in which power involves the body and strategy. First of all, power is "rooted deep in the social nexus," and the roots of the network of social relations go no deeper than the social body itself. Second, power involves the selection of means to secure an advantage over others. These means are strategically indirect: they afford an indirect structuring effect on the field of other possible actions.[170] For Foucault the term 'strategy' implies improvisational, expedient, or the minimum form of rationality needed.[171]

Foucault's analysis of the body and the close workings of power is an analysis of the strategies by which power relations are put into play in the very constitution of the social body. He does not depict the appropriation of the body by something outside it. Rather, the social body is the micronetwork of power relations, but not in terms of a reflection of larger social institutions or as some sort of social homunculus that contains a blueprint for them. The social body is the active site of "dispositions, maneuvers, tactics, techniques, functionings," it is a "network of relations, constantly in tension" for which the proper metaphor would be a "perpetual battle" rather than "the conquest of a territory."[172] He is concerned with how power relations both penetrate and constitute the body in depth, bypassing the subject's own representations, and even any process of internalization in consciousness.[173]

Quite unlike the approach of Douglas described earlier, the social body for Foucault "is the effect not of consensus [or coherence or control] but of the materiality of power operating on the very bodies of individuals."[174] The social body—as the shifting network of power relations "between a man and a woman, between the members of a family, between a master and his pupil, between every one who knows and every one who does not"—is, simultaneously, the "concrete, changing soil" out of which the sovereigns's power is constituted and out of which the individual and his or her power strategies are constituted.[175] Foucault goes so far as to locate the very generation of individuality, the subject, and subjectivity within this network of strategic power relations. "It is already one of the prime effects of power that certain bodies, certain gestures, certain discourses, certain desires, come to be identified and constituted as individuals," he asserts. "The individual, that is, is not the vis-à-vis of power; it is, I believe, one of its prime effects. The individual is an effect of power, and at the same time, or precisely to the extent to which it is that effect, it is the element of its articulation. The individual which power has constituted is at the same time its vehicle."[176] It would be more in keeping with his broader treatment of power for Foucault to rephrase the sentence just quoted to the effect that the individual so constituted is not so much a vehicle of power as that very microcluster of relations that constitutes power itself. "Power constitutes the individual," and the individual is the root of the constitution of power.[177]

Intrinsic to this mutual constitution and maintenance of the individual/social body and the microphysics of power is the freedom and resistance to power mentioned previously. From this angle as well, the fact that there are no relations of power without resistance means that the body is not appropriated by power and neither is consciousness.[178] Rather, the body and consciousness, and any distinction between them, are constituted by those relations of domination and resistance that are the play of power.[179]

Foucault's analytics of power is a provocative retreatment that has received much attention and a fair amount of criticism. While many find it not entirely satisfactory to do away with coercion, I am convinced that his treatment of power as embedded in the social bodies and interactions of persons opens up an important dimension of power hitherto underemphasized. In terms of this dimension of power, to extend Lukes's list, we can elaborate an analysis of ritualization that goes well beyond the social solidarity thesis and significantly nuances the definition of reality thesis. The language of this analytics of power also enables us to begin to answer the question of this chapter: Under what general conditions is ritualization an effective social strategy? It is in ritual—as practices that act upon the actions of others, as the mute interplay of complex strategies within a field structured by engagements of power, as the arena for prescribed sequences of repetitive movements of the body that simultaneously constitute the body, the person, and the macro- and micronetworks of power—that we can see a fundamental strategy of power. In ritualization, power is not external to its workings; it exists only insofar as it is constituted with and through the lived body, which is both the body of society and the social body. Ritualization is a strategic play of power, of domination and resistance, within the arena of the social body.[180]

Ritual Empowerment: Effects and Limits

It is useful to recapitulate some basics before proceeding further. First, ritualization involves the differentiation and privileging of particular activities. Theoretically, these activities may differentiate themselves by a variety of features; in practice, some general tendencies are obvious. For example, these activities may use a delineated and structured space to which access is restricted; a special periodicity for the occurrence and internal orchestration of the activities; restricted codes of communication to heighten the formality of movement and speech; distinct and specialized personnel; objects, texts, and dress designated for use in these activities alone;

verbal and gestural combinations that evoke or purport to be the ways things have always been done; preparations that demand particular physical or mental states; and the involvement of a particular constituency not necessarily assembled for any other activities. These are not universal features, however. At best, ritualization can be defined only as a 'way of acting' that makes distinctions like the foregoing ones by means of culturally and situationally relevant categories and nuances. When such culturally specific strategies are generalized into a universal phenomenon, much of the logic by which these ritual strategies do what they do is lost. This becomes particularly clear in recalling that the situational and strategic nature of ritualization affects even the degree to which such ritualized acts differentiate themselves at all from other forms of activity. In other words, an essential strategy of ritualization is how it clarifies or blurs the boundaries that identify it as a specific way of acting.

For example, Wuthnow has explored what he calls the "ritual aspects" of left-hand turn signals and the mass viewing of the television series "Holocaust."[181] Given the analysis advanced in this chapter, however, the first case is not one of ritualized activities, merely regularized (rule-bound) behavior that functions as a signal of intentions in the context of driving. Why? The answer is cultural. In this culture, such legally articulated modes of regularized behavior are insufficient to count as 'ritual' for most people. In the second case, the network and general media undoubtedly used a variety of strategies to heighten the sense that people were viewing a unique and profound event, that the television was a medium of communal participation with other viewers for witnessing an important simulation of reality, and to dramatize the solemnity of the broadcast in contrast to the usual television fare. Indeed, there was sufficient evocation of ritual ways of acting that many people probably reacted with some of the conventions of consent used in ritual—"If it is this unique and important I should watch and accept," and the like. Nonetheless, in this culture, viewing the series was not likely to be judged ritual for those involved due to cultural distinctions among ways of acting, distinctions vital to any analysis of social action.

The evocation of ritualizing strategies by activities that do not wish to be considered religious ritual is a very common feature particularly in the secularism of American society. Courtroom procedures and public school graduation exercises, congressional hearings and AA meetings—all ritualize to a strategic degree. As a way of acting that can be put to different purposes, ritualization will sometimes be used to the point of creating certain impressions, but then stop short of provoking a controversy about its appropriateness. For other purposes, usually those of political opposition or artistic experimentation, ritualization will deliberately mime religious symbols and activities in order to create controversy, as in a formal gathering on the steps of the Supreme Court to burn the flag instead of raising it. Hence, cultural and situational forms of ritualization are strategies in the repertoire of any moderately socialized person, and one of the most basic of these strategies concerns the degree of ritualization used to distinguish or blur activities.

The deployment of ritualization, consciously or unconsciously, is the deployment of a particular construction of power relationships, a particular relationship of domination, consent, and resistance. As a strategy of power, ritualization has both positive and effective aspects as well as specific limits to what it can do and how far it can extend. While it may be an effective way of acting in certain places at certain times, under other conditions it may be useless or counterproductive. It is necessary to explore the relationships of power constituted through ritualization and the circumstances in which these relationships are effective or ineffective forms of social interaction.

As a strategy for the constitution of power relations that appears to be 'instinctive' to the socialized agent, ritualization involves two basic dimensions. The first dimension is that of the dynamics of the social body, its projection and embodiment of a structured environment. Ritualization in this dimension, as we have seen, is a process that works below the level of discourse. It produces and objectifies constructions of power (via the schemes that organize its environment), which the social agent then reembodies. Ritualized agents do not see themselves as projecting schemes; they see themselves only acting in a socially instinctive response to how things are. Thus, the production and objectification of structured and structuring schemes in the environment involve a misrecognition of the source and arbitrariness of these schemes. These schemes tend to be experienced as deriving from powers or realities beyond the community and its activities, such as god or tradition, thereby depicting and testifying to the ultimate organization of the cosmos.[182] The process of objectification is one in which participants themselves physically effect the construction of a set of relationships, in the guise of participating in organizational schemes that appear to be mandated by the nature of the environment itself. This misrecognition involves another in turn: participants do not recognize that the objectified schemes which they reembody have been orchestrated so that the patterns of dominance and subordination they contain generate the sense of integrated totality and embracing holism experienced by the participants. Participants misrecognize both the source of the schemes and the changes these schemes undergo in the temporal process of projection and embodiment. These schemes are drawn from each agent's socialized instincts; when objectified they produce an environment that is itself a complex pattern, or objectification, of power relations. This structured and structuring environment that the participants have created and with which they interact inevitably nuances the disposition of schemes that each agent repossesses as a practical knowledge of the world. Relationships of power are drawn from the social body and then reappropriated by the social body as experience. Specific relations of domination and subordination are generated and orchestrated by the participants themselves simply by participating. Within the intricacies of this objectification and embodiment lies the ability of ritualization to create social bodies in the image of relationships of power, social bodies that *are* these very relationships of power. If it is at all accurate to say that ritualization controls—by modeling, defining, molding, and so on—it is this type of control that must be understood.

A second dimension to the ritual construction of power, however, involves dynamics whereby the power relations constituted by ritualization also empower those who may at first appear to be controlled by them. This second dimension illustrates the actual limits of most ritual practices as a means of domination and control; it is the flip side of their strategic effectiveness. Integral to the processes of objectification and embodiment described earlier are concomitant processes of consent, resistance, and negotiated appropriation. In a very basic way, one consents to participation by a variety of internal discriminations about one's relation to what is going on. A person's involvement in ritual activities—as a particular instance of his or her involvements with very specific people, groups, places, and events—is never an indiscriminate openness to what is going on. A participant, as a ritualized agent and social body, naturally brings to such activities a self-constituting history that is a patchwork of compliance, resistance, misunderstanding, and a redemptive personal appropriation of the hegemonic order.

The 'consent' that such participation involves cannot be deemed a mere illusion or something artificially manufactured.[183] It may be based in great part on material needs, as the need for employment will encourage many to consent to various ritualized activities at the workplace, or there may be other less material reasons. However, the notion of consent cannot mean 'false consciousness' or ideological colonization of the participant's consciousness since power as such does not reside outside the relationships constituted by and constitutive of the participants. 'Resistance' similarly constitutes relationships of power in defining participants themselves. A participant pressured to attend a political ritual in a totalitarian state might assert that her physical presence is consenting to what is going on, but her mind is resisting. Such participation creates the relations and the very hold of power within her person in terms of a consenting physical body experienced as distinct from a resisting mind.

Just as participation is negotiated, so are the processes of objectification and embodiment. Embodiment, like consensual participation in the objectification processes of the rite, is *experienced* as a negotiated appropriation, not as a total and indiscriminate absorption or social molding. As we have seen, the ritualized agent already possesses schemes that he or she can deploy, more or less effectively, to produce actions that are more or less coherent with each other and with a larger view of the whole of life. It is by virtue of these schemes that agents also orchestrate and appropriate for their own purposes the hegemonic order reconstituted in ritual. They do so in ways that open up for them some personal and provisional understanding of how the immediate universe works and how they as individuals fit into it. One appropriates and thereby constructs a version (usually neither very explicit nor coherent) of the hegemonic order that promises a path of personal redemption, that gives one some sense of relative dominance in the order of things, and thereby some ability to engage and affect that order.[184]

When forced into verbal formulations, a person's view of this will probably not match those of other participants or of specialists. Ritualization, as the interaction of the social body with a structured and structuring environment, specifically affords the opportunity for consent and resistance and negotiated appropriation on a variety of levels.

One of the most interesting ethnographies to situate ritual activities within the social organization of power is Jean Comaroff's study of the Tshidi of South Africa before and after colonialization. Although Comaroff does not develop a specific notion of power or the ritual construction of power relations, she focuses closely on the role of the body and ritual strategies of resistance within the context of political domination. She argues that the body "mediates" all action upon the world: through the schemes of classification inscribed in it, reworked whenever the person needs to be remade, the body effectively constitutes both the self and the universe of which it is a part. Ritual, by focusing on the making and remaking of the body, reproduces the sociopolitical context in which it takes place while also attempting to transform it.[185]

Comaroff argues that the imagery of physical affliction and healing so central to the postcolonial ritual practices of the Zionist churches—in which the body, at war with itself, must be simultaneously healed and reintegrated into the community—actualizes a position of protest and resistance to the intrusion of the colonial hegemonic order into the Tshidi sense of the natural world. Zionist rituals of baptism and healing construct a social body not as an icon or microcosm of the sociocosmic order, as found in precolonial ritual, but as a matter of parts in fractured relation to the whole. In so doing, these rites define a universe that is also afflicted, at war with itself, but amenable to healing. While such metaphors accept the fact of white political dominance and replicate various dimensions of that power, they simultaneously resist and discourage wholesale acceptance of the order of domination and subordination politically in place in South Africa. The Tshidi reproduce that hegemonic order by appropriating it in a way that empowers them to envision redemption, to seek healing and domination over the forces of disease and fragmentation.[186]

Comaroff does not look for similar power dynamics of consent and resistance in the precolonial ritual practices of the Tshidi. Indeed, she tends to see precolonial ritual in terms of a more monolithic ideological molding. In contrast to postcolonial practices, precolonial initiation rituals inscribed the hegemonic order within the body of the adult and impressed it upon the body of the child. All levels of social experience—body, home, community, and cosmos—were brought into a reinforcing conformity with each other. In the process, however, symmetrical schemes of complementary opposition, such as gender relations or the individual vis-à-vis the collective, were overlaid with asymmetrical schemes of dominance that emphasized centrism, control, and the authority of the ruler. Comaroff does call attention, in a Geertzian fashion, to a variety of structural tensions expressed in this overlay of schemes: tension between an unambiguous system of cultural classifications and a rather ambiguous network of actual social relations on the one hand, and tension between the social organization and the forms of material production and competition on the other.[187] According to the Geertzian formula, she tends to see such tensions mediated or resolved by their ritual expression, which in precolonial idiom worked to "reinforce" the system of so-called natural categories of the world, whereas postcolonial idiom worked to "reform" or "reconstruct" them.[188] Yet, despite the formula and the tendency to see a simpler molding process in precolonial ritual, Comaroff's careful data suggest that the ritual definition and reinforcement of the natural order was neither fixed nor nonstrategic.

Ritualization both implies and demonstrates a relatively unified corporate body, often leading participants to assume that there is more consensus than there actually is. It leads all to mistake the minimal consent of its participants for an underlying consensus or lack of conflict, even when some conflict is objectified and reembodied. Most of all, ritualization leads participants to mistake the group's reformulation of itself as a straightforward communication and performance of its most traditional values.

The misrecognitions of ritualization affect both those who dominate and those who are dominated. Moreover, the misrecognitions that make ritualization so effective for the creation and maintenance of certain power relations simultaneously set the limits of ritualization's social efficacy. These limits are rooted in several interrelated features: first, there is the need to presume at least an illusion of consensus among participants; second, this involves the necessity of encouraging or inducing consent, usually by stressing the personal advantages to be had or costs to be incurred by not consenting; and third, to induce the consent of participants by whatever means also affords the participants the opportunity to appropriate and/or resist in negotiated ways.

Although it is difficult to address in narrative succession relationships that are simultaneous and meant to elude the structure of explicit articulation, a variety of perspectives taken up in turn may provide more specificity about the way in which power is negotiated in ritual and how ritual strategies construct distinct forms of domination and resistance. The following four perspectives are essentially artificial but useful devices: (1) how ritualization empowers those who more or less control the rite; (2) how their power is also limited and constrained; (3) how ritualization dominates those involved as participants; and (4) how this domination involves a negotiated participation and resistance that also empowers them.

How ritualization empowers those who control or regulate ritual practices is probably the most documented aspect of the study of ritual. Bourdieu reflects a consensus of sorts when he suggests that those who control ritualization are in command of a particularly powerful form of objectification, especially in cultures where there are relatively few other institutionalized structures to rival it.[189] Bloch also views ritualization as a more or less institutionalized medium of objectification, one that constitutes traditional forms of authority through techniques of formalization that render this authority relatively invulnerable to casual challenge. Echoing Weber, Bloch demonstrates how ritualization depersonalizes authority, lodging the power of the specialist in an office or formal status, not in the person. In this way, a whole system or social order based on office and status is also reinforced. The ritual construction of authority is a stabilization of power and therein a specific augmentation of power. For if power is demonstrated as bestowed on the proper person by external sources, such as ancestors or deities, that power comes to be seen as vast, legitimate, and accessible only to those in the appropriate offices. In describing the perfection of such a form of "rule through ritual" in Asia, Lucien Pye characterizes this delineation of power as "the highest kind" in terms of sheer scope, justification, and limited accessibility.[190] Geertz, as noted earlier, also described the political empowerment of ritual "display" in very similar terms.

These studies yield at least three ways in which the empowerment of those who most control ritualization is constituted: the objectification of office, the hierarchization of practices, and traditionalization. Yet this should not be taken as a definitive list of the strategies of this form of empowerment. Nor should the potential efficacy of such strategies obscure the real limits of the power so constituted. Despite his observations as to its scope, Pye readily acknowledges that empowerment through ritual can be very unwieldy and constraining. Indeed, more than a few scholars have noted some of the specific limits of this form of power through ritualization. In essence, their insights appear to develop one of the conclusions that Gluckman reached in his analyses of the ritual containment of conflict—the intrinsically and categorically conservative nature of ritual. For example, both Bloch and Pye find that the ritual construction of traditional authority is very inflexible and diffuse. It is often a liability that so much authority is so loosely attached to the person, while being so tightly attached to office. Pye goes on to note that when power is seen as external to the actor, it can render cause and effect so complicated that the process is nearly invisible. Such power can establish authority, but not for any precision of purpose or application. Serving as "a rather blunt tool," this form of power cannot in itself generate an agenda of problem-solving plans or specific policy decisions.[191]

Bloch similarly observes that such traditional authority is ultimately disconnected from the real world. In the case of the Merina, he describes how the power and authority created by the highly structured patterns and impoverished language of formal oratory also render that authority unable to deal with specific problems, creating the need for another level of nonformalized discourse.[192] Just as the belief structures that may undergird ritual power can be neither proved nor disproved, so the successes and failures of the application of this power are also beyond real proof or disproof. Such power is vindicated only by general and continued well-being; it is indicted by widespread and sustained social problems.[193]

Just as contractual authority must be renewed (implying the periodic option of choice) and coercive force must be constantly vigilant in maintaining its threat, in the same way power constituted through ritualization must regularly sustain itself through the re-creation of tradition, the reobjectification of office, and the reproduced display of its magnificence.[194] A breakdown in the cycle of rites that create ritualized power, or a breakdown in the semblance of conformity to traditional models, can quickly fragment the illusion of social cohesion. As noted earlier, the criteria for and the value of coherence with tradition can be quite different in oral and literate societies, but the constraint on ritual remains roughly the same: it must be legitimated and authenticated by those whom it affects, as Valeri has described so vividly for the Hawaiian system of kingship.[195] The criteria for authentification are nothing less than a satisfying sense of adherence to precedent in addition to a close resonance with lived experience—in other words, a collective confidence in the continued well-being of the society along with an individual sense of participation in a process of redemptive activity.

However, if the ritual construction of power on the higher levels of social organization builds on the microrelations of power that shape daily life on the lower levels of the society, changes in the latter level can precipitate a crisis in which the demands of ritual to conform to traditional models clash with the ability of those rites to resonate with the real experiences of the social body. This is certainly a well-known and widespread phenomenon, and the very type addressed by Geertz in his analysis of the Javanese funeral analyzed in Part I. In Fernandez's study of the Bwiti, a reform cult among the Fang, the constituency of an old ritual master pressed him in vain for new rites of a type like the innovations of other nearby groups. With his refusal they deserted him to join other cults. Eventually he had to swallow his pride in order to be part of the community and their new activities.[196] The traditionalism, authority, and dramaturgy of ritual power can be as fragile as they can be impressive and enduring.

How people are controlled or manipulated by ritual, as noted at the beginning of this section, is also well represented in the literature. Here, however, I do not wish to pursue how the strategies of domination implemented in ritual *appropriate* minds and bodies, but rather how they *engage* them in a set of tensions that involve both domination and resistance. This engagement, as Foucault has argued, must also be understood as constitutive of the persons so engaged.

In a basic sense, when nonspecialist ritual participants are differentiated from ritual specialists, a differentiation displayed in and produced through ritual, lay participants lose direct control over a major medium of symbolic production and objectification. The result, of course, is that they can affect only indirectly the constructions of 'reality' or 'the ideal' objectified through ritualized activities. Other social media may be more directly available to the laity, if only to balance the power of ritual specialists, but the social stratification that attends the presence of ritual specialists often implies a more general division of labor that limits access to other such media as well. The lack of direct access to collective methods of objectification means that the struggle to define the world in ways most useful to the interests of the laity will be a covert one, both dependent upon specialists and resistant to them.

A very simple example is the way in which most American Catholics do not agree with or practice the position on birth control authoritatively pronounced by the papacy in Rome. Their subversion always comes as a bit of a surprise to everyone but Catholics. Outsiders tend to assume that Catholics have internalized the authority of the pope, especially since the papacy looms as the single most distinctive institution of Catholicism and a classic instance of traditional authority. Yet Catholics tend to think of their faith and church in terms of longstanding and idiosyncratic processes of appropriation, many of which may have little reference to Rome but great reference to the more immediate issues of local communities.[197] The 1987 visit of Pope John Paul to the United States is a good example: the pope was consistently greeted with the truly enthusiastic fanfare of popular devotion, which is clear evidence of an experience or a willingness to experience the charisma of office and its person. Yet this devotion does not imply unreserved or nonnegotiable obedience. Catholicism is a consent to papal power and a resistance to it at the same time. Moreover, those seen as controlled by ritual authority are not simply able to resist or limit this power; they are also empowered by virtue of being participants in a relationship of power.

Bloch and others have drawn attention to the way in which ritualization catches people up in its own terms, asking little more than a mere consent to the forms while relegating anything but the most concerted challenge to the non-threat of rudeness. "You cannot argue with a song," Bloch writes.[198] The only real alternative to negotiated compliance is either total resistance or asocial self-exclusion. Insofar as ritual is objectified as a distinct way of acting it provides a fairly resistant surface to casual disagreement. At the same time, negotiated compliance offers manifold opportunities for strategic appropriation, depending on one's mastery of social schemes, even to the point of subversion. Nonetheless, any discussion of freedom and resistance in the ritual construction of power, although a corrective to theories of ritual control, should not minimize how ritualization does appropriate and culturally school the social body. Negotiated consent, such as the resisting participant in a totalitarian rally, or the pursuit of alternative ritual activities, such as the home churches of disaffected Catholics, may qualify and nuance the socialization effected by the dominant ritual activities, but this relativizing and its tensions still shape the personhood and the microdynamics of power within and among those involved. The orchestrated construction of power and authority in ritual, which is deeply evocative of the basic divisions of the social order, engage the social body in the objectification of oppositions and the deployment of schemes that effectively reproduce the divisions of the social order. In this objectification lie the resonance of ritual and the consequences of compliance. As Bourdieu and Bloch suggest, one might retain one's limited and negotiated involvement in the activities of ritual, but bowing or singing in unison imperceptibly schools the social body in the pleasures of and schemes for acting in accordance with assumptions that remain far from conscious or articulate.

Yet it is crucial to demonstrate that the efficacy of ritualization as a power strategy lies not only in the domination it affords, but in the resistance as well. Ritual mastery, that sense of ritual which is at least a basic social mastery of the schemes and strategies of ritualization, means not only that ritualization is the appropriation of a social body but that the social body in turn is able to appropriate a field of action structured in great measure by others. The circularity of this phenomenon is intrinsic to it. Ritual mastery is itself a capacity for and relationship of relative domination. It does not merely socialize the body with schemes that structure and reproduce parts (large or small) of the social order, nor does it merely construct the social person with versions of these schemes as the order of its subjectivity and consciousness. To do all that it must also enable the person to deploy schemes that can manipulate the social order on some level and appropriate its categories for a semicoherent vision of personal identity and action. Socialization cannot be anything less than the acquisition of schemes that can potentially restructure and renuance both self and society. As a "discursive practice," ritual activity concerns knowledge (ritual mastery) that is "reproduced through practices made possible by the framing assumptions of that knowledge." These practices are "a very practical knowledge," which "disciplines the body, regulates the mind, and orders the emotions in such a way that the ranking, hierarchy and stratification which ensues from these practices is not just the blind reproduction of a transcendent traditional order." The practical knowledge that emerges by and through ritualization, what I have referred to as ritual mastery or the sense of ritual, which structures and fixes meanings in historical forms, is an "accomplishment of power."[199]

As a strategic embodiment of schemes for power relationships—schemes that hierarchize, integrate, define, or obscure—ritualization can promote social solidarity. It can promote solidarity particularly in a fairly homogeneous group with general recognition of key symbols, where a sense of unity can be achieved through consent to the forms, and where most subgroups benefit in some way from the simultaneous integration and differentiation of the social order. This is *not* a matter of simply reinforcing shared beliefs or instilling a dominant ideology. At the same time, as a strategic embodiment of schemes for power relationships—schemes that can hierarchize, subordinate, integrate, define, and obscure—ritualization can also promote the forces that have been traditionally thought to work against social solidarity and control. Indeed, one aspect of ritual mastery surely acquired in the processes of consent, resistance, and appropriation may be schemes for the differentiation of private and social selves. Some scholars, as noted earlier, have seen ritual as a mechanism for the integration of the individual and society, or the individual and social dimensions of the self; others, such as Tambiah and Bloch, have noted the opposite. The formalization of ritual often appears to involve a distancing within actors of their private and social identities. Tambiah suggests that such distancing may be integral to what ritual does on the one hand (i.e., its elaboration of the symbolic), but also problematic if taken too far. The result could be disassociation and disaffection, as well as the cultural perception of empty ritualism and hypocrisy.[200] It is possible that ritualization itself can generate and deploy such bifurcations of the self as that described by Durkheim as "two beings facing in different and almost contrary directions."[201] If so, it would be a feature of ritualization in a particular historical and cultural setting, a setting in which such schemes would have some efficacious value outside the ritual. And indeed, something of the modern world and the modern self is heard very forcibly in Durkheim's account of religion. Such schemes of bifurcation of self, if present at all, may have worked very differently in precolonial Tshidi and Hawaiian communities. Certainly Foucault concluded that in the emergence of meticulous rituals of corporal incarceration in the nineteenth century, we can witness the historical germination of the modern 'soul'.[202] The strategies of ritualization clearly generate forms of practice and empowerment capable of articulating an understanding of the personal self vis-à-vis community, however these might be understood. The results might well be seen in terms of the continuity between self and community, or in terms of an autonomous identity. However, the result might also be the formation of a subjectivity that polarizes thought and action, the personal self and the social body. To take these possibilities seriously is to recognize that practice can give rise to thoughts, cognitive categories, and modes of perception. In this analysis, ritual is not devised to join what the modern world experiences as divided; rather, ritualization is one set of cultural practices that contributes to the formation of such experiences. Clearly, for the Tshidi of the Zionist churches of the colonial era, ritualization strategies facilitated a perception that Durkheim claimed to be a universal one—"the antithesis which all men have more or less clearly conceived between the body and the soul, the material and the spiritual beings who coexist within us."[203] And such schemes of disassociation enabled them to resist (i.e., work out some form of dominance and appropriation of) the oppressive definitions of the colonial order.

For Durkheim, "The believer who has communicated with his god is not merely a man who sees new truths of which the unbeliever is ignorant; he is a man who is *stronger*. He feels within him more force, either to endure the trials of existence, or to conquer them."[204] Durkheim's perception has been analyzed for too long only in terms of the so-called illusions generated by affective states of social enthusiasm. Yet as the foregoing analysis suggests, his statement may accurately capture the truth of ritually constructed power relations, not the delusions of collective emotion. The person who has prayed to his or her god, appropriating the social schemes of the hegemonic order in terms of an individual redemption, may be stronger because these acts are the very definitions of power, personhood, and the capacity to act.

The variety of evidence examined here has attempted to demonstrate that ritualization necessitates and engenders both consent and resistance. It does not assume or implement total social control; it is a flexible strategy, one that requires complicity to the point of public consent, but not much more than that. Ultimately, the resistance it addresses and produces is not merely a limit on the rite's ability to control; it is also a feature of its efficacy.

It is not totally inappropriate, or unexpected, that the end of this exploration of ritual should return to one of the original questions with which it began, however altered the relationship with it may be. In Part I of this book I demonstrated the coherent, closed, and circular discourse that results when ritual is cast as a mechanism for the integration of thought and action, or self and society. In this final part I find a coherent and circular closing in the suggestion that ritual practices themselves can generate the culturally effective schemes that yield the categories with which to differentiate self and society, thought and action. This is not to say that ritualization is the only form of practice that defines the self. Hardly. It is that form of practice where the definition is simultaneously embedded in the social body and its environment, negotiated, and rendered prestigious by the privileged status that ritualized activities claim.

Conclusion

The preceding analyses do not add up to a new theory of ritual. This is deliberate, and for several reasons. First, I do not wish to imply or designate some independently existing object, named ritual, with a set of defining features that characterize all instances of ritual. Such an approach also implies that ritual so defined is readily amenable to objective analysis and formulation without suffering any distortion in the process. In addition, a theory of ritual would also have to distinguish ritual from ceremony and ceremony from magic and social etiquette, and so on—leading to a whole galaxy of independent and pure entities with static features. A second major reason to avoid a theory of ritual is to free this analysis from the required format of demonstrating the originality, systematicity, and general applicability that a claim for a new theory would warrant. Many aspects of this study are intentionally experimental, developed as an exploration of ways of *not* thinking about ritual as well as ways of rethinking the idea and the data. Many of the discrete points made here have been made before by others; the construct of originality often obscures rather than reveals the lines of thinking about the issue. It is also probable that many of the arguments I have laid out here replicate the structures they attempt to discern and discard. This may have its virtues as a form of further evidence of the real constraints on thinking about acting and of the strategies of argument-building. Although a writer cannot evade the blindnesses that are the flip side of his or her insights, both can be made useful to the reader.

What I have attempted to do is forge a framework for reanalyzing the types of activities usually understood as ritual. At a fundamental level, this framework attempts to return such ritual activities to the context of human action in general. Ritual is not assumed to exist as a natural category of human practice. Within this interpretive framework some activities are performed in culturally relevant ways to generate the perception that these activities are both intrinsically different from other acts and privileged in their significance and ramifications. The framework proposed here focuses, therefore, on the generation of what we call ritual as a way of acting, namely, the ritualization of activity. It is possible that further progress along this line will yield sufficient detail to generalize more effectively about cultural strategies of ritualization vis-à-vis other strategies, but that is beyond the scope of this initial study. Some preliminary generalizations have, nonetheless, been suggested. Within the framework of ac-

tivity, specifically the context formed by the cultural spectrum of
ways of acting and what they imply, several features emerge as
very common to ritualization: strategies of differentiation
through formalization and periodicity, the centrality of the body,
the orchestration of schemes by which the body defines an environment and is defined in turn by it, ritual mastery, and the negotiation of power to define and appropriate the hegemonic
order.

When returned to the context of human activity in general, so-
called ritual acts must be seen first in terms of what they share with
all activity, then in terms of how they set themselves off from other
practices. Ritualization is fundamentally a way of doing things to
trigger the perception that these practices are distinct and the associations that they engender are special. A great deal of strategy
is employed simply in the degree to which some activities are ritualized and therein differentiated from other acts. While formalization and periodization appear to be common techniques for
ritualization, they are not intrinsic to 'ritual' per se; some ritualized
practices distinguish themselves by their deliberate informality, although usually in contrast to a known tradition or style of ritualization. Hence, ritual acts must be understood within a semantic
framework whereby the significance of an action is dependent upon
its place and relationship within a context of all other ways of
acting: what it echoes, what it inverts, what it alludes to, what it
denies.

Aside from the strategic and privileged distinctions established
by ritualization, another primary way it acts is through a focus on
the body, specifically the interaction of the body within a highly
structured environment. I have suggested that the body of the socialized participant structures an environment but sees only the
body's response to a supposedly preexisting set of structures. The
physical movements of the socialized body within this demarcated
space and time generate an endlessly circular run of oppositions
that come to be loosely homologized to each other, deferring their
significance to other oppositions so that the meaning of any one
set of symbols or references depends upon the significance of others.
By virtue of movement and stillness, sound and silence, through
which the body produces and reabsorbs these oppositional schemes,
an orchestration is effected in which some schemes come to dom-

inate and interpret others. The ability to produce schemes that
hierarchize and integrate in complex ways is part and parcel of the
practical knowledge acquired in and exercised through ritualization.
The ultimate purpose of ritualization is neither the immediate goals
avowed by the community or the officiant nor the more abstract
functions of social solidarity and conflict resolution: it is nothing
other than the production of ritualized agents, persons who have
an instinctive knowledge of these schemes embedded in their bodies,
in their sense of reality, and in their understanding of how to act
in ways that both maintain and qualify the complex microrelations
of power. Such practical knowledge is not an inflexible set of assumptions, beliefs, or body postures; rather, it is the ability to
deploy, play, and manipulate basic schemes in ways that appropriate and condition experience effectively. It is a mastery that
experiences itself as relatively empowered, not as conditioned or
molded.

With these same schemes the activities of ritualization generate
historical traditions, geographical systems, and levels of professionals. Just as a rite cannot be understood apart from a full spectrum of cultural forms of human action in general, so it must also
be seen in the context of other ritualized acts as well. The construction of traditions and subtraditions, the accrual of professional and
alternative expertise—all are effected by the play of schemes invoked through ritualization.

When placed within this framework, the work accomplished
through ritualization is very inadequately grasped by the notion of
social control. Ritualization is not a matter of transmitting shared
beliefs, instilling a dominant ideology as an internal subjectivity, or
even providing participants with the concepts to think with. The
particular construction and interplay of power relations effected by
ritualization defines, empowers, and constrains. Ritualized practices, of necessity, require the external consent of participants while
simultaneously tolerating a fair degree of internal resistance. As
such they do not function as an instrument of heavy-handed social
control. Ritual symbols and meanings are too indeterminate and
their schemes too flexible to lend themselves to any simple process
of instilling fixed ideas. Indeed, in terms of its scope, dependence,
and legitimation, the type of authority formulated by ritualization
tends to make ritual activities effective in grounding and displaying

a sense of community *without* overriding the autonomy of individuals or subgroups. Ritualization as any form of social control, however indirectly defined, will be effective only when this control can afford to be rather loose. Ritualization will not work as social control if it is perceived as not amenable to some degree of individual appropriation. If practices negate all forms of individual choice, or *all* forms of resistance, they would take a form other than ritualization. Basic to what makes Foucault's "rites of penal discipline" a matter of ritualization rather than the use of a metaphor is the form of consent and resistance still afforded the subjugated participant even if it be no more than a recognition of the limits placed on the activities of the subjugator. For example, the court-ordered flogging of an accused thief would play up its own ritual nature (ritualize its activities) in a display of power that simultaneously recognized its own limits—in the number of strokes, their intensity, the personal uninvolvement of the officer doing the flogging, and so on. Ritualization cannot turn a group of individuals into a community if they have no other relationships or interests in common, nor can it turn the exercise of pure physical compulsion into participatory communality. Ritualization can, however, take arbitrary or necessary common interests and ground them in an understanding of the hegemonic order; it can empower agents in limited and highly negotiated ways.

Ultimately, the notion of ritual is constructed in the image of the concerns of a particular cultural era. Certainly, analyzing the social and cultural import of ritual activities is a form of practice known only to secular societies that make a distinction between the pursuit of objective knowledge and the practice of religion. The study of ritual is surely a cultural corollary to the antiritualism that Douglas finds common in secular societies. It might be more: A strategic dichotomizing of thought and action may well be basic to the pragmatic negotiations of 'self' and 'society' in such secular cultures. The formal study of ritual itself, therefore, may be more than a simple *reflection* of secularism; it might be yet another arena for negotiating the relations between the practice of knowledge and the practice of religion.

Any new theory, even a new framework, overstates its case. Usually it is best understood as a corrective to the problems inherent in a preceding set of emphases. 'Ritualization' attempts to correct the implications of universality, naturalness, and an intrinsic structure that have accrued to the term 'ritual'. Some of these accretions are a consequence of the way in which 'ritual' corrected notions like liturgy and magic. While this framework's emphasis on ritual as a differentiated strategy of social action may effectively reintepret our data for a while, it is also likely that its extremes, particularly its limits on generalization, will need to be addressed in turn.

III. Notes

Introduction

1. Valeri cites Bergson's notion of ritual as a type of social "drill" (p. 344).
2. See Lane, who uses the work of Nancy Munn, Terence Turner, and Sherry B. Ortner, among others, to develop a fairly nuanced description of the modeling process (p. 17 in particular).
3. David I. Kertzer, *Ritual, Politics and Power* (New Haven: Yale University Press, 1988), p. 2.

Chapter 7

4. Kertzer, p. 62.
5. Lukes, "Political Ritual and Social Integration," pp. 293–96; Edward Shils and Michael Young, "The Meaning of the Coronation," *Sociological Review*, n.s. 1 (1953): 63–81; W. Lloyd Warner, *The Living and the Dead: A Study of the Symbolic Life of Americans* (New Haven: Yale University Press, 1959); Robert N. Bellah, "Civil Religion in America," in *Religion in America*, ed. William G. McLoughlin and Robert N. Bellah (Boston: Houghton Mifflin, 1968), pp. 3–23; and Verba, pp. 348–60.
6. Lukes, "Political Rituals and Social Integration," pp. 289–91, 300, and 305.
7. Gluckman, *Order and Rebellion in Tribal Africa*, pp. 110–36.
8. Gluckman, *Politics, Law and Ritual in Tribal Society*, p. 265.
9. Lane, pp. 2, 4–5.
10. Edelman, pp. 21–22.

11. V. Turner, *The Forest of Symbols,* p. 30.
12. Gluckman notes the "fit" with Freudian theory, but he asserts that a "social" interpretation is being advanced (*Politics, Law and Ritual in Tribal Societies,* p. 259).
13. Durkheim, p. 298.
14. See Robert G. Hamerton-Kelly, ed., *Violent Origins: Walter Burkert, René Girard, and Jonathan Z. Smith on Ritual Killing and Cultural Formation* (Stanford: Stanford University Press, 1987).
15. Hamerton-Kelly, pp. 7–9; and René Girard, *Violence and the Sacred,* trans. Patrick Gregory (Baltimore: John Hopkins Press, 1977).
16. Walter Burkert, *Homo Necans: The Anthropology of Ancient Greek Sacrificial Ritual and Myth,* trans. Peter Bing (Berkeley: University of California Press, 1983), p. 27.
17. In an analysis of Freud's approach to ritual, Volney Gay argues that Freud saw ritual not as pathologically "repressive," as Freud's well-known comparison of ritual with obsessive disorders might imply, but as nonpathologically "suppressive." Suppression, according to Gay, is freely chosen by the ego from "among alternative actions which can help it avoid or reduce interpersonal conflict yet also offer drive satisfaction" (*Freud on Ritual* [Missoula, Mont.: Scholars Press, 1979], p. 185).
18. Heesterman, pp. 3–5, 28–29, 90–91, 101–7. Also see Brian K. Smith's review of this argument in the context of Heesterman's earlier work, "Ideals and Realities in Indian Religion," *Religious Studies Review* 14, no. 1 (1988): 1–10, and p. 3 in particular.
19. B. K. Smith, *Reflections on Resemblance, Ritual and Religion,* pp. 42–43. Smith makes a useful comparison here with Jonathan Z. Smith's notion of ritual as the performance of things as they ought to be in tension with things as they are (p. 45 note 53).
20. Valeri, pp. 67–70.
21. Mack, "Introduction: Religion and Ritual," pp. 1–72.
22. See his "Preface" in Bourdillon and Fortes. It is probably the influence of theological categories which leads Fortes, among others, to see "sacrifice" as the most central ritual institution for all but a minority of humankind, despite "the great diversity and flexibility, material, situational, and symbolical of sacrifice in different cultures" (pp. v and xiii).
23. This generalization is most clearly seen in the work of T. Turner, particularly "Transformation, Hierarchy and Transcendence," pp. 59–61.
24. Lukes, "Political Ritual and Social Integration," pp. 301–2.

25. These contrasting approaches to ritual are also noted, in a different context, by Delattre, p. 283.
26. Geertz, *Negara*, pp. 123–24, 130–31.
27. Bloch, *Political Language and Oratory*, pp. 3–4.
28. Bourdieu, *Outline of a Theory of Practice*, pp. 94–95.
29. Such a role for ritual does little to explicate particular acts but much to constitute a discourse structured around the resolution of dichotomies or the embodiment of fundamental contradictions. Ultimately, theories of ritual as social control tend to define ritual and control and society in terms that do not merely complement each other but magnetically draw each other into a tight knot of deferred significations.
30. Bourdieu, *Outline of a Theory of Practice*, p. 207 note 74.
31. Gluckman, *Politics, Law and Ritual*, p. 265.
32. Gluckman, *Essays on the Ritual of Social Relations*, pp. 38, 49–50; and *Politics, Law and Ritual*, pp. 261ff. Kertzer also discusses this point (p. 177).
33. Gluckman considers the "spectacles" of modern secular society to be potential analogies to the role of ritual in tribal societies in his essay "On Drama, and Games and Athletic Contests" (in *Secular Ritual*, ed. Sally F. Moore and Barbara G. Myerhoff [Amsterdam: Van Gorcum, 1977], pp. 227–43). Also see his discussion of the cleavages, and ceremonials, among relationships in a modern Cambridge college where ritualization failed to materialize even when it was needed. Aside from the segregation of groups and conflicts, Gluckman does not allude to other reasons for the absence of ritual in modern secular societies, although he does note an ethos of antiritualism which engenders self-consciousness about recourse to anything like "tribal-type rituals" (*Essays on the Ritual of Social Relations*, pp. 43–45, 48).
34. Lane and Edelman, noted above, are good examples.
35. Douglas, *Natural Symbols*, pp. 41–58.
36. Douglas, *Natural Symbols*, p. 42–43. See Basil Bernstein, *Class Codes and Control, Vol. 1: Theoretical Studies Towards a Sociology of Language* (London: Routledge and Kegan Paul, 1971); or his useful summary, "Social Class, Language and Socialization" in *Current Trends in Linguistics*, vol. 12, part 3, ed. A. S. Abramson (The Hague: Mouton, 1974), pp. 1545–62; also reprinted in *Power and Ideology in Education*, ed. Jerome Karabel and A. H. Halsey (New York: Oxford University Press, 1977), pp. 473–86.
37. Douglas, *Natural Symbols*, pp. 33–37. On secular tribal societies, also see Morris, pp. 227–30; and Moore and Myerhoff, pp. 19–20.

38. See Douglas, *Natural Symbols,* pp. 33, 103, 178–79; on group and grid, see p. 50 for one formulation, as well as pp. 9, 41–56ff.

39. Douglas, *Natural Symbols,* pp. 26–27, 72, 103, 113–14.

40. Leach, "Ritual," p. 523.

41. Bloch, *Political Language and Oratory,* p. 3.

42. Valeri, p. 134.

43. John Comaroff, "Talking Politics: Oratory and Authority in a Tswana Chiefdom," in *Political Language and Oratory in Traditional Society,* ed. M. Block (New York: Academic Press, 1975), p. 155. It seems far from clear to me that Douglas does not do this.

44. Douglas, *Natural Symbols,* p. 93. The body, as part of a system, is used to express the nature of the social order as a system; that is, the body symbolizes the whole and the relationship of the part to the whole (p. 112).

45. Douglas, *Natural Symbols,* p. 112.

46. Douglas, *Natural Symbols,* pp. 136–52.

47. Victor Turner, *Forest of Symbols,* p. 90.

48. Valeri, p. 340. Emphasis added.

49. Valeri, pp. 270, 340.

50. Valeri, p. 344.

Chapter 8

51. This is the position of Rodney Needham, in particular, who argues that belief is an individual mental state and is best left to psychology. Social analysis may address how society induces and shapes such mental states, but it does not have the ability to determine what a person's mental state is and whether it constitutes a state of "belief" as such. Even if beliefs refer to cultural views, statements made about what is believed, by both informants and ethnographers, can rarely be demonstrated to be true in the sense that they are believed by all or most people in the society. Furthermore, Needham cautions, people do not necessarily believe what they have been taught to say and many will privately question what their society holds to be a belief. For these reasons and others, Needham is not alone is recommending that the word "belief" be dropped in anthropological studies. See Rodney Needham, *Belief, Language and Experience* (Chicago: University of Chicago Press, 1972).

52. Martin Southwold critiques assumptions that belief is an individual mental state or subject to judgments of truth or falsity. He makes a case for the social nature of belief—as a matter of activities, such as

assenting, affirming, or making formal obeisances, and social relationships—rather than some disembodied state of mind. See Martin
Southwold, "Religious Belief," *Man*, n.s. 14, no. 4 (1978): 628–44,
especially pp. 625, 628, 632, 637–38, and 643 note 5. While agreeing
with Needham that beliefs are rarely absolute in their hold on individuals or groups, Abner Cohen finds that they are much more
powerful for what they *do* socially (*Two-Dimensional Man: An Essay
on the Anthropology of Power and Symbolism in Complex Society*
[Berkeley: University of California Press, 1976], p. 83).

53. For a basic analysis of these and other approaches, see Mary B. Black,
"Belief Systems," in *Handbook of Social and Cultural Anthropology*,
ed. John J. Honigmann (Chicago: Rand McNally, 1973), pp. 509–
77; and Kenneth Thompson, *Beliefs and Ideology* (London: Tavistock Publications, 1986), pp. 11–26, for a discussion of this
approach.

54. Southwold, p. 633. Among the Singhalese, for example, Southwold
found that no judgments of truth or falsity were made about such
tenets as the Buddha's attainment of nirvana or the karmic determination of existence. However, there was a readiness to question
the effectiveness of various rituals, the need for the services of Buddhist monks, and the existence of lesser deities. He concludes that
basic religious beliefs are not concerned with issues that we associate
with factual truth, and they probably never could be and still act
as religious truths. Leach also notes the ambiguity and "essential
vagueness of all ritual statements" (*Political Systems of Highland
Burma*, p. 286).

55. Southwold, pp. 629–34. Tambiah also finds that ritual is meant to
express not mental orientations of individuals, but attitudes of institutionalized discourse ("A Performative Approach to Ritual,"
pp. 124–25).

56. Southwold, p. 634.

57. James W. Fernandez, "Symbolic Consensus in a Fang Reformative
Cult," *American Anthropologist* 67 (1965): 902–29. Goody also
notes that it is quite common for participants to need the details of
rites explained to them ("Against 'Ritual'," p. 31).

58. Fernandez even finds that effective communication was resisted so
as to continue ritual activity ("Symbolic Consensus," p. 922).

59. Fernandez does the same thing that Geertz did in setting up his
categories in his analysis of the Javanese funeral: ritual is defined as
social action as opposed to cultural beliefs. However, whereas Geertz
argues that (successful) ritual also integrates action and belief, society
and culture, ethos and worldview, Fernandez ends up opposing the

social to the cultural, activity to concept, significance to meaning, sign to symbol, social solidarity to cultural disjunction, etc. ("Symbolic Consensus," pp. 912–21). Indeed, by characterizing the unity achieved through the patterned and regularized activities of ritual as unity on a social level, not on a cultural level, Fernandez explicitly distances belief from what is fundamental to ritual ("Symbolic Consensus," pp. 902, 907, 911–14).

60. David Jordan, "The jiaw of Shigaang (Taiwan): An Essay in Folk Interpretation," *Asian Folklore Studies* 35, no. 2 (1976): 81–107; and Peter Stromberg, "Consensus and Variation in the Interpretation of Religious Symbolism: A Swedish Example," *American Ethnologist* 8 (1981): 544–59. Stromberg also finds sources other than ritual for promoting solidarity.

61. David K. Jordan and Daniel L. Overmyer, *The Flying Phoenix: Aspects of Chinese Sectarianism in Taiwan* (Princeton: Princeton University Press, 1986), pp. 270, and 267–74 passim. This idea echoes Southwold's analysis.

62. Watson, "Standardizing the Gods," pp. 323–24.

63. Also see Kertzer (pp. 69–75) on the "virtues of ambiguity."

64. See Abner Cohen, "Political Symbolism," *Annual Review of Anthropology* 8 (1979): 87, 102.

65. V. Turner, *The Forest of Symbols*, pp. 28–29. Also see Cohen's discussion of Turner's notion of symbolism in "Political Symbolism," p. 100.

66. Clifford Geertz, *Islam Observed* (Chicago: University of Chicago Press, 1968), p. 97, cited by Wuthnow, p. 46. Several earlier studies analyze the ease with which beliefs are changed to rationalize behavior and reduce "cognitive dissonance." See Leon Festinger, *A Theory of Cognitive Dissonance* (Evanston, Ill.: Row, Peterson, 1957); and Bruno Bettelheim, *The Informed Heart* (Glencoe, Ill.: Free Press, 1960).

67. Philip Converse, "The Nature of Belief Systems in Mass Publics," in *Ideology and Discontent*, ed. David Apter (New York: Free Press, 1964), pp. 206–61.

68. Converse rejects the notion of "ideology" as too muddy for use and adopts "belief systems" (pp. 207–9). On this point, also see Black, "Belief Systems," pp. 509–11.

69. Converse, pp. 229–31.

70. Converse also discusses the "economy" of simple dichotomies like liberal–conservative and how they function in public discourse, making many of the same points about the expediency of such oppositions that Bourdieu has made (pp. 214 and 227 in particular).

71. Converse, p. 261 note 62.
72. Suzanne W. Barnett and John K. Fairbanks, *Christianity in China: Early Protestant Missionary Writings* (Cambridge, Mass.: Harvard University Press, 1985), p. 55.
73. A good example is Evans-Pritchard's famous confrontation with Azande reasoning. Logical analysis of the effects of termites on the granary, while apparent and relevant to Azande reckoning, was unable to account adequately for the specificity of the granary killing the particular people sitting underneath it. See E. E. Evans-Pritchard, *Witchcraft, Oracles and Magic Among the Azande* (Oxford: Clarendon Press, 1965), pp. 63–70, especially p. 69.
74. Converse calls attention to those pockets of the population, most common in the rural hinterlands of the Soviet Union or the People's Republic of China, where people often have little sense of belonging to a larger nation. The "nation" as such is an abstract entity that they do not experience in daily life (p. 237). National rituals, which do not penetrate far into such communities, would not receive much support if forced, given the dearth of any concrete experience of the nation as such. Even the "synchronization" of local rites across the nation or the standardization of local forms to conform to a model for national celebrations have little effect on isolated communities.
75. Rappaport, p. 193.
76. Kertzer, p. 95. Kertzer is concerned (p. 92) to distinguish ritual from political demonstrations, despite the fact that the social demonstrations he analyzes appear to be determined to collapse such distinctions.
77. Kertzer, p. 72.
78. A practical example of their interrelationship is seen in the very different work of Geertz and Bourdieu, each of whom proposes descriptions of religion and ideology on separate occasions that are remarkably similar. Compare Geertz's "Religion as a Cultural System" with his "Ideology as a Cultural System," both reproduced in *The Interpretation of Cultures*.
79. J. G. Merquior, *The Veil and the Mask: Essays on Culture and Ideology* (London: Routledge and Kegan Paul, 1979), p. 14; Kenneth Thompson, *Beliefs and Ideology*, p. 12; Jorge Larrain, in particular, provides a good discussion of the history of criticism of religion and how it shaped Marx's exploration of ideology (*The Concept of Ideology* [Athens: University of Georgia Press, 1979], pp. 24–32).
80. In addition to Williams, Larrain, K. Thompson, Geuss, and Merquior, all cited earlier, also see Zygmunt Bauman, *Culture as Praxis* (London: Routledge and Kegan Paul, 1973); and John B. Thompson,

Studies in the Theory of Ideology (Berkeley: University of California Press, 1984).

81. This perspective is sometimes used for homogeneous tribal societies in contrast to the second approach, which is seen to fit the social stratification of more complex and pluralistic societies. Comaroff notes the explicit coexistence of "worldview" and "ideology" in precolonial Tswana (p. 125).

82. The negative side of this perspective, however, is that it leads to the assumption that culture is a separate realm of metasocial phenomena. Analysis must then attempt to show how the more abstract features of social life are linked to its concrete features. As seen in the work of structural Marxists like Althusser, Godelier, and Bloch, culture as ideology serves to create a level of social processes that supposedly mediates opposing material and idealist levels of human existence. See Ortner, "Theory in Anthropology," p. 140.

83. J. B. Thompson critiques the tendency to see ideology as social cement (p. 5). For K. Thompson, ideology as such is embedded in rituals (pp. 23–24 and 72). Merquior critiques Althusser's structural Marxism for how he assumes that power pervades society in the guise of belief (*The Veil and the Mask*, p. 36).

84. For Althusser, for example, ideology expresses the collective, but it does so as a mystification that is essential for social reproduction. See Dowling, p. 83; also Jacques Ranciere, "On the Theory of Ideology (The Politics of Althusser)," *Radical Philosophy* 7 (1974): 2–3. Ortner argues that in this extreme view ritual, myth and taboo merely maintain the status quo ("Theory in Anthropology Since the Sixties," pp. 140–41).

85. K. Thompson is representative of this criticism, specifically arguing that ideologies do not necessarily promote consensus or social solidarity (p. 33).

86. Merquior, *The Veil and the Mask*, pp. 5–7.

87. J. B. Thompson, pp. 4–5. On the same principle, he argues that language, ideology, and power are thoroughly intertwined (pp. 2 and 8).

88. Merquior, *The Veil and the Mask*, pp. 11–14.

89. Merquior, *The Veil and the Mask*, pp. 28–29 and 35, where he also discusses the ramifications of the impact of linguistic deprivation on class consciousness, using the work of Bernstein.

90. See J. B. Thompson, p. 63; also see K. Thompson, p. 86, on the difference between legitimacy and consent.

91. J. B. Thompson, pp. 62–63.

92. Merquior, *The Veil and the Mask*, p. 38.

93. Unless we do so, he argues, we will not understand ideology. Merquior wishes to pursue a less "mentalist" and more "behavioristic" approach and does so by "seeing ideology as part of the empirical mechanics of power" (*The Veil and the Mask*, p. 15).

94. According to K. Thompson, Gramsci's notion of "negotiation" avoids the deficiencies of theories of culture as social control or social expression (p. 102). On the dialogic notion of ideology or hegemonic discourse, see Jameson, *The Political Unconscious*, pp. 83–84; Dowling, pp. 130–31; and K. Thompson, pp. 101–2.

95. Merquior, pp. 28–30. The term "manipulation of bias" was first coined by E. E. Schattschneider (*The Semi-Sovereign People: A Realist's View of Democracy in America* [New York: Holt, Rinehart and Winston, 1960] but became central to the debates on the nature of power with its use by Peter Bachrach and Morton S. Baratz (*Power and Poverty: Theory and Practice* [Oxford: Oxford University Press, 1970]). For a good overview of these debates and the place of this term, see Clegg, pp. 1–20, especially p. 12.

96. Merquior, *The Veil and the Mask*, pp. 27–29. Bourdieu also argues that ideologies function primarily to integrate the dominant class while simultaneously distinguishing it from other groups ("Symbolic Power," p. 114).

97. Merquior, *The Veil and the Mask*, p. 35.

98. Merquior, *The Veil and the Mask*, pp. 26–27.

99. See J. B. Thompson's discussion of Bourdieu's theory of complicity, which he challenges as "too consensual" (pp. 44–46, 58–59, 62). Thompson suggests that the dominated class may misrecognize the dominant value system in some form as the only workable value system, particularly if the alternatives remain unformulated or incoherent. They may also misrecognize how the value system of the dominant class actually divides, even when it disguises itself as a means of communication and consensus among the whole (in this regard, see Bourdieu, "Symbolic Power," pp. 114–15). Thus, the dominated classes may accept at face value a status hierarchy that rigidly and arbitrarily divides and ranks because the hierarchy proclaims that such a clear system allows anyone to ascend and change status.

100. Bourdieu, "Symbolic Power," p. 115.

101. Bourdieu, "Symbolic Power," p. 114.

102. The terms are drawn from Comaroff, pp. 4–6. See Bourdieu on the pitfalls of a dualism of practice and ideology (*Outline of a Theory of Practice*, p. 179).

103. See Michael Mann, *The Sources of Social Power*, vol. 1 (Cambridge: Cambridge University Press, 1986), pp. 2–3.

104. For similar views concerning the dialogic and social process aspects of ideologies, see Goran Therborn, *The Ideology of Power and the Power of Ideology* (London: Verso, 1980), p. vii.

105. J. B. Thompson, pp. 14, 17, 34.

106. Geuss, pp. 61ff.

107. Hebdige, p. 133.

108. See Clegg, p. 16, who is alluding to the theories of E. Laclau and C. Mouffe in *Hegemony and the Socialist Strategy* (London: Verso, 1985).

109. One advantage of a focus on ideology instead of belief is the readiness of ideology studies to attempt to analyze the ways in which the individual is addressed, involved, or constituted. Althusser has made famous the notion that ideologies "interpellate" persons or communities as subjects: in being addressed an identity is constituted. K. Thompson, however, contrasts this rather mechanistic description with Gramsci's emphasis on how people negotiate their identities (p. 25, as well as pp. 15–16, 32, and 50).

110. See Larrain, who discusses the various ways in which force and ideology have been opposed from Machiavelli to Gramsci (p. 19).

111. Jameson, *The Political Unconscious*, p. 289; and Dowling, pp. 31 and 83–84.

112. Bourdieu, *Outline of a Theory of Practice*, pp. 159–70; also J. B. Thompson, pp. 49–52.

113. Bourdieu, *Outline of a Theory of Practice*, p. 164.

114. On constraint, see Converse, p. 211.

115. Based on Geuss, pp. 71–74.

116. James G. Frazer, *The Golden Bough*, 3rd ed. (London: Macmillan, 1935, first published in 1890), and A. M. Hocart, *Kingship* (Oxford: Clarendon, 1927).

117. Geertz, *Negara*, pp. 122–36 passim.

118. Howard J. Wechsler, *Offerings of Jade and Silk: Ritual and Symbol in the Legitimation of the T'ang Dynasty* (New Haven: Yale University Press, 1985), pp. 5–6.

119. Wechsler, pp. 6–7.

120. Geertz, *Negara*, pp. 122–23.

121. Geertz, *Negara*, p. 136.

122. David Cannadine, "Introduction: Divine Right of Kings," in *Rituals of Royalty: Power and Ceremonial in Traditional Societies,* ed. David Cannadine and Simon Price (Cambridge: Cambridge University Press, 1987), pp. 1–19; and Bloch, "The Ritual of the Royal Bath," pp. 271–97.

123. Cannadine, "Introduction," in Cannadine and Price, pp. 17–19.

124. Also see Eric Hobsbawn, "Introduction: Inventing Traditions," in *The Invention of Tradition,* ed. Eric Hobsbawn and Terence Ranger (Cambridge: Cambridge University Press, 1983), pp. 1–14.

125. Reinhard Bendix, *Kings or People: Power and the Mandate to Rule* (Berkeley: University of California Press, 1978), p. 17; also cited in Hok-lam Chan, *Legitimation in Imperial China: Discussions under the Jurchin-Chin Dynasty (1115–1234)* (Seattle: University of Washington Press, 1984), p. 10.

126. Chan, p. 3.

127. Wei-ming Tu, "Iconoclasm, Holistic Vision, and Patient Watchfulness: A Personal Reflection on the Modern Chinese Intellectual Quest," *Daedalus* 116, no. 2 (1987): 84.

128. Chan, p. 11.

129. Bloch, "The Ritual of the Royal Bath," p. 294.

130. Geertz, *Negara*, pp. 102, 123; Bloch, "The Ritual of the Royal Bath," pp. 296–97.

131. Geertz, *Negara*, p. 102.

132. Geertz, *Negara*, pp. 123–35 passim.

133. Geertz, *Negara*, p. 136.

134. Cannadine, "Introduction," in Cannadine and Price, p. 19.

135. Cohen, "Political Symbolism," p. 89.

136. Kertzer also replicates the perspective that Geertz wants to overcome when he argues that it is crucial that power be "expressed through symbolic guises" (p. 174).

Chapter 9

137. See Colin Gordon, "Afterword," in Michel Foucault, *Power/Knowledge: Selected Interviews and Other Writings 1972–77* (New York: Pantheon, 1980), pp. 234–35.

138. Merquior discusses the "traditional distinction" between power (intended) and social control (inherent) (*The Veil and the Mask,* p. 17). This distinction is also assessed by Steven Lukes in *Power: A Radical View* (New York: Macmillan, 1974), pp. 28–33.

139. Cannadine, "Introduction," in Cannadine and Price, p. 9.

140. For example, see Burridge's reworking of Weber's notion of charisma in terms of particular social relationships (pp. 155–58).

141. Clegg, pp. 3–5; quote from p. 4, where it draws on Lukes, *Power,* p. 24.

142. Lukes, *Power,* p. 25. Lukes's analysis is also discussed by Merquior, *The Veil and the Mask,* p. 23.

143. Lukes, *Power,* pp. 11–15. See Robert A. Dahl, "The Concept of Power," *Behavioral Science* 2 (1957): 201–15; and *Who Governs? Democracy and Power in an American City* (New Haven: Yale University Press, 1961).
144. Lukes, *Power,* pp. 16–20. See Peter Bachrach and Morton S. Baratz, "The Two Faces of Power," *American Political Science Review* 56 (1962): 947–52; and "Decisions and Nondecisions: An Analytical Framework," *American Political Science Review* 57 (1963): 641–51. Bachrach and Baratz's four types of power are also discussed by Merquior (*The Veil and the Mask,* pp. 21–22).
145. Lukes, *Power,* pp. 21–25.
146. Roderick Martin, *The Sociology of Power* (London: Routledge and Kegan Paul, 1977). See Merquior, *The Veil and the Mask,* pp. 20–22. Martin has redefined power as a function of relations based on an asymmetric dependence and the lack of any alternatives for those subordinated by the relationship.
147. Bourdieu, "Symbolic Power," p. 117.
148. Cohen, *Two-Dimensional Man,* pp. 18ff.
149. Bourdieu, *Outline of a Theory of Practice,* p. 164.
150. As described by Clegg (p. 5), this tradition would include Gramsci and the more recent work of Callon, Laclau, and Mouffe in particular. For both Clegg and Zygmunt Bauman (*Legislators and Interpreters* [Cambridge: Polity Press, 1987]), the two traditions rooted in Hobbes on the one hand and Machiavelli on the other are also differentiated by the fact that the latter wrote "to fix and serve" power, whereas the former wrote simply to "interpret" power (p. 5).
151. Gordon, "Afterword," in Foucault, *Power/Knowledge,* p. 235.
152. Foucault's approach is radical by virtue of his refusal to furnish a "theory" of power, that is, a context-free, ahistorical, and objective description that could be generalized for application to all times and places. His alternative "analytics of power" attempts to sidestep the rhetoric of theory that implies some 'thing,' called power, which exists. If this 'thing-ness' is granted, then one is "obliged to view it as emerging at a given place and time and hence to deduce it, to reconstruct its genesis." See Foucault, *Power/Knowledge,* pp. 198–99.
153. In this way, Foucault regards "power" as a "perspective concept" (*Power/Knowledge,* p. 245) instead of a thing. On his "analytics of power," see Foucault, *The History of Sexuality,* vol. 1, p. 82–83; Sheldon S. Wolin, "On the Theory and Practice of Power," in *After Foucault: Humanistic Knowledge, Postmodern Challenges,* ed. Jonathan Arac (New Brunswick, N.J.: Rutgers University Press, 1988),

pp. 179–201; J. G. Merquior, *Foucault* (Berkeley: University of California Press, 1985), pp. 108–18; G. Wickham, "Power and Power Analysis," *Economy and Society* 12, no. 4 (1983): 468–98; M. Cousins and A. Hussain, *Michel Foucault* (New York: Macmillan, 1984), pp. 225–61.

154. Michel Foucault, "The Subject and Power," in *Michel Foucault: Beyond Structuralism and Hermeneutics,* 2nd ed., ed. Hubert L. Dreyfus and Paul Rabinow (Chicago: University of Chicago Press, 1983), pp. 220–21.

155. Foucault, *Power/Knowledge,* p. 198.

156. Foucault, "The Subject and Power," pp. 222–24.

157. Foucault, *Power/Knowledge,* pp. 96, 187–88.

158. Foucault, *Power/Knowledge,* pp. 199–200.

159. Foucault, *Power/Knowledge,* p. 200–201.

160. Foucault, "The Subject and Power," p. 221. Compare this point to Lukes's thesis (versus Poulantzas) that to exercise power per se one must be able to choose to do otherwise (Lukes, *Power,* p. 55).

161. Foucault, "The Subject and Power," p. 221.

162. Foucault, "The Subject and Power," p. 225.

163. Foucault, "The Subject and Power," p. 225.

164. Foucault, "The Subject and Power," p. 225.

165. Particular examples from Foucault's *Discipline and Punish* include the following: penal ceremony as the rite that "concluded the crime" (p. 9), rituals of execution (p. 11), penal ritual (p. 18), a ritual of public torture (p. 28), the liturgy of punishment (pp. 34, 49), legal ceremonial (p. 35), penal liturgy (p. 47), the ritual of armed law (p. 50), public execution ritualized as a political operation (p. 53), power recharged in a ritual display of its reality (p. 57), and power relations ritualized (p. 68). For other examples, see his *History of Sexuality,* vol. 1, and "Nietzsche, Genealogy, History," in *The Foucault Reader,* ed. Paul Rabinow (New York: Pantheon, 1984).

166. Dreyfus and Rabinow, p. 110.

167. Dreyfus and Rabinow, p. 111.

168. Foucault, *Discipline and Punish,* p. 25.

169. Foucault, *Discipline and Punish,* p. 28.

170. For Foucault's understanding of strategy, see "The Subject and Power," pp. 224–25. Ultimately, power relationships are not really even relationships—the power relationship "is no more a 'relationship' than the place where it occurs is a place; and, precisely for this reason, it is fixed, throughout its history, in rituals, in meticulous procedures that impose rights and obligations" (Foucault, "Nietzsche, Genealogy, History," p. 85).

171. Foucault, *Power/Knowledge*, pp. 202, 206.

172. Foucault, *Discipline and Punish*, p. 26.

173. Foucault, *Power/Knowledge*, p. 186.

174. Foucault, *Power/Knowledge*, p. 55. The spirit of these ideas is not totally foreign to a perspective within cultural anthropology that has pushed toward just such an analysis of the cultural construction of perception, awareness, and individuality. Yet Foucault's analysis of these constructions in terms of power is challenging. Ultimately his agenda goes beyond an attempt to explore the dynamism of social life from within its own terms; it includes a recognition of the involvement of the theoretical enterprise itself and of the interrelationships among techniques of objectification, knowledge, discourse, truth, and power.

175. Foucault, *Power/Knowledge*, p. 187.

176. Foucault, *Power/Knowledge*, p. 98. Foucault's discussions of subjectivity and the individualizing as well as totalizing power of the state make clear that power relations may be constituted on a variety of levels, among which subjectivity/subjectivization and individuality/individualization may figure. See Foucault, *Power/Knowledge*, pp. 239, 255; *Discipline and Punish*, p. 99; and Dreyfus and Rabinow, pp. 120, 139, 143.

177. Foucault, *Power/Knowledge*, p. 98.

178. Again, compare Lukes, who argues that power is not something that is "exercised" as such—i.e., brought to bear on people consciously or unconsciously in an intentional ways (*Power*, pp. 39–40).

179. For examples of the resistance of the constituted body, see Foucault, *Power/Knowledge*, pp. 56–57.

180. Foucault, *Discipline and Punish*, pp. 23–31, 47–57, 68–69; *Power/Knowledge*, pp. 55–62.

181. Wuthnow, pp. 111–14, 124–28.

182. The schemes may also derive in part from the existence of larger social organizations in which the smaller ritual community is embedded.

183. Clegg, p. 166.

184. Lukes notes how ritual provides the sense that the individual's needs and wants are being transformed in public or social policy. See Lukes, "Political Ritual and Social Integration," pp. 304–5.

185. Comaroff, pp. 6–8, 81, 124–27. As noted in Part II, her analysis falls into some of the problems attending notions of ritual as "mediating" structure and event (or history and practice) and "resolving" contradictions between cultural categories and social experiences.

186. Comaroff, pp. 197–98, 251, 260–61.

187. Comaroff, pp. 52–53, 60–62.

188. Comaroff, p. 228.

189. Bourdieu, *Outline of a Theory of Practice,* pp. 41, 184.

190. Lucien W. Pye, *Asian Power and Politics: The Cultural Dimensions of Authority* (Cambridge, Mass.: Harvard University, 1985), p. 39.

191. Pye, pp. 39–46, especially p. 40.

192. Bloch, "Symbols, Song, Dance and Features of Articulation," pp. 62–65 and 77.

193. Sangren, for example, argues that for the Chinese such culturally constituted power can be authenticated only by history itself (p. 231).

194. On the "dramaturgy" of power, see Abner Cohen, *The Politics of Elite Cultures* (Berkeley: University of California Press, 1981), pp. 14–16, 200–213; and Geertz on the "symbology" or "symbolics" of power in *Negara,* pp. 98–109, and *Local Knowledge,* pp. 121–46.

195. Valeri, p. 74.

196. Fernandez, "Symbolic Consensus," pp. 914–15.

197. Douglas's description of the stubborn Catholicism of the Bog Irish, which maintains a tight and highly differentiated community, is a good demonstration of this (*Natural Symbols,* pp. 59–76).

198. Bloch, "Symbols, Song, Dance and Features of Articulation," p. 71. Kertzer cites a similar sentiment expressed by Walter Bagehot, "Now no man can argue on his knees" (p. 97). Bourdieu generalizes the principle when he notes that "the most successful ideological efforts are those which have no need of words, and ask no more than complicitous silence" (*Outline of a Theory of Practice,* p. 188).

199. Clegg, pp. 152–53.

200. Tambiah, "A Performative Approach to Ritual," pp. 124–25, 163.

201. Durkheim, p. 298.

202. Foucault, *Discipline and Punish,* p. 29.

203. Durkheim, p. 298.

204. Cited by Wuthnow, p. 368 note 59 (as cited in Robert N. Bellah, ed., *Emile Durkheim on Morality and Society* [Chicago: University of Chicago Press, 1973], pp. ix–lv).

Bibliography

Ahern, Emily M. "The Problem of Efficacy: Strong and Weak Illocutionary Acts." *Man*, n.s. 14, no. 1 (1979): 1–17.

Alexander, Bobby C. "Ceremony." In Mircea Eliade et al., eds. *The Encyclopedia of Religion*, vol. 3. New York: Macmillan, 1987, pp. 179–83.

Althusser, Louis. *For Marx*. Translated by Ben Brewster. London: Verso, 1977.

Althusser, Louis, and Etienne Balibar. *Reading Capital*. Translated by Ben Brewster. London: Verso, 1979.

Apter, David. *Ideology and Discontent*. New York: Free Press, 1964.

Arac, Jonathan, ed. *After Foucault: Humanistic Knowledge, Postmodern Challenges*. New Brunswick, N.J.: Rutgers University Press, 1988.

Augé, Marc. *The Anthropological Circle: Symbol, Function and History*. Cambridge: Cambridge University Press, 1982.

Austin, J. L. *How to Do Things with Words*, 2nd ed. Cambridge, Mass.: Harvard University Press, 1975.

Bachrach, Peter, and Morton S. Baratz. "Decisions and Nondecisions: An Analytical Framework." *American Political Science Review* 57 (1963): 641–51.

Bachrach, Peter, and Morton S. Baratz. *Power and Poverty: Theory and Practice*. Oxford: Oxford University Press, 1970.

Bachrach, Peter, and Morton S. Baratz. "The Two Faces of Power." *American Political Science Review* 56 (1962): 947–52.

Baird, Robert D. *Category Formation and the History of Religions*. The Hague: Mouton, 1971.

Barnes, Andrew E. "Review Essay: Religious Reform and the War Against Ritual." *Journal of Ritual Studies* 4, no. 1 (1990): 127–33.

Barnett, Suzanne W., and John K. Fairbanks. *Christianity in China: Early*

Protestant Missionary Writings. Cambridge, Mass.: Harvard University Press, 1985.

Bateson, Gregory. *Naven,* 2nd ed. Stanford: Stanford University Press, 1958. Originally published in 1936.

Bateson, Mary Catherine. "Ritualization: A Study in Texture and Texture Change." In Irving I. Zaretsky and Mark P. Leone, eds., *Religious Movements in Contemporary America.* Princeton: Princeton University Press, 1974, pp. 150–65.

Bauman, Zygmunt. *Culture as Praxis.* London: Routledge and Kegan Paul, 1973.

Bauman, Zygmunt. *Legislators and Interpreters.* Cambridge: Polity Press, 1987.

Beattie, John H. M. "On Understanding Ritual." In Brian R. Wilson, ed., *Rationality.* Oxford: Basil Blackwell, 1970, pp. 240–68.

Beattie, John H. M. *Other Cultures.* New York: Free Press, 1964.

Beattie, John H. M. "Ritual and Social Change." *Man* 1 (1966): 60–74.

Becker, A. L. "Text-Building, Epistemology, and Aesthetics in Javanese Shadow Theater." In A. L. Becker and Aram A. Yengoyan, eds., *The Imagination of Reality: Essays in Southeast Asian Coherence Systems.* Norwood, N.J.: Ablex, 1979, pp. 211–43.

Bell, Catherine. "Ritual, Change and Changing Rituals," *Worship* 63, no. 1 (1989): 31–41.

Bell, Catherine. "Ritualization of Texts and Textualization of Ritual in the Codification of Taoist Liturgy." *History of Religions* 27, no. 4 (1988): 366–92.

Bellah, Robert N. "Civil Religion in America." In William G. McLoughlin and Robert N. Bellah, eds., *Religion in America.* Boston: Houghton Mifflin, 1968, pp. 3–23.

Bendix, Reinhard. *Kings or People: Power and the Mandate to Rule.* Berkeley: University of California Press, 1978.

Bendix, Reinhard. *Max Weber: An Intellectual Portrait.* Berkeley: University of California Press, 1977. Originally published in 1960.

Benthall, Jonathan, and Ted Polhemus, eds. *The Body as a Medium of Expression.* New York: Dutton, 1975.

Bergesen, Albert. *The Sacred and the Subversive: Political Witch Hunts as National Rituals.* Storrs, Conn.: Society for the Social Scientific Study of Religion, 1984.

Bernstein, Basil. *Class, Codes and Control, Vol. 1: Theoretical Studies Towards a Sociology of Language.* London: Routledge and Kegan Paul, 1971.

Bernstein, Basil. "Social Class, Language and Socialization." In A. S. Abramson, ed., *Current Trends in Linguistics,* vol. 12, part 3. The

Hague: Mouton, 1974, pp. 1545–62. Reprinted in Jerome Karabel and A. H. Halsey, eds., *Power and Ideology in Education.* New York: Oxford University Press, 1977, pp. 473–86.

Bernstein, Basil, H. L. Elvin, and R. S. Peters. "Ritual in Education." In Sir Julian Huxley, ed., "A Discussion on Ritualization of Behavior in Animals and Man." *Philosophical Transactions of the Royal Society,* series B, 251 (1966): 429–36.

Bettelheim, Bruno. *The Informed Heart.* Glencoe, Ill.: Free Press, 1960.

Black, Mary B. "Belief Systems." In John J. Honigmann, ed., *Handbook of Social and Cultural Anthropology.* Chicago: Rand McNally, 1973, pp. 509–77.

Blackburn, Stuart H. *Singing of Birth and Death: Texts in Performance.* Philadelphia: University of Pennsylvania Press, 1988.

Blacking, John. "Towards an Anthropology of the Body." In John Blacking, ed., *Anthropology of the Body.* London: Academic Press, 1977, pp. 1–28.

Bloch, Maurice, ed. *Political Language and Oratory in Traditional Society.* New York: Academic Press, 1975.

Bloch, Maurice. "The Ritual of the Royal Bath in Madagascar." In David Cannadine and Simon Price, eds., *Rituals of Royalty: Power and Ceremonial in Traditional Societies.* Cambridge: Cambridge University Press, 1987, pp. 271–97.

Bloch, Maurice. "Symbols, Song, Dance and Features of Articulation: Is Religion an Extreme Form of Traditional Authority?" *Archives Européenes de Sociologie* 15 (1974): 55–81.

Blondeau, Anne-Marie, and Kristofer Schipper, eds. *Essais sur le rituel.* Louvain: Peeters, 1988.

Boon, James A. *Other Tribes, Other Scribes.* Cambridge: Cambridge University Press, 1982.

Bossy, John. *Christianity in the West, 1400–1700.* Oxford: Oxford University Press, 1985.

Bottomore, Tom, ed. *A Dictionary of Marxist Thought.* Oxford: Basil Blackwell, 1983.

Bourdieu, Pierre. *Distinctions: A Social Critique of the Judgment of Taste.* Translated by Richard Nice. Cambridge, Mass.: Harvard University Press, 1984.

Bourdieu, Pierre. *Outline of a Theory of Practice.* Translated by Richard Nice. Cambridge: Cambridge University Press, 1977.

Bourdieu, Pierre. "Symbolic Power." Translated by Colin Wringe. In Denis Gleeson, ed., *Identity and Structure: Issues in the Sociology of Education.* Driffield, England: Nafferton Books, 1977, pp. 112–19.

Bourdieu, Pierre, and Jean-Claude Passeron. *Reproduction in Education,*

Society and Culture. Translated by Richard Nice. Beverly Hills, Calif.: Sage Publications, 1977.

Bourdillon, M. F. C., and Meyer Fortes, eds. *Sacrifice.* New York: Academic Press, 1980.

Bowra, Sir Maurice. "Dance, Drama, and the Spoken Word." In Sir Julian Huxley, ed., "A Discussion on Ritualization of Behavior in Animals and Man." *Philosophical Transactions of the Royal Society,* series B, 251 (1966): 387–92.

Brown, Peter. *The Body and Society: Men, Women, and Sexual Renunciation in Early Christianity.* New York: Columbia University Press, 1988.

Brown, Peter. *The Making of Late Antiquity.* Cambridge, Mass.: Harvard University Press, 1978.

Burke, Kenneth. *The Philosophy of Literary Form,* 3rd ed. Berkeley: University of California Press, 1973. Originally published in 1941.

Burkert, Walter. *Homo Necans: The Anthropology of Ancient Greek Sacrificial Ritual and Myth.* Translated by Peter Bing. Berkeley: University of California Press, 1983.

Burnett, Jacquetta Hill. "Ceremony, Rites, and Economy in the Student System of an American High School." *Human Organization* 28 (1969): 1–10.

Burridge, Kenelm. *New Heaven, New Earth: A Study of Millenarian Activity.* New York: Schocken Books, 1969.

Cameron, Averil. "The Construction of Court Ritual: The Byzantine *Book of Ceremonies.*" In David Cannadine and Simon Price, eds., *Rituals of Royalty: Power and Ceremonial in Traditional Societies.* Cambridge: Cambridge University Press, 1987, pp. 106–36.

Cannadine, David, and Simon Price, eds. *Rituals of Royalty: Power and Ceremonial in Traditional Societies.* Cambridge: Cambridge University Press, 1987.

Cesara, Manda. *Reflections of a Woman Anthropologist—No Hiding Place.* London: Academic Press, 1982.

Chan, Hok-lam. *Legitimation in Imperial China: Discussions under the Jurchin-Chin Dynasty (1115–1234).* Seattle: University of Washington Press, 1984.

Cixous, Hélène. "The Laugh of the Medusa." *Signs* 1, no.4 (1976): 875–93.

Clarke, John, Stuart Hall, Tony Jefferson, and Brian Roberts. "Subcultures, Cultures and Class: A Theoretical Overview." In Stuart Hall and Tony Jefferson, eds., *Resistance Through Rituals: Youth Subcultures in Post-war Britain.* London: Hutchinson and Company, 1976, pp. 9–74.

Clegg, Stewart R. *Frameworks of Power*. London: Sage Publications, 1989.

Clifford, James. *The Predicament of Culture: Twentieth-Century Ethnography, Literature and Art*. Cambridge, Mass.: Harvard University Press, 1988.

Clifford, James, and George E. Marcus, eds. *Writing Culture: The Poetics and Politics of Ethnography*. Berkeley: University of California Press, 1986.

Cohen, Abner. "Political Symbolism." *Annual Review of Anthropology* 8 (1979): 87–113.

Cohen, Abner. *The Politics of Elite Cultures*. Berkeley: University of California Press, 1981.

Cohen, Abner. *Two-Dimensional Man: An Essay on the Anthropology of Power and Symbolism in Complex Society*. Berkeley: University of California Press, 1976.

Comaroff, Jean. *Body of Power, Spirit of Resistance*. Chicago: University of Chicago Press, 1985.

Comaroff, John. "Talking Politics: Oratory and Authority in a Tswana Chiefdom." In Maurice Bloch, ed., *Political Language and Oratory in Traditional Society*. New York: Academic Press, 1975, pp. 141–62.

Combs-Schilling, M. E. *Sacred Performances: Islam, Sexuality, and Sacrifice*. New York: Columbia University Press, 1989.

Comstock, W. Richard, Robert D. Baird, Alfred Bloom, Janet K. O'Dea, Thomas F. O'Dea, and Charles J. Adams, eds. *Religion and Man: An Introduction*. New York: Harper and Row, 1971.

Converse, Philip. "The Nature of Belief Systems in Mass Publics." In David Apter, ed., *Ideology and Discontent*. New York: Free Press, 1964, pp. 206–61.

Cousins, M., and A. Hussain. *Michel Foucault*. New York: Macmillan, 1984.

Culler, Jonathan. *The Pursuit of Signs: Semiotics, Literature and Deconstruction*. Ithaca, N.Y.: Cornell University Press, 1981.

Dahl, Robert A. "The Concept of Power." *Behavioral Science* 2 (1957): 201–15.

Dahl, Robert A. *Who Governs? Democracy and Power in an American City*. New Haven: Yale University Press, 1961.

d'Aquili, Eugene. "The Myth–Ritual Complex: A Biogenetic Structural Analysis," *Zygon* 18, no. 3 (1983): 247–69.

d'Aquili, Eugene G., Charles D. Laughlin, Jr., and John McManus, with Tom Burns, Barbara Lex, G. Ronald Murphy, S.J., and W. John Smith, eds. *The Spectrum of Ritual: A Biogenetic Structural Analysis*. New York: Columbia University Press, 1979.

de Certeau, Michel. *The Practice of Everyday Life.* Translated by Steven Rendell. Berkeley: University of California Press, 1984.

Delattre, Roland A. "Ritual Resourcefulness and Cultural Pluralism." *Soundings* 61, no. 3 (1978): 281–301.

Deleuze, Gilles, and Félix Guattari. *Anti-Oedipus: Capitalism and Schizophrenia.* Translated by Robert Hurley, Mark Seem, and Helen R. Lane. Minneapolis: University of Minnesota Press, 1983. Originally published in 1972.

Derrida, Jacques. *Dissemination.* Translated by Barbara Johnson. Chicago: University of Chicago Press, 1981.

Derrida, Jacques. *Writing and Difference.* Translated by Alan Bass. Chicago: University of Chicago Press, 1978.

Diamond, Stanley. "Anthropology in Question." In Dell Hymes, ed., *Reinventing Anthropology.* New York: Random House, 1969, pp. 401–29.

DiMaggio, Paul. "Review Essay: On Pierre Bourdieu." *American Journal of Sociology* 84, no. 6 (1979): 1460–74.

Dix, Gregory. *The Shape of the Liturgy.* New York: Seabury Press, 1983. Originally published in 1945.

Doroszewki, W. "Quelques rémarques sur les rapports de la sociologie et de la linguistique: Durkheim et F. de Saussure." *Journal de Psychologie* 30 (1933): 82–91.

Doty, William G. *Mythography: The Study of Myths and Rituals.* University: University of Alabama Press, 1986.

Douglas, Mary. *Natural Symbols.* New York: Random House, 1973.

Douglas, Mary. *Purity and Danger.* New York: Praeger, 1960.

Dowling, William C. *Jameson, Althusser, Marx.* Ithaca, N.Y.: Cornell University Press, 1984.

Dreyfus, Hubert L., and Paul Rabinow. *Michel Foucault: Beyond Structuralism and Hermeneutics,* 2nd ed. Chicago: University of Chicago Press, 1983.

Dudbridge, Glen. *The Legend of Miao-shan.* London: Ithaca Press, 1978.

Durkheim, Emile. *The Elementary Forms of the Religious Life.* Translated by J. W. Swain. New York: Free Press, 1965. Originally published in 1915.

Durkheim, Emile, and Marcel Mauss. *Primitive Classification.* Translated by Rodney Needham. Chicago: University of Chicago Press, 1967. Originally published in 1902.

Edelman, Murray. *Politics as Symbolic Action.* Chicago: Markham Publishing Company, 1971.

Eisenstein, Elizabeth. *The Printing Press as an Agent of Change.* Cambridge: Cambridge University Press, 1979.

Eliade, Mircea. *Cosmos and History.* New York: Harper and Row, 1959.

Eliade, Mircea. *The Sacred and the Profane.* New York: Harcourt, 1959.

Erikson, Erik. *Toys and Reasons: Stages in the Ritualization of Experience.* New York: Norton, 1977.

Evans-Pritchard, E. E. *The Nuer.* Oxford: Oxford University Press, 1940.

Evans-Pritchard, E. E. *Nuer Religion.* Oxford: Oxford University Press, 1956.

Evans-Pritchard, E. E. *Theories of Primitive Religion.* Oxford: Clarendon Press, 1965.

Evans-Pritchard, E. E. *Withcraft, Oracles and Magic among the Azande.* Oxford: Clarendon Press, 1965. Originally published in 1937.

Fabian, Johannes. *Time and the Other: How Anthropology Makes Its Object.* New York: Columbia University Press, 1983.

Febvre, Lucien, and Henri-Jean Martin. *The Coming of the Book: The Impact of Printing 1450–1800.* Translated by David Gerard. London: NLB, 1976. Originally published in 1958.

Feher, Michel, with R. Naddaff and N. Tazi, eds. *Fragments for a History of the Human Body.* 3 vols. New York: Zone, 1989.

Fenn, Richard K. *Liturgies and Trials: The Secularization of Religious Language.* New York: Pilgrim Press, 1982.

Fernandez, James W. "The Performance of Ritual Metaphors." In J. David Sapir and J. Christopher Crocker, eds., *The Social Use of Metaphor: Essays on the Anthropology of Rhetoric.* Philadelphia: University of Pennsylvania Press, 1977, pp. 100–131.

Fernandez, James W. "Persuasions and Performances: Of the Beast in Every Body...And the Metaphors of Everyman." *Daedalus* 101, no. 1 (1972): 39–60. Also in Clifford Geertz, ed., *Myth, Symbol and Culture.* New York: Norton, 1971, pp. 39–60.

Fernandez, James W. "Symbolic Consensus in a Fang Reformative Cult." *American Anthropologist* 67 (1965): 902–29.

Festinger, Leon. *A Theory of Cognitive Dissonance.* Evanston, Ill.: Row, Peterson, 1957.

Foucault, Michel. *The Archeology of Knowledge.* Translated by A. M. Sheridan. New York: Pantheon, 1972.

Foucault, Michel. "Body/Power." In *Power/Knowledge: Selected Interviews and Other Writings 1972–77.* Edited by Colin Gordon. New York: Pantheon, 1980, pp. 55–62.

Foucault, Michel. *Discipline and Punish: The Birth of the Prison.* Translated by Alan Sheridan. New York: Vintage Books, 1979.

Foucault, Michel. *The History of Sexuality, Vol. 1: An Introduction.* Translated by Robert Hurley. New York: Vintage Books, 1980.

Foucault, Michel. *Language, Counter-Memory, Practice.* Translated by Donald F. Bouchard and Sherry Simon. Ithaca, N.Y.: Cornell University Press, 1977.

Foucault, Michel. "Nietzsche, Genealogy, History." In Paul Rabinow, ed., *The Foucault Reader.* New York: Pantheon, 1984, pp. 76–100.

Foucault, Michel. *The Order of Things.* Translated by Alan Sheridan. New York: Pantheon, 1970.

Foucault, Michel. *Power/Knowledge: Selected Interviews and Other Writings 1972–77.* Edited by Colin Gordon. New York: Pantheon, 1980.

Foucault, Michel. "The Subject and Power." In Hubert L. Dreyfus and Paul Rabinow, eds., *Michel Foucault: Beyond Structuralism and Hermeneutics,* 2nd ed. Chicago: University of Chicago Press, 1983, pp. 208–26.

Fox, James J. "The Ceremonial System of Savu." In A. L. Becker and Aram A. Yengoyan, eds., *The Imagination of Reality: Essays in Southeast Asian Coherence Systems.* Norwood, N.J.: Ablex, 1979, pp. 145–73.

Frazer, James G. *The Golden Bough.* 3rd ed. London: Macmillan, 1935. Originally published in 1890.

Fustel de Coulanges, N. D. *The Ancient City.* Translated by Willard Small. New York: Doubleday, 1963. Originally published in 1864.

Gadamer, Hans-Georg. *Truth and Method,* 2nd rev. ed. Translated by Joel Weinsheimer and Donald G. Marshall. New York: Crossroad, 1989. Originally published in 1960.

Gager, John G. *Kingdom and Community: The Social World of Early Christianity.* Englewood Cliffs, N.J.: Prentice-Hall, 1975.

Gallop, Jane. *Thinking Through the Body.* New York: Columbia University Press, 1988.

Gay, Volney P. *Freud on Ritual.* Missoula, Mont.: Scholars Press, 1979.

Geertz, Clifford. *The Interpretation of Cultures.* New York: Basic Books, 1973.

Geertz, Clifford. *Islam Observed.* Chicago: University of Chicago Press, 1968.

Geertz, Clifford. *Local Knowledge: Further Essays in Interpretive Anthropology.* New York: Basic Books, 1983.

Geertz, Clifford. *Negara: The Theatre State in Nineteenth Century Bali.* Princeton: Princeton University Press, 1980.

Geertz, Clifford, ed. *Myth, Symbol and Culture.* New York: Norton, 1971.

Gelber, Steven M., and Martin L. Cook. *Saving the Earth: The History of a Middle-Class Millenarian Movement.* Berkeley: University of California Press, 1990.

Geuss, Raymond. *The Idea of a Critical Theory.* Cambridge: Cambridge University Press, 1981.

Giddens, Anthony. *Central Problems in Social Theory: Action, Structure and Contradiction.* Berkeley: University of California Press, 1979.

Giddens, Anthony. *The Constitution of Society: Outline of a Theory of Structuration.* Berkeley: University of California Press, 1984.

Giddens, Anthony. "The Politics of Taste." *Partisan Review* 53, no. 2 (1986): 300–305.

Gilbert, Sandra M., and Susan Gubar. *The Madwoman in the Attic.* New Haven: Yale University Press, 1979.

Girard, René. *Violence and the Sacred.* Translated by Patrick Gregory. Baltimore: John Hopkins Press, 1977.

Gluckman, Max. *Essays on the Ritual of Social Relations.* Manchester: Manchester University Press, 1962.

Gluckman, Max. "On Drama, and Games and Athletic Contests." In Sally F. Moore and Barbara G. Myerhoff, eds., *Secular Ritual.* Amsterdam: Van Gorcum, 1977, pp. 227–43.

Gluckman, Max. *Order and Rebellion in Tribal Africa.* Glencoe, Ill.: Free Press, 1963.

Gluckman, Max. *Politics, Law and Ritual in Tribal Society.* Chicago: Aldine, 1965.

Goffman, Erving. *Asylum.* Chicago: Aldine, 1962.

Goffman, Erving. *Interaction Ritual.* Garden City, N.Y.: Doubleday, 1967.

Goffman, Erving. *Strategic Interaction.* Philadelphia: University of Pennsylvania Press, 1969.

Goody, Jack. "Against 'Ritual': Loosely Structured Thoughts on a Loosely Defined Topic." In Sally F. Moore and Barbara G. Myerhoff, eds., *Secular Ritual.* Amsterdam: Van Gorcum, 1977, pp. 25–35.

Goody, Jack. *The Logic of Writing and the Organization of Society.* Cambridge: Cambridge University Press, 1986.

Goody, Jack. "Religion and Ritual: The Definitional Problem." *British Journal of Sociology* 12 (1961): 142–64.

Goody, Jack, and Ian Watt. "The Consequences of Literacy." In Jack R. Goody, ed., *Literacy in Traditional Societies.* Cambridge: Cambridge University Press, 1968, pp. 27–68.

Gouldner, Alvin W. *The Function of Intellectuals and the Rise of the New Class.* New York: Seabury Press, 1979.

Graham, William A. *Beyond the Written Word: Oral Aspects of Scripture in the History of Religions.* Cambridge: Cambridge University Press, 1987.

Gramsci, Antonio. *The Modern Prince and Other Writings*. Translated by Louis Marks. New York: International Publishers, 1957.

Greenblatt, Stephen. "Filthy Rites." *Daedalus* 111, no. 3 (1982): 1–16.

Grimes, Ronald L. *Beginnings in Ritual Studies*. Washington, D.C.: University Press of America, 1982.

Grimes, Ronald L. "Defining Nascent Ritual." *Journal of the American Academy of Religion* 50, no. 4 (1982): 539–55.

Grimes, Ronald L. *Research in Ritual Studies*. Metuchen, N.J.: Scarecrow Press and The American Theological Library Association, 1985.

Grimes, Ronald L. *Ritual Criticism: Case Studies in Its Practice, Essays on Its Theory*. Columbia: University of South Carolina Press, 1990.

Grimes, Ronald L. "Ritual Criticism and Reflexive Fieldwork." *Journal of Ritual Studies* 2, no. 2 (1988): 217–39.

Grimes, Ronald L. "Ritual Studies." In Mircea Eliade et al., eds., *The Encyclopedia of Religion*, vol. 12. New York: Macmillan, 1987, pp. 422–25.

Grimes, Ronald L. "Sources for the Study of Ritual." *Religious Studies Review* 10, no. 2 (1984): 134–45.

Guttmann, Allen. *From Ritual to Record: The Nature of Modern Sports*. New York: Columbia University Press, 1978.

Hall, Stuart, and Tony Jefferson, eds. *Resistance Through Rituals: Youth Subcultures in Post-war Britain*. London: Hutchinson and Company, 1976.

Hamerton-Kelly, Robert G., ed. *Violent Origins: Walter Burkert, Rene Girard, and Jonathan Z. Smith on Ritual Killing and Cultural Formation*. Stanford: Stanford University Press, 1987.

Hayes, James. "Specialists and Written Materials in the Village World." In David Johnson, Andrew J. Nathan, and Evelyn S. Rawski, eds., *Popular Culture in Late Imperial China*. Berkeley: University of California Press, 1985, pp. 75–111.

Hebdige, Dick. *Subculture: The Meaning of Style*. London: Methuen, 1979.

Heesterman, J. C. *The Inner Conflict of Tradition*. Chicago: University of Chicago Press, 1985.

Hertz, Robert. "The Pre-eminence of the Right Hand: A Study in Religious Polarity." Translated by Rodney Needham. In Rodney Needham, ed., *Right and Left: Essays on Dual Symbolic Classification*. Chicago: University of Chicago Press, 1973, pp. 3–31. Originally published in 1909.

Hill, Carole E., ed. *Symbols and Society: Essays on Belief Systems in Action*. Athens, Ga.: Southern Anthropological Society, 1975.

Hobsbawn, Eric. "Mass-Producing Traditions: Europe, 1870–1914." In

Eric Hobsbawn and Terence Ranger, eds., *The Invention of Tradition*. Cambridge: Cambridge University Press, 1983, pp. 263–307.

Hobsbawn, Eric, and Terence Ranger, eds. *The Invention of Tradition*. Cambridge: Cambridge University Press, 1983.

Hocart, A. M. *Kingship*. Oxford: Clarendon Press, 1927.

Homans, George C. "Anxiety and Ritual: The Theories of Malinowski and Radcliffe-Brown." *American Anthropologist* 43 (1941): 164–72.

Horton, Robin. "A Definition of Religion, and Its Uses." *Journal of the Royal Anthropological Institute* 90 (1960): 201–26.

Hubert, Henri, and Marcel Mauss. *Sacrifice: Its Nature and Function*. Translated by W. D. Hall. Chicago: University of Chicago Press, 1981. Originally published in 1898.

Huxley, Sir Julian. "Introduction: A Discussion on Ritualization of Behavior in Animals and Man." In Sir Julian Huxley, ed., "A Discussion on Ritualization of Behavior in Animals and Man." *Philosophical Transactions of the Royal Society*, series B, 251 (1966): 249–71.

Hymes, Dell. "Breakthrough into Performance." In Dan Ben-Amos and Kenneth S. Goldstein, eds., *Folklore: Performance and Communication*. The Hague: Mouton, 1975, pp. 11–74.

Hymes, Dell, ed. *Reinventing Anthropology*. New York: Random House, 1969.

Jaggar, Alison M., and Susan R. Bordo, eds. *Gender/Body/Knowledge: Feminist Reconstructions of Being and Knowing*. New Brunswick, N.J.: Rutgers University Press, 1988.

James, E. O. *The Nature and Functions of the Priesthood*. London: Thames and Hudson, 1955.

Jameson, Fredric. "The Ideology of the Text." *Salmagundi* 31–32 (Fall 1975/Winter 1976): 204–46.

Jameson, Fredric. *The Political Unconscious*. Ithaca, N.Y.: Cornell University Press, 1981.

Jameson, Fredric. *The Prison-House of Language*. Princeton: Princeton University Press, 1972.

Jennings, Theodore. "On Ritual Knowledge." *Journal of Religion* 62, no. 2 (1982): 111–27.

Johnson, Mark. *The Body in the Mind*. Chicago: University of Chicago Press, 1987.

Jones, Ann Rosalind. "Writing the Body: Toward an Understanding of *l'Ecriture feminine*." *Feminist Studies* 7, no. 2 (1981): 247–63. Reprinted in Elaine Showalter, ed. *The New Feminist Criticism*. New York: Pantheon, 1985, pp. 361–78.

Jordan, David K. "The jiaw of Shigaang (Taiwan): An Essay in Folk Inter-
    pretation." *Asian Folklore Studies* 35, no. 2 (1976): 81–107.
Jordan, David K., and Daniel L. Overmyer. *The Flying Phoenix: Aspects
    of Chinese Sectarianism in Taiwan.* Princeton: Princeton University
    Press, 1986.
Josipovici, Gabriel. *Writing the Body.* Princeton: Princeton University
    Press, 1982.
Kertzer, David I. *Ritual, Politics and Power.* New Haven: Yale University
    Press, 1988.
Keyes, Charles F. "Buddhist Pilgrimage Centers and the Twelve-Year Cycle:
    Northern Thai Moral Order in Space and Time." *History of Religions*
    15, no. 1 (1975): 71–89.
Kuhn, Thomas. *The Structure of Scientific Revolutions,* 2nd rev. ed. Chi-
    cago: University of Chicago Press, 1970.
Kuipers, Joel C. *Power in Performance: The Creation of Textual Authority
    in Weyewa Ritual Speech.* Philadelphia: University of Pennsylvania
    Press, 1990.
Laclau, E., and C. Mouffe. *Hegemony and the Socialist Strategy.* London:
    Verso, 1985.
Laing, R. D. "Ritualization and Abnormal Behavior." In Sir Julian Huxley,
    ed., "A Discussion on Ritualization of Behavior in Animals and Man."
    Philosophical Transactions of the Royal Society, series B, 251 (1966):
    331–35.
Laitin, David D. *Hegemony and Culture: Politics and Religious Change
    Among the Yoruba.* Chicago: University of Chicago Press, 1986.
Lakoff, George. *Women, Fire and Other Dangerous Things.* Chicago: Uni-
    versity of Chicago Press, 1987.
Lane, Crystal. *The Rites of Rulers: Ritual in Industrial Society—The Soviet
    Case.* Cambridge: Cambridge University Press, 1981.
Larrain, Jorge. *The Concept of Ideology.* Athens: University of Georgia
    Press, 1979.
Laughlin, Charles D. "Ritual and the Symbolic Function: A Summary of
    Biogenetic Structural Theory." *Journal of Ritual Studies* 4, no. 1
    (1990): 15–39.
Lawson, E. Thomas, and Robert N. McCauley. *Rethinking Religion: Con-
    necting Cognition and Culture.* Cambridge: Cambridge University
    Press, 1990.
Leach, Edmund. *Culture and Communication.* Cambridge: Cambridge
    University Press, 1976.
Leach, Edmund. *The Political Systems of Highland Burma,* 2nd ed. Lon-
    don: Athlone Press, 1964.
Leach, Edmund. *Rethinking Anthropology.* London: Athlone Press, 1961.

Leach, Edmund R. "Ritual." In David L. Sills, ed., *International Encyclopedia of the Social Sciences*, vol. 13. New York: Macmillan, 1968, pp. 520–26.

Leach, E. R. "Ritualization in Man in Relation to Conceptual and Social Development." In Sir Julian Huxley, ed., "A Discussion on Ritualization of Behavior in Animals and Man." *Philosophical Transactions of the Royal Society*, series B, 251 (1966): 403–8.

Leertouwer, L. "Inquiry into Religious Behavior: A Theoretical Reconnaissance." In P. van Baaren and H. J. W. Drijvers, eds., *Religion, Culture and Methodology*. The Hague: Mouton, 1973, pp. 79–98.

Levering, Miriam, ed. *Rethinking Scripture*. Albany: State University of New York Press, 1989.

Lévi-Strauss, Claude. "French Sociology." In George Gurvitch and Wilbert E. Moore, eds., *Twentieth Century Sociology*. New York: The Philosophical Library, 1945, pp. 503–37.

Lévi-Strauss, Claude. *The Naked Man: Introduction to a Science of Mythology*, vol. 4. Translated by John Weightman and Doreen Weightman. New York: Harper and Row, 1981.

Lévi-Strauss, Claude. *The Savage Mind*. Translated by George Weidenfeld and Nicolson Ltd. Chicago: University of Chicago Press, 1966.

Lévi-Strauss, Claude. "The Scope of Anthropology." *Current Anthropology* 7 (1966): 112–23.

Lévi-Strauss, Claude. *Tristes Tropiques*. Translated by John Weightman and Doreen Weightman. New York: Atheneum, 1975.

Lewis, Gilbert. *Day of Shining Red: An Essay on Understanding Ritual*. Cambridge: Cambridge University Press, 1980.

Lincoln, Bruce. *Discourse and the Construction of Society*. New York: Oxford University Press, 1989.

Lobkowicz, Nicholas. *Theory and Practice: History of a Concept from Aristotle to Marx*. Notre Dame, Ind.: University of Notre Dame Press, 1967.

Lukes, Steven. "Political Ritual and Social Integration." *Sociology: Journal of the British Sociological Association* 9, no. 2 (1975): 289–308.

Lukes, Steven. *Power: A Radical View*. New York: Macmillan, 1974.

Lyotard, Jean-François. *The Postmodern Condition: A Report on Knowledge*. Translated by Geoff Bennington and Brian Massumi. Minneapolis: University of Minnesota Press, 1984.

MacAloon, John J. *Rite, Drama, Festival, Spectacle: Rehearsals Toward a Theory of Cultural Performance*. Philadelphia: Institute for the Study of Human Issues, 1984.

McMullen, David. "Bureaucrats and Cosmology: The Ritual Code of T'ang

China." In David Cannadine and Simon Price, eds., *Rituals of Royalty: Power and Ceremonial in Traditional Societies*. Cambridge: Cambridge University Press, 1987, pp. 181–236.

Mack, Burton. "Introduction: Religion and Ritual." In Robert G. Hamerton-Kelly, ed. *Violent Origins*. Stanford: Stanford University Press, 1987, pp. 1–70.

Mann, Michael. *The Sources of Social Power*, vol. 1. Cambridge: Cambridge University Press, 1986.

Marcus, George E., and Michael M. J. Fischer. *Anthropology as Cultural Critique*. Chicago: University of Chicago Press, 1986.

Marks, Elaine, and Isabelle de Courtivron, eds. *New French Feminisms*. Amherst: University of Massachusetts Press, 1980.

Martin, Roderick. *The Sociology of Power*. London: Routledge and Kegan Paul, 1977.

Mauss, Marcel. *The Gift: Forms and Functions of Exchange in Archaic Societies*. Translated by Ian Cunnison. New York: Norton, 1967.

Mauss, Marcel. "Techniques of the Body." In Rodney Needham, ed., *Right and Left: Essays on Dual Symbolic Classification*. Chicago: University of Chicago Press, 1973. Originally published in 1936.

Merquior, J. G. *Foucault*. Berkeley: University of California Press, 1985.

Merquior, J. G. *The Veil and the Mask: Essays on Culture and Ideology*. London: Routledge and Kegan Paul, 1979.

Moore, Robert L., Ralph Wendell Burhoe, and Philip J. Hefner, eds. "Ritual in Human Adaptation." *Zygon* 18, no. 3 (1983): 209–350.

Moore, Sally F., and Barbara G. Myerhoff, eds. *Secular Ritual*. Amsterdam: Van Gorcum, 1977.

Morris, Brian. *Anthropological Studies of Religion*. Cambridge: Cambridge University Press, 1987.

Munn, Nancy D. "Symbolism in a Ritual Context." In John J. Honigmann, ed., *Handbook of Social and Cultural Anthropology*. Chicago: Rand McNally, 1973, pp. 579–612.

Naquin, Susan. "Funerals in North China: Uniformity and Variations." In James L. Watson and Evelyn S. Rawski, eds., *Death Ritual in Late Imperial and Modern China*. Berkeley: University of California Press, 1988, pp. 37–70.

Needham, Rodney. *Belief, Language, and Experience*. Chicago: University of Chicago Press, 1972.

Needham, Rodney. "Percussion and Transition." *Man*, n.s. 2 (1967): 606–15.

Norris, Christopher. *Deconstruction: Theory and Practice*. London: Methuen, 1982.

Ortner, Sherry B. *High Religion: A Cultural and Political History of Sherpa Buddhism.* Princeton: Princeton University Press, 1989.

Ortner, Sherry B. *Sherpas Through Their Rituals.* Cambridge: Cambridge University Press, 1978.

Ortner, Sherry B. "Theory in Anthropology Since the Sixties." *Comparative Studies in Society and History* 26 (1984): 126–65.

Parsons, Talcott. *The Structure of Social Action,* 2nd ed. New York: Free Press, 1966. Originally published in 1937.

Parsons, Talcott, and Edward Shils, eds. *Toward a General Theory of Action.* New York: Harper and Row, 1962.

Peacock, James L. "Weberian, Southern Baptist, and Indonesian Muslim Conceptions of Belief and Action." In Carole E. Hill, ed., *Symbols and Society: Essays on Belief Systems in Action.* Athens: University of Georgia Press, 1975, pp. 82–92.

Penner, Hans. "Language, Ritual and Meaning." *Numen* 32, no. 1 (1985): 1–16.

Pitts, Walter. "Keep the Fire Burnin': Language and Ritual in the Afro-Baptist Church." *Journal of the American Academy of Religion* 56, no. 1 (1988): 77–97.

Pye, Lucien W. *Asian Power and Politics: The Cultural Dimensions of Authority.* Cambridge, Mass.: Harvard University Press, 1985.

Rabinow, Paul, ed. *The Foucault Reader.* New York: Pantheon, 1984.

Raheja, Gloria Goodwin. *The Poison in the Gift.* Chicago: University of Chicago Press, 1988.

Ranciere, Jacques. "On the Theory of Ideology (The Politics of Althusser)." *Radical Philosophy* 7 (1974): 2–15.

Rappaport, Roy A. *Ecology, Meaning and Religion.* Richmond, Calif.: North Atlantic Books, 1979.

Ricoeur, Paul. "The Model of the Text: Meaningful Action Considered as a Text." *Social Research* 38 (Autumn 1971): 529–62.

Rorty, Richard. *Philosophy and the Mirror of Nature.* Princeton: Princeton University Press, 1979.

Sahlins, Marshall. *Culture and Practical Reason.* Chicago: University of Chicago Press, 1976.

Sahlins, Marshall. *Historical Metaphors and Mythical Realities.* Ann Arbor: University of Michigan Press, 1981.

Said, Edward W. *Orientalism.* New York: Pantheon, 1978.

Said, Edward W. *The World, the Text, and the Critic.* Cambridge, Mass.: Harvard University Press, 1983.

Sangren, P. Steven. *History and Magical Power in a Chinese Community.* Stanford: Stanford University Press, 1987.

Schattschneider, E. E. *The Semi-Sovereign People: A Realist's View of*

Democracy in America. New York: Holt, Rinehart and Winston, 1960.

Schechner, Richard. *Between Theater and Anthropology.* Philadelphia: University of Pennsylvania Press, 1985.

Schechner, Richard. *Essays on Performance Theory 1970–1976.* New York: Drama Book Specialists, 1977.

Schechner, Richard. "The Future of Ritual." *Journal of Ritual Studies* 1, no. 1 (1987): 5–33.

Schechner, Richard, and Willa Appel, eds. *By Means of Performance: Intercultural Studies of Theatre and Ritual.* Cambridge: Cambridge University Press, 1989.

Schipper, Kristofer. "Vernacular and Classical Ritual in Taoism." *Journal of Asian Studies* 45, no. 1 (1985): 21–57.

Searle, John R. *Speech Acts.* Cambridge: Cambridge University Press, 1969.

Sheridan, Alan. *Michel Foucault: The Will to Truth.* London: Methuen, 1980.

Shils, Edward. "Ideology: The Concept and Function of Ideology." In David L. Sills, ed., *International Encyclopedia of the Social Sciences,* vol. 7. New York: Macmillan, 1968, pp. 66–76.

Shils, Edward. "Ritual and Crisis." In Donald R. Cutler, ed., *The Religious Situation: 1968.* Boston: Beacon Press, 1968, pp. 733–49. This is a revised version of the abridged contribution with the same name included in Sir Julian Huxley, ed., "A Discussion on Ritualization of Behavior in Animals and Man." *Philosophical Transactions of the Royal Society,* series B, 251 (1966): 447–50.

Shils, Edward, and Michael Young. "The Meaning of the Coronation." *Sociological Review,* n.s. 1 (1953): 63–81.

Showalter, Elaine. *The New Feminist Criticism.* New York: Pantheon, 1985.

Singer, Milton, "The Cultural Pattern of Indian Civilization." *Far Eastern Quarterly* 15 (1955): 23–35.

Singer, Milton, ed. *Traditional India: Structure and Change.* Philadelphia: American Folklore Society, 1959.

Skinner, Quentin, ed. *The Return to Grand Theory in the Human Sciences.* Cambridge: Cambridge University Press, 1985.

Skorupski, John. *Symbol and Theory: A Philosophical Study of Theories of Religion in Social Anthropology.* Cambridge: Cambridge University Press, 1976.

Smith, Brian K. "Ideals and Realities in Indian Religion." *Religious Studies Review* 14, no. 1 (1988): 1–10.

Smith, Brian K. *Reflections on Resemblance, Ritual and Religion.* New York: Oxford University Press, 1989.

Smith, Jonathan Z. "The Bare Facts of Ritual." In *Imagining Religion: From Babylon to Jonestown*. Chicago: University of Chicago Press, 1982, pp. 53–65.

Smith, Jonathan Z. "The Domestication of Sacrifice." In Robert G. Hamerton-Kelly, ed., *Violent Origins*. Stanford: Stanford University Press, 1987, pp. 191–205.

Smith, Jonathan Z. *Imagining Religion: From Babylon to Jonestown*. Chicago: University of Chicago Press, 1982.

Smith, Jonathan Z. *To Take Place: Toward Theory in Ritual*. Chicago: University of Chicago Press, 1987.

Smith, Pierre. "Aspects de l'organisation des rites." In Michel Izard and Pierre Smith, eds., *La fonction symbolique*. Paris: Gallimard, 1979, pp. 139–70.

Smith, W. Robertson. *The Religion of the Semites*. New York: Schocken Books, 1972. Originally published in 1894.

Sontag, Susan. "The Anthropologist as Hero." In *Against Interpretation and Other Essays*. New York: Farrar, Straus and Giroux, 1961, pp. 69–81.

Southwold, Martin. "Religious Belief." *Man*, n.s. 14, no. 4 (1978): 628–44.

Sperber, Dan. *On Anthropological Knowledge*. Cambridge: Cambridge University Press, 1985.

Sperber, Dan. *Rethinking Symbolism*. Cambridge: Cambridge University Press, 1974.

Staal, Frits. *Agni: The Vedic Ritual of the Fire Altar*, 2 vols. Berkeley, Calif.: Asian Humanities Press, 1983.

Staal, Frits. "The Meaninglessness of Ritual." *Numen* 26, no. 1 (1975): 2–22.

Staal, Frits. "The Sound of Religion: Parts I–III." *Numen* 33, no. 1 (1986): 33–64.

Staal, Frits. "The Sound of Religion: Parts IV-V." *Numen* 33, no. 2 (1986): 185–224.

Stegmüller, Wolfgang. *The Structure and Dynamic of Theories*. New York: Springer-Verlag, 1976.

Stock, Brian. *The Implications of Literacy*. Princeton: Princeton University Press, 1983.

Stromberg, Peter. "Consensus and Variation in the Interpretation of Religious Symbolism: A Swedish Example." *American Ethnologist* 8 (1981): 544–59.

Sullivan, Lawrence E. "Body Works: Knowledge of the Body in the Study of Religion." *History of Religions* 30, no. 1 (1990): 86–99.

Sullivan, Lawrence E. "Sound and Senses: Toward a Hermeneutics of Performance." *History of Religions* 26, no. 1 (1986): 1–33.

Tambiah, Stanley J. *Buddhism and the Spirit Cults in North-East Thailand.* Cambridge: Cambridge University Press, 1970.

Tambiah, Stanley J. "The Magical Power of Words." *Man,* n.s. 3, no. 2 (1968): 175–208.

Tambiah, Stanley J. "A Performative Approach to Ritual." *Proceedings of the British Academy* 65 (1979): 113–69.

Taussig, Michael T. *The Devil and Commodity Fetishism in South America.* Chapel Hill: University of North Carolina Press, 1980.

Therborn, Goran. *The Ideology of Power and the Power of Ideology.* London: Verso, 1980.

Thompson, Bard. *Liturgies of the Western Church.* New York: New American Library, 1961.

Thompson, John B. *Studies in the Theory of Ideology.* Berkeley: University of California Press, 1984.

Thompson, Kenneth. *Beliefs and Ideology.* London: Tavistock Publications, 1986.

Thorpe, W. H. "Ritualization in Ontogeny, Part 1: Animal Play." In Sir Julian Huxley, ed., "A Discussion on Ritualization of Behavior in Animals and Man." *Philosophical Transactions of the Royal Society,* series B, 251 (1966): 311–20.

Tu, Wei-ming. "Iconoclasm, Holistic Vision, and Patient Watchfulness: A Personal Reflection on the Modern Chinese Intellectual Quest." *Daedalus* 116, no. 2 (1987): 75–94.

Turner, Bryan S. *The Body and Society.* New York: Basil Blackwell, 1984.

Turner, Terence S. "Dual Opposition, Hierarchy and Value." In Jean-Claude Galey, ed., *Différences, valeurs, hiérarchie: Textes offerts à Louis Dumont.* Paris: Ecole des Hautes Etudes en Sciences Sociales, 1984, pp. 335–70.

Turner, Terence S. "Transformation, Hierarchy and Transcendence: A Reformulation of Van Gennep's Model of the Structure of Rites of Passage." In Sally F. Moore and Barbara G. Myerhoff, eds., *Secular Ritual.* Amsterdam: Van Gorcum, 1977, pp. 53–70.

Turner, Victor. *Dramas, Fields and Metaphors.* Ithaca, N.Y.: Cornell University Press, 1974.

Turner, Victor W. *The Drums of Affliction.* Oxford: Oxford University Press, 1968.

Turner, Victor. *Forest of Symbols: Aspects of Ndembu Ritual.* Ithaca, N.Y.: Cornell University Press, 1967.

Turner, Victor. *From Ritual to Theater: The Human Seriousness of Play.* New York: Performing Arts Journal Publications, 1982.

Turner, Victor W. "Ritual as Communication and Potency: An Ndembu Case Study." In Carole E. Hill, ed. *Symbols and Society: Essays on Belief Systems in Action.* Athens: University of Georgia Press, 1975, pp. 58–81.

Turner, Victor W. *The Ritual Process: Structure and Anti-Structure.* Chicago: Aldine, 1966.

Turner, Victor. *Schism and Continuity in African Society.* Manchester: Manchester University Press, 1957.

Turner, Victor. "Variations on a Theme of Liminality." In Sally F. Moore and Barbara G. Myerhoff, eds., *Secular Ritual.* Amsterdam: Van Gorcum, 1977, pp. 36–52.

Valeri, Valerio. *Kingship and Sacrifice: Ritual and Society in Ancient Hawaii.* Chicago: University of Chicago Press, 1985.

van Baaren, P., and H. J. W. Drijvers, eds. *Religion, Culture and Methodology.* The Hague: Mouton, 1973.

Van Gennep, Arnold. *The Rites of Passage.* Translated by M. B. Vizedom and G. L. Caffee. Chicago: University of Chicago Press, 1960. Originally published in 1909.

Verba, Sidney. "The Kennedy Assassination and the Nature of Political Commitment." In Bradley S. Greenberg and Edwin P. Parker, eds., *The Kennedy Assassination and the American Public.* Stanford: Stanford University Press, 1965, pp. 348–60.

Wach, Joachim. *Sociology of Religion.* Chicago: University of Chicago Press, 1971. Originally published in 1944.

Wagner, Roy. *The Invention of Culture,* rev. ed. Chicago: University of Chicago Press, 1981.

Wallace, Anthony F. C. *Religion: An Anthropological View.* New York: Random House, 1966.

Warner, W. Lloyd *The Living and the Dead: A Study of the Symbolic Life of Americans.* New Haven: Yale University Press, 1959.

Watson, James L. "Funeral Specialists in Cantonese Society: Pollution, Performance, and Social Hierarchy." In James L. Watson and Evelyn S. Rawski, eds., *Death Ritual in Late Imperial and Modern China.* Berkeley: University of California Press, 1988, pp. 109–34.

Watson, James L. "Standardizing the Gods: The Promotion of T'ien Hou ('Empress of Heaven') Along the South China Coast, 960–1960." In David Johnson, Andrew J. Nathan, and Evelyn S. Rawski, eds., *Popular Culture in Late Imperial China.* Berkeley: University of California Press, 1985, pp. 292–324.

Watson, James L. "The Structure of Chinese Funerary Rites." In James L. Watson and Evelyn S. Rawski, eds., *Death Ritual in Late Imperial and Early Modern China*. Berkeley: University of California Press, 1988, pp. 3–19.

Weber, Max. *The Sociology of Religion*. Translated by Ephraim Fischoff. New York: Beacon Press, 1963. Originally published in 1922.

Wechsler, Howard J. *Offerings of Jade and Silk: Ritual and Symbol in the Legitimation of the T'ang Dynasty*. New Haven: Yale University Press, 1985.

Wickham, G. "Power and Power Analysis." *Economy and Society* 12, no. 4 (1983): 468–98.

Williams, Raymond. *Marxism and Literature*. London: Oxford University Press, 1977.

Wolin, Sheldon S. "On the Theory and Practice of Power." In Jonathan Arac, ed., *After Foucault: Humanistic Knowledge, Postmodern Challenges*. New Brunswick, N.J.: Rutgers University Press, 1988, pp. 179–201.

Woodward, Mark R. "The *Slametan:* Textual Knowledge and Ritual Performance in Central Javanese Islam." *History of Religions* 28, no. 1 (1988): 54–89.

Wuthnow, Robert. *Meaning and Moral Order*. Berkeley: University of California Press, 1987.

Zuesse, Evan M. "Ritual." In Mircea Eliade et al., eds., *The Encyclopedia of Religion*, vol. 12. New York: Macmillan, 1987, pp. 405–22.

Zuesse, Evan M. *Ritual Cosmos: The Sanctification of Life in African Religions*. Athens: Ohio University Press, 1979.

Index

Political Unconscious, The (Jameson),
12n.16, 64n.116, 78, 148n.46
*Politics, Law and Ritual in Tribal
Societies* (Gluckman), 225n.12
Poulantzas, Nicos, 236n.160
Power, 8, 232n.95
and body, 201–4, 237n.174,
237n.176, 237n.178
defined, 197–204, 234n.138,
235n.146, 235n.150, 235n.152,
236n.160, 237n.178
and freedom, 200–201, 203–4
and ideology, 192–93, 198, 199,
232n.93
legitimation of, 8, 193–95, 221–22
relationships of, 201, 206–8, 216,
221, 236n.170, 237n.176,
237n.182, 237n.184
and ritual, 193–94, 195–96, 201–2,
204, 206–7, 211–13, 215, 218,
220, 234n.136, 236n.165,
236n.170, 238n.193
Power: A Radical View (Lukes), 198,
234n.138, 236n.160, 237n.178
*Power and Poverty: Theory and
Practice* (Bachrach and Baratz),
232n.95
Power/Knowledge (Foucault),
235n.152
Practice, 148–49n.57. *See also* Practice
theory
defined, 75–76, 81
as misrecognition, 81, 82–83, 86,
108–10, 156n.171
as 'redemptive hegemony,' 81, 83–
88, 149–50n.70, 150n.71
as situational, 81
as strategic, 81, 82, 149n.61,
149n.69
Practice of Everyday Life, The (de
Certeau), 149n.61
Practice theory, 74–81, 85–86, 147–
48n.43, 148n.56, 151n.99. *See
also* Practice
and other approaches, 146–47n.34
problems with, 76–78, 147n.42
Price, Simon, 85

*Printing Press as an Agent of Change,
The* (Eisenstein), 163n.244
*Pursuit of Signs: Semiotics, Literature
and Deconstruction, The* (Culler),
64n.116
Pye, Lucien W., 211, 212

Rabinow, Paul, 159n.190
Radcliffe-Brown, A. R., 59n.34
Raheja, Gloria Goodwin, 155n.151
Ranciere, Jacques, 231n.84
Ranger, Terence, 119, 120, 124,
160n.199
Rappaport, Roy A., 72, 89, 101,
151n.105, 152n.107
on body, 99–100
ecological rationalism of, 108–9,
126
on ritual, 112, 119–20, 126–27
on myth, 186
and performance theory, 43
*Reflections of a Woman
Anthropologist—No Hiding Place*
(Cesara), 65–66n.143
*Reflections on Resemblance, Ritual
and Religion* (Smith), 164n.252,
166n.267
Religion, 23, 171, 185, 187. *See also*
Belief
Durkheim on, 15, 20, 23, 91, 217–
18
Geertz on, 26, 230n.78
and ideology, 187, 230n.78
and literacy, 163–64n.246, 166–
67n.270
and ritual, 14–15, 19, 25, 40, 55n.6,
56n.8, 205–6, 222
Religion: An Anthropological View
(Wallace), 145–46n.25
"Religion as a Cultural System"
(Geertz), 230n.78
"Religious Belief" (Southwold), 227–
28n.52
Ricoeur, Paul, 44, 50–52, 64n–65n.123
Rites. *See* Ritual
Ritual, 20, 21, 22, 230n.74. *See also*
Ritual theory; Ritualization